THE KINDNESS OF STRANGERS

THE KINDNESS OF STRANGERS

Bernard Braden

Hodder & Stoughton
LONDON SYDNEY AUCKLAND TORONTO

British Library Cataloguing in Publication Data

Braden, Bernard *1916–*
   The kindness of strangers.
   1. Acting. Biographies
   I. Title
   792.028092

   ISBN 0-340-52527-4

First published in Great Britain 1990

Published by Hodder and Stoughton,
a division of Hodder and Stoughton Ltd,
Mill Road, Dunton Green, Sevenoaks, Kent TN13 2YA
Editorial Office: 47 Bedford Square, London WC1B 3DP

Photoset by Rowland Phototypesetting Ltd
Bury St Edmunds, Suffolk
Printed and bound in Great Britain by
Butler and Tanner Ltd, Frome, Somerset

DEDICATION

A man bought a car and offered to take his friend for a ride.
"What do you think of it?" he said.

His friend pointed out that the bonnet was bright green, the boot was yellow, the nearside was purple and the offside was blue. "It's not what I'd call an artistic triumph," he said.

"Ah," said the owner, "but when I have an accident you should hear the witnesses contradict each other."

Anon

This book is dedicated to all those witnesses who remember it differently.

FOREWORD

Autumn 1950

Barbara and I attended a new play at the Duchess Theatre. In the foyer she said, "Don't look now, but guess who's standing over there?" Naturally I turned to look immediately, just in time to lip-read Lord Mountbatten saying to Lady Edwina, "That's Bernard Braden and Barbara Kelly." My spine froze. "My God!" I thought, "we're not just entertainers, we're important, like them."

Autumn 1988

Coincidence took us to two wedding receptions in two days. The first was at a hotel near Arundel Cathedral for Mr and Mrs Derek Jameson. Celebrities abounded, as did photographers. Some of these photographers I've come to know through the years and we chatted in a friendly way.

In the car on the way home, Barbara and I agreed that while the photographers were friendly and asked after the children, none of them seemed to point a camera in our direction.

The following night we went to Langan's Brasserie where there was a wedding reception for London's best-known showbiz agent, Dennis Selinger, and Mrs Selinger. Even more celebrities and photographers. Again I chatted with the photographers, mostly about the wedding reception we'd all attended the day before. Again, no cameras were pointed in my direction. At one point while I was chatting with Michael Caine and Roger Moore a photographer approached me and whispered that he'd be grateful if I'd get out of the shot he wanted to take of Michael and Roger.

As Barbara and I left we were faced outside with even more photographers, none of whom offered to take our picture, but one of them did offer to get me a taxi. When we were in it, Barbara said, "You know, I think we've entered a new phase in our lives. We've moved into another category. We now belong to the EFVIPs."

"What's that?"

"Elderly Former Very Important Persons."

◆　　◆　　◆

"THE KINDNESS OF STRANGERS"

Prologue

A party in Toronto in 1948. Two female voices raised in anger, the sound of smashing glass, then one lady threatening the other with a broken tumbler, and screaming, "My husband's a better actor than your husband!"

On the way home my wife said, "That settles it. We have to get out of this town. This country."

We were actors.

In English-speaking Canada at that time, people who engaged in cultural pursuits were considered odd . . . rather like homosexuals. In fact, most of them were thought to *be* homosexuals. To say you were an actor was to be effete, unless of course it was a hobby. If you claimed to be a professional, you evoked laughter, or an embarrassed change of subject. A friend of mine who was called up during the war filled in the usual form, and was faced with a sergeant who said, "What the hell have you put down here?"

"Actor. It says 'trade or profession'."

"It *means* 'What do you do for a living?' "

"What would you expect Clark Gable to put down?"

"Actor. But he's an American."

That was the crux of it. An actor in Canada was an amateur by definition. If he was any good he'd have emigrated to the United States or England.

And quite right, too. Most Canadians were still from first or second generation pioneer stock. The country had to be settled, all five thousand miles of it, east to west, then consolidated. Agriculture, railways and business. It was a mammoth task for a small population, and churches were built before theatres.

When theatres *were* built they played host to touring companies from New York to England. In due course a few businessmen became rich and were persuaded by their wives to subsidise "Little" theatres for amateur productions, ballet companies and even symphony orchestras. But no one was expected to make a living out of them. That might come later. How much later nobody knew, or seemed interested in finding out.

In Toronto today there are half a hundred fringe theatres, displaying excellent Canadian talent, and two large theatres downtown playing host to touring companies from New York and London.

In 1948, the only professional outlet for Canadian actors was radio, but Canadians preferred to listen to Bob Hope and Jack Benny on American networks, and who could blame them? For us – the Canadian writers, directors and actors – there was a chilling anonymity that turned us into a kind of sullen defence mechanism, huddling together at parties, where a woman could only scream, "My husband's a better actor than your husband!" There was no one else to pass judgement, or even offer an opinion.

Hence, "That settles it. We have to get out of this town . . . this country!"

◆   ◆   ◆

But where to go? If I've suggested that Canadian performers were ignored by their compatriots, this doesn't mean we weren't able to earn a living. The Canadian Broadcasting Corporation provided a very good living for up to a hundred writers, directors and actors. Under its Charter it was required to. The trouble was that the Charter didn't require citizens to listen to this radio. At one point, under a brilliant director called Andrew Allan, the Canadian Broadcasting Corporation was producing a Sunday night live drama series which won awards in competition with the best American shows. It had a higher listening figure in the state of New York than in the whole of Canada.

So, where to go? Before I was married I'd spent some time in Los Angeles working as an announcer for a local radio station and hoping to break into films. The job came my way purely because the chief announcer at Station KNX was a Canadian I'd known in Vancouver. After several months another and better Canadian announcer called on my boss. He hired him immediately, and fired me. End of Hollywood career.

Just after the war, a Canadian comedian called Alan Young was invited to do a summer season for NBC in New York as a replacement for Eddie Cantor. Alan insisted that I accompany him as his producer, and I used the opportunity to flog my performing wares at all the big networks. One day I had an appointment with a major CBS drama producer. During the interview, he was called out of his office, and I took the opportunity to read a card on his desk. The card was from an actor I considered the best radio actor in the world, and it said, "Call me anything, but call me". If Everett Sloane was reduced to this kind

10

of hustling, it was too much of a rat race for me. As soon as I could arrange to get out of my commitments, I returned to Toronto.

In the summer of 1947 I'd spent two months in London preparing a post-war documentary radio series called *These English*. On the basis of that experience I persuaded Barbara that London was "where to go".

On February 10th, 1949 we were in New York, booked to sail on the *Queen Mary* to Southampton the following morning. A friend was trying to get us tickets for the opening performance that evening of Arthur Miller's *Death of a Salesman*. Late in the afternoon, she called to say she'd been unsuccessful but *could* get us seats for the 500th performance of *A Streetcar Named Desire* by Tennessee Williams. We were grateful, but disappointed. By the 500th performance the actors are usually just going through the motions.

As the house lights dimmed and the curtain rose, we basked on a winter's evening in the steamy atmosphere of a summer day in New Orleans, emanating from the stage. Initially, there was a confusion of voices and images, then on to the scene burst a muscular young man so full of vitality that I couldn't look at anyone else. As suddenly as he'd arrived he was gone, and to me the stage was empty. Was he a bit player, or would he come back? He came back with a vengeance!

This was my introduction to the young Marlon Brando. I've never seen a performance to approach it, before or since. It was as if someone had seen him delivering ice or coal to the stage door and had said, "Look, our leading man's ill, and his understudy's just broken a leg. Will you go on in his place?"

"But I've never been on the stage. I've never been in a theatre!"

"Doesn't matter. Just go on and do or say whatever comes into your head."

That's what it looked and sounded like to me, and in a 500th performance! There's a lot of humour in *Streetcar*, and much of it came from Brando, but he seemed to kill laughs deliberately. Not by riding over them, but by looking straight into the audience . . . at me . . . as if to say, "You may find that funny, but I don't, and if you're not careful, I'll come out there and tear you apart!" Laughs died in my throat.

Jessica Tandy, Kim Hunter and Karl Malden undoubtedly gave splendid performances that night, but to me the play belonged to Stanley. Not Brando. But Stanley. That character up there treating a stage like a real place, and the other characters as if they were real people.

After the performance, we had a farewell dinner with friends at

11

the Algonquin Hotel, then on to a jazz club to hear a favourite group, but I remember little about any of it. Not the food, not the name of the group, not even who the friends were. My mind was still on that stage. Later I found I'd committed whole scenes of the play to memory on the basis of one performance.

◆　　◆　　◆

Five days on the *Queen Mary* gave Barbara and me time to think of what we'd actually done in response to her heartfelt plea to get out of Canada. We'd sold our house and most of our belongings, cut ourselves off from lucrative work with every chance that it wouldn't be there to go back to, and left our three children with my widowed father, seven thousand miles away in Vancouver. The youngest was less than three months old.

Not everything was on the debit side. Selling the house had given us enough money to live comfortably in London for a year without actually working. Also, I still had a contract with the Canadian Broadcasting Corporation to record five programmes a week at the BBC for Canadian consumption. This would ensure that the children would have a couple to look after them so that my father would have a minimum of inconvenience, and the opportunity to enjoy them when he wanted to. My mother's death in 1947 had left him alone, and we felt he might feel less lonely with children in the house. I think we were also aware that to some extent this was a rationale for selfishness.

Meantime, I'd acquired a loan from an investment house in Vancouver for the purpose of studying the film industry in Britain, with a view to making films in Canada. It was my folly to think that by making films with Canadian talent we could stop the export of that talent to other countries. Folly or not, it helped ease Barbara's guilt about leaving the children. "We'll go home within a year," I told her.

That's why we were relatively carefree when we stepped off the boat-train in London to be met by an old friend, Peggy Hassard, who took us straight to the Westminster Theatre to see *Home of the Brave*, a play starring Richard Attenborough, with Peggy's husband, Arthur Hill, in a supporting role. After the show we went backstage to see Arthur and meet the rest of the cast. I remember a warm welcome, a sense of excitement and Richard Attenborough taking us outside to see something he'd acquired that very day . . . a 1934 Bentley. He couldn't wait to drive it home.

The Hills and the Bradens then moved on to the Albany Club in

12

Albemarle Street for dinner. We were prepared for austerity in post-war Britain, but not for the Albany Club. On the ground floor was a superb bar, and downstairs a large but intimate dining room where a happy group of people were eating lobster, smoked salmon, sirloin steaks and Black Forest gâteau. At one end of the room was a bandstand with a seven-piece orchestra, and from time to time someone would get up from a table and do an act. There was a little man called Chaz Chase who seemed to enjoy eating innumerable lighted cigarettes, then a comedian and straight man, who kept us convulsed for about fifteen minutes, followed by five more comedians who insulted each other, the establishment and the guests. I expressed surprise that one night-club could afford so much talent and Arthur explained that they weren't paid. All these people worked elsewhere. This was their favourite place for relaxing after a show, and their contributions were purely voluntary. The comedian and the straight man were Sid Field and Jerry Desmonde, and the other group belonged to something called "The Crazy Gang". Barbara and I had never heard of them.

After dinner Peggy and Arthur went home, and we took a taxi to our hotel which, on the basis of my previous visit to London, I'd chosen very carefully. It was the Regent Palace, off Piccadilly Circus. As soon as we'd checked in, I suggested a walk before bed and as we moved into the Circus, still dimly lit, because of what some Londoners called "The Brown Out", Barbara stopped, took a deep breath, looked at me, and said, "I'm home!"

We then walked along Coventry Street, around Leicester Square and back to the hotel. It was after midnight, but you could do that in 1949, although the streets were full. During the war a song had been written called "I'm Gonna Get Lit Up When the Lights Come on in London". By 1950 neon and electric signs were still forbidden and cars were not allowed anything but dipped lights. Streetlights were still mainly gas. Hence the term "Brown Out".

I'd chosen the Regent Palace because it was at the centre of London night life. That is to say the haunt of prostitutes and their clients. From our window we looked down on the scene, and listened to the ribaldry, all of it good-natured. At one point a young woman lifted her skirt, under which she wore nothing, and directed a stream of urine on to the pavement, laughing raucously, and cheered by the group around her, which included a policeman. We'd certainly come a long way from Toronto. The following morning after breakfast in bed I watched Barbara carefully as she read the only newspaper I'd ordered. As she turned the pages her eyes widened. She finally looked at me and said, "Is this really England? Is this what goes on all the time?"

It was Sunday, and I'd ordered the *News of the World*.

◆   ◆   ◆

Within a week we'd found a first-floor flat in Lower Sloane Street, furnished, including a grand piano. Eight pounds a week. It consisted of one large reception room, with high windows facing the street, a small kitchen, and a bedroom at the back. Halfway up the landing was a tiny bathroom with a toilet and stand-up bath. The only heating was one of those honeycomb gas fires in the bedroom.

We, used to below zero temperatures in Toronto, had never been so cold in our lives. Each morning one of us would finally get up the courage to jump out of bed, turn on the gas fire, then dive back under the covers until the room was warm enough to dress in. That could be as late as noon.

There was a good reason for that. Our first child was born nine months to the day after our marriage. From that moment we were a family rather than a couple. Barbara had two children before she was twenty. And now there was a third. Life, for her, had been children, a husband and a desire for fame. Three times she'd won the award as best radio actress in Canada, but that was not fame. It was a challenge to prove she could achieve the same kind of recognition in another country. So . . . for the first time in our married life she was not pregnant or looking after children in tandem with seeking a career. That's why we spent most of those first winter mornings under the covers in Lower Sloane Street. We were reliving our pre-marital relationship without shame and enjoying it thoroughly.

But something was bothering her. It took weeks of prompting for me to find out what. One morning as we lay together she started to cry. I insisted on an explanation and she finally said: "I'll never make it. I'm too old." She was twenty-four.

◆   ◆   ◆

She'd just turned sixteen when I first met her. It was shortly before Christmas 1940.

The Canadian Broadcasting Corporation in Vancouver was about to embark on its first production of the York and Chester Mysteries, to be performed live on Christmas Day with a full symphony orchestra, a chorus of thirty-two and a cast of forty.

14

The only problem was that, having tested virtually every actress in Vancouver, our producer had failed to find a Virgin Mary he thought could do justice to the part, and rehearsals were less than a week away.

Then one of our actors went to see an amateur production at the Vancouver Little Theatre, phoned the producer and said, "I've found her." The next day she was given a private audition and we heard that the part had been cast. Her name was Barbara Kelly, she'd just left school to take up modelling and was rumoured to be engaged to a young naval officer. She was also said to be blonde and beautiful.

I was sceptical. A model who could act? An amateur who'd never been in a radio play? A kid of sixteen? A likely story! I was twenty-three years old at the time, going on twenty-four and trying to look thirty. There was a reason for this. Having spent a year in bed with tuberculosis in 1937 I wasn't eligible for the armed forces. To avoid embarrassment I grew a moustache,

Me and mike

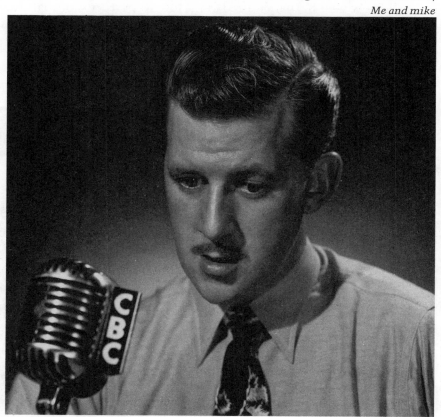

smoked a pipe and, dressed in tweeds and brown brogues, tried to look as much as possible like a foreign correspondent. Outdoors I added a snap-brimmed trilby and a trench-coat with the collar turned up.

On the morning of the first readthrough all eyes were on the young stranger in our midst. I feigned indifference but conceded to myself that she was an attractive child and noted that she was not wearing an engagement ring. For one so young she was amazingly unselfconscious and showed no sign of nerves.

When she began to read the entire male cast looked first at her then at each other in astonishment. She read the lines beautifully with an instinctive feel for scansion, but it was the voice that caused a hush. The range was incredible. It moved from that of a young girl responding to the prophesy of the Angel that she would bear the child of God, to a deep contralto as she reassured Joseph that all would be well. I thought it phenomenal. So did everyone else. The live Christmas Day performance was a triumph.

In the new year Barbara joined our Radio Repertory Company at the CBC, but still found time to work as a fashion model at the Hudson Bay Company department store. She also seemed to lead a hectic social life. All the unmarried men in our group asked her out, including the producer, and she accepted every invitation, but played no favourites. Somehow she managed to repel all

Barbara Kelly – Fletcher Markle

sexual advances without offending. Perhaps because I stayed well out of it (much too old), they confided in me. Apparently she was wonderful company; happy to go bowling, dancing, to a cinema or a football game. Gregarious, a good mixer in any company . . . just didn't seem interested in "the goodnight kiss". Must have something to do with the young naval officer.

Her most frequent escort was the actor who'd discovered her at the Little Theatre, a brilliant young man of nineteen. He was a fine actor, an excellent writer, and would eventually become a well-known director of Hollywood films. He confided in me too. Barbara was driving him mad. She appeared to enjoy his company immensely, but firmly resisted all physical overtures . . . Would I take her to lunch or tea and try to find out what was wrong? He wasn't asking me to put his case, just discover why she didn't respond.

At the time I was the proud owner of a Morris 8 roadster, circa 1937, delivered to Vancouver at a cost of less than £150. I invited Barbara to join me for a drive and we stopped for Vienna coffee at an inn on what was then a scenic drive around Point Gray. Still playing the older man I put my questions as obliquely as possible. Yes, she liked my friend, but his attempts at seduction only made her laugh. Yes, there was a young naval officer who wanted to marry her, but she hadn't made up her mind.

On the journey home – it was spring and the roadster's top was down – I asked if she'd ever been in love. "Oh, yes!" she said, and explained that she'd been head over heels with a West Vancouver boy who "looked like Tyrone Power and played the violin". While still at school they'd attempted to buy a marriage licence and elope across the American border. They were thwarted by two insurmountable obstacles. One, they had no money. Two, they were both under eighteen. So they'd gone back to school and the romance seemed to have petered out.

And so my courtship began. It had to be conducted carefully, but I'd fallen in love, and this was the girl I wanted to marry. We went out regularly and before long our relationship became physical . . . up to a point. There was no "pill" in those days and conventionally brought up young people tended not to go "all the way". There was also the fact that Barbara was below the age of consent. Frustrating but formidable. We'd go to a cinema in downtown Vancouver, then drive across the bridge to West Vancouver and stop for a hamburger at a place called the Tomahawk where the food was brought to your car. We'd tune the radio to a Los Angeles station and listen to Stan Kenton and his orchestra "Live from the beautiful Balboa Inn in downtown Los

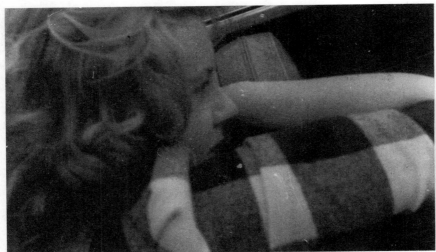

Barbara

Angeles". Then I'd drive to a spot about fifty yards short of Barbara's home, which was on a hill. Some time later when the car windows were thoroughly steamed up we'd stop to look at the time (always much later than we expected), Barbara would get out of the car and walk down to her driveway. When she waved I'd take off the handbrake and coast well past the house before turning on the engine or the lights.

After several months Barbara's parents suggested it was time I met the family, so one Sunday I showed up for tea. Mrs Kelly was the soul of charm, but Mr Kelly acknowledged my presence with a grunt and returned to his Sunday paper. After a brief embarrassed pause he said, "Well . . . I see you finally got him into the house." After I'd left Barbara asked what he thought of me. "Dirty fingernails," he muttered, "and shoes not properly polished for a Sunday."

Still, I was invited back for dinner and continued to see Barbara at every opportunity. There was the occasional hiccup when the young naval lieutenant was on leave, but I was very careful not to show jealousy. Given the opportunity I'd have killed him.

One evening we dined at a restaurant called Scott's, and during the meal the electricity was cut off. Candles were brought to each table, which suited me fine. It wasn't till we left the restaurant that we realised the power cut had blacked out the entire city. Policemen with torches were roaming the streets insisting that all cars be driven with parking lights only. As we made our way slowly towards the bridge that would take us to West Vancouver we found ourselves in a long line of traffic that eventually came to a dead halt. A policeman walked along the queue explaining that the bridge was closed for the night.

I turned the car round, wondering what we were going to do now. Barbara said, "Why don't we go to your place? Perhaps it's time I met *your* parents."

It was a long slow journey to Kerrisdale, the Vancouver suburb where I lived. We arrived about 2.00 a.m. to find candles burning in the window. Barbara was warmly welcomed, and it was only then we learned what it was all about. Apparently an enemy submarine had been sighted off Vancouver Island and an official blackout had been ordered . . . the only one we ever had in Vancouver.

Since my father was a clergyman I suggested he be nominated to phone Barbara's parents and explain she'd be staying the night.

"No, thank you," said Barbara. "I'll do it." And she did. Without any fuss she phoned her father and explained the situation coolly and calmly. There was no problem.

Now that everyone knew about us, including our parents, Barbara and I went everywhere together. I took great pride in introducing her, whatever the company, because of her ability to mix and adapt. Sometimes, out of her hearing, I'd ask someone to guess her age. Estimates ranged from seventeen (based on her face and figure) to twenty-four (based on her maturity).

The first time we went swimming together I watched her stride into the cold Pacific Ocean, launch herself at a wave and move into a smooth Australian crawl. No tentative toe in the water. No girlish giggles. I think that's when I decided to test our relationship.

One night in the parked car I said, "This naval lieutenant of yours . . ."

"He's been promoted," she said.

"Why do you keep going out with him?"

"Because he's good company."

"Is that all?"

"Well – nobody else has offered to slip a ring on my finger."

I reached into my pocket and pulled out a little blue box, then opened it. "How about trying this one on for size?"

The ring was a perfect fit. The diamond was infinitesimal. We hurried home to Mr and Mrs Kelly who pretended to admire this minute stone, holding it up to the light but politely refraining from reaching for a magnifying glass.

We were married by my father on April 13th, 1942. Before the service he said to Barbara, "You don't want to obey, do you? We'll make it 'love, honour and cherish'." I wondered whose side he

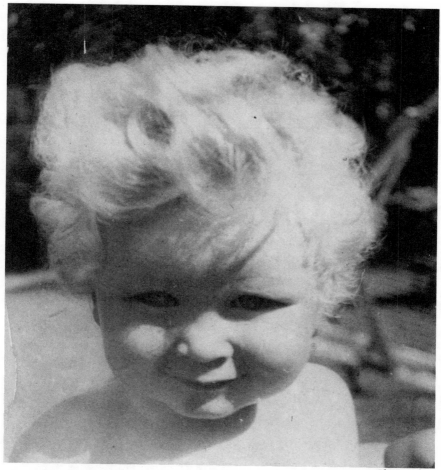

Christopher

was on! Certainly Barbara stuck to her vow. In forty-eight years of marriage she has yet to obey.

When we next performed the York and Chester Mysteries on Christmas Day it was deemed sensible for Barbara to sit at a table during the show. Members of the orchestra and chorus were taking bets as to whether the Christ-child would arrive before ours . . . Christopher was born on January 10th, 1943.

A week after our wedding I came home to find Barbara pretending to be upset because she'd "accidentally" dropped her engagement ring down the sink. It wasn't until our twenty-fifth anniversary that I was able to buy her a ring she *didn't* lose down the sink.

♦   ♦   ♦

Barbara with final engagement ring

The late winter and early spring of 1949 were to most people in the United Kingdom simply the beginning of another year of austerity for which they were starting to blame the Labour government. Those who could afford a brief trip to France were only too aware that, however unstable the French economy, and regardless of the constant change of leadership, the French had recovered their lifestyle. The British visitor would be complimented by his French host on the fact that Britain had accepted its responsibility for *winning* the war.

"We do admire you," he'd say, "for rationing your food so that everyone gets his fair share. Do have some more butter with your bread. We are so grateful you protected our General de Gaulle during our tribulations under the Vichy government. More cream on the mushrooms? We suffered, but you continue to suffer voluntarily. It is so brave, and so British . . . please have another glass of cognac."

Others were simply too young to understand. David Frost was ten years old . . . Neil Kinnock was seven, so was Paul McCartney. Andrew Lloyd Webber was a year old and Prince Charles a babe in arms.

Barbara and I were younger than they are now, and imbued with a sense of adventure.

Part of our fascination with Britain was that although Winston Churchill had unquestionably led the country successfully through a devastating war, the electorate had chucked him out at the end of it, and that the vote of the armed forces had contributed substantially to his defeat. What kind of people reacted in that way?

Not that we felt qualified to criticise. As we watched Londoners queuing everywhere and going about their business in what appeared to be a state of apathy we were acutely aware that these were the same people who had weathered the Blitz, displayed incredible personal bravery and had never given up. Indeed we watched them with a sense of awe, mainly because ours had been a totally vicarious war. Canadian troops had taken part, yes, Canadian lives had been lost and few Canadian people had been untouched by the conflict. Our petrol had been rationed, but not all that severely, and so had liquor, but there was always food in abundance.

Now, four years after the end of the war, Clement Attlee was Prime Minister, Herbert Morrison Leader of the House, Ernest Bevin Foreign Secretary, Sir Stafford Cripps Chancellor of the Exchequer, Aneurin Bevan Minister of Health, Emanuel Shinwell Secretary of State for War, and Harold Wilson President of the Board of Trade. The Archbishop of Canterbury earned the staggering salary of £7,500 per annum.

The wage for the average man in 1949 was just over ten new pence per hour; for a woman about half that. Miners earned less than £10 a week. Dockers just over £5.

We were coming to terms with the fact that the bacon ration had just been reduced to two ounces per week, and that of the one-shilling-per-person meat ration, one ounce would have to be tinned. As we wandered about, familiarising ourselves with the Sloane Square area, it was a shock to learn that we must register with one butcher only and surrender our meat coupons or ration book to him. Meats, fats, tea, cheese, sugar: all these were rationed, and a host of other goods simply unavailable. There was government price control over a wide range of goods.

Restaurants were not allowed to charge more than five shillings for a three-course meal. Guests staying in hotels for more than five nights had to surrender their ration books so the management could cut out the appropriate coupons.

The British were so used to this situation that when clothes rationing ended most people kept their coupons. They thought it might be a trick.

Our enthusiasm about being in London did not diminish.

Meantime there were contacts to be renewed and new ones to be made. We'd met Leslie Mitchell of the BBC when he visited Canada the previous year. The same was true of Laurence Gilliam, Head of BBC Radio Features. Our other BBC contact was an unknown and irascible man who had spent several years during the war as the BBC's under-representative to the Canadian Broadcasting Corporation, a position from which he'd been recalled in disgrace. His name was Gilbert Harding.

Then, of course, there were our friends the Arthur Hills, who seemed to know everything that was going on in the theatre. Arthur told me there was talk – just talk – that *A Streetcar Named Desire* was about to be produced in London and that casting would start soon.

My first job, though, was to make contact with the Rank Organisation on behalf of the Vancouver investment house who'd advanced me a sum of money to investigate the possibility of making films in Canada.

I had a letter to Mr Bernard Slidel who was with the PR Department, and immediately invited Barbara and me out to Pinewood Studios where we could watch films being made and meet some Very Important People who were experimenting with a process called "Independent Frame".

Mr Slidel was as good as his word. He picked us up one cold morning in February in an open car and drove us at an alarming rate of speed, talking all the way. Sometimes he turned round to the back seat where I was sitting and addressed a few words to me. Fortunately, the car seemed to know the route very well and we arrived shaken but safe.

Mr Slidel's conversation had nothing to do with films. His sole interest seemed to be placing the proper bets on the upcoming

Lincoln and Grand National races. His policy was to choose a horse in each race and if the first one won, he let the winnings ride on his choice in the National. So far he'd won one or the other, but never both. This year his hopes were high because he'd met a jockey who claimed to have the right answers.

From Reception at Pinewood we were taken into a film studio, and introduced to actors we'd known only from the screen in Canada. There were Derek Bond, Derek Farr, Muriel Pavlov, Diana Dors, Lana Morris, Honor Blackman and Rona Anderson. All very heady!

What puzzled us was that they were not working in sets, but bits of sets. There was an enormous entrance to a staircase that only had three steps. When someone rested an arm on a balustrade, the balustrade ended just beyond his fingers. Somebody else was standing behind half an armchair.

I looked enquiringly at Mr Slidel who whispered, "This is Independent Frame", but offered no further explanation.

Eventually I was taken away to an office where an architect undertook to explain Independent Frame. He was one of a group of architects who'd been hired by J. Arthur Rank to find a way of distributing Rank films to foreign countries without having to dub them into different languages. The theory was that by building bits of sets and installing enormous tunnels on all sides of the studio you could back-project the rest of the set with mathematical precision to incorporate the rest of the staircase, balustrade and chair. Meantime, lighting experts had been employed to position lights for each scene on a drawing-board. This, said the gentleman with great enthusiasm, was a great time-saver because most of the time on the shooting day was taken up with the lighting cameraman arranging his lights. They'd invited the leading lighting cameramen on to an Independent Frame set and asked them to light it their way. In every case they'd been forced into the exact lighting prescribed in advance on the drawing-board.

He then waited for me to respond and all I could think of to say was, "What's the point?"

"Ah," he said, "that's the beauty of it. When the film is complete we pack up all the bits of sets and the back-projected film, fit them into a single trunk and send that trunk, with the drawings, to, for example, Rio de Janeiro. They will then make their own version of the film in their own language! Simple isn't it?"

I said our idea in Canada was to make our own films and export them to other countries.

"Exactly!" he said. "We send out one of our architects to draw up the plan of your film in advance, you make the film in Independent Frame, then put it in a trunk and export it just the way we do."

I was slightly puzzled, because, apart from talent, all we had to offer in Canada were spectacular locations, such as the Rocky Mountains and the Pacific Ocean. I asked the gentleman if they'd run into any problems.

"We have one slight hiccup. Our top directors, such as David Lean, Carol Reed and Ronald Neame, will have nothing to do with it. They've grown used to depending on and taking the advice of their lighting cameramen through the years, and they flatly refuse to work in Independent Frame."

I don't know if those directors were right or wrong, but very few films were ever released on Independent Frame, and the huge tunnels constructed for back-projection were taken away and destroyed.

I had several other meetings with the protagonists of Independent Frame over the next two months, but couldn't come to terms with either the principles involved, or the enthusiasm of the men who'd invented it. I gave up my concept of starting a film industry in Canada, and returned the money advanced to the investment house in British Columbia.

It was to be the only setback of the year.

Bernard Slidel phoned me with his tips for the Lincoln and the Grand National, but I didn't bet on them, which was a shame, because they both won.

◆   ◆   ◆

The following Sunday, Leslie Mitchell and his then wife Phyllis took us to the Olde Bell at Hurley for a Sunday lunch . . . also in an open car. Virtually everyone we met that late winter and spring drove an open car, if they had a car. Driving home, it occurred to Leslie that it might be a matter of minor interest if he were to interview us as Canadian actors on his television programme, *Picture Page*. We agreed with alacrity.

On the appointed day we turned up at Alexandra Palace where in 1949 all television programmes originated. The atmosphere was friendly and cosy from top to bottom. We were introduced to Norman Collins, then Head of BBC Television, and his assistant, Cecil McGivern.

The studio itself seemed to be in a state of chaos, and at some point during the proceedings the producer said there wouldn't be time to interview us both, that Miss Kelly seemed the more photogenic of the two, but that if Mr Kelly would like to join him in the control room he would be made welcome. A story grew from this that I had said, "If there's no Mr Braden, there'll be no Miss Kelly". But it wasn't true. I sat meekly in the control room while Miss Kelly was interviewed.

In those days, with cameras at a premium, only the interviewee appeared in shot. The interviewer (in this case Leslie) stood beside the camera and directed his questions from a distance of about fifteen feet. Since the show was live, if the person interviewed said something unacceptable, the interviewer was totally helpless. At one point Leslie asked, "Miss Kelly, I'm aware that you don't have television yet in Canada, but if this was a Canadian radio broadcast, would it be different in any way?"

Barbara said in all innocence, "The only difference would be that if we were in Canada, this programme would be sponsored by Kelloggs Cornflakes, or Shredded Wheat, or Persil, or Johnson's Wax or . . ."

Barbara's first TV interview

Unaware of Leslie's horrified eyes she managed to name more than a dozen products before he could interrupt her with another question. Now in 1949 the only products that could be named on the BBC were Rolls-Royce and Coca-Cola, the former because it was considered invincible, and the latter because it was accepted as inevitable.

There were less than fifty thousand television sets in Britain at the time, but Barbara's inadvertent faux pas made the front page of every national daily the next morning.

One of those television sets had been installed that very day in the bar of the Arts Theatre in Great Newport Street. Watching it were Alec Clunes, director of the theatre, his wife Stella Richman and the man who was to direct their next play, Roy Rich.

The play was *The Male Animal* by James Thurber and Elliott Nugent, it was American, and they were desperate for a leading lady. The following morning the BBC forwarded a telegram from

Roy Rich to Barbara and after an audition the next day it was agreed she would star in the play opposite our friend Arthur Hill.

It didn't bother me. The grapevine had it that *A Streetcar Named Desire* was soon to start casting, and that auditions would be held for an actor to play Stanley. I couldn't wait.

♦   ♦   ♦

With Barbara in rehearsal for *The Male Animal* I found myself with time on my hands and spent most of it listening to the radio and reading. I took particular interest in radio because that was the one thing I thought I knew something about. Since 1946 I'd done less and less acting and more producing and writing. The Canadian Broadcasting Corporation, which had started out very much like the BBC, had long since given up resisting a commercial income. Given that we already had commercial radio in competition with the CBC, most Canadians could pick up American radio stations as easily as they could Canadian.

Radio Luxembourg apart, the BBC had a monopoly. The war had given it a special role, particularly in Europe, but now the war was over and, overseas services aside, the BBC had settled into a routine. It consisted of the Third Programme, the Home Service and the Light Programme. The Third Programme was aimed at intellectuals, the Home Service tried for a cross-section, and the Light Programme was for the general public, and in my view, totally patronising. "We must cater for the majority, who are basically stupid, therefore we shall give them what we think they want."

My assessment was that given different production values twenty per cent of what was heard on the Third could be comfortably accommodated in the Home Service, and forty per cent of the Home Service could be happily transferred to the Light Programme. I was to learn as I went along.

Newspapers and magazines concerned themselves mainly with austerity because that was the main subject of the day. I was particularly taken by *Picture Post* because I'd never seen anything like it. I suppose in these sophisticated days it would never occur to a magazine to have the President of the Board of Trade interviewed by a housewife.

The President of the Board of Trade at that time was Harold Wilson and here are some extracts from that interview.

HOUSEWIFE: How can you explain how I paid nearly £3 for a pair of shoes the other day? Before the war they would have cost me just over £1.

28

WILSON: Well, one of the main reasons is the high cost of raw materials which we have to import, and in shoes you've chosen a very good example. Out of that £3, nearly a third goes in raw leather. The other materials – things like packing – take another 2s 3d and labour nearly 10s. So before you've begun to count the manufacturer's overhead or profit, or the retailer's share, you're well above your £1. Actually out of that £3 only 2s 5d goes in profit to the manufacturer, and by the time the shoe reaches the retailer, it's already cost more than £2.

HOUSEWIFE: Well, doesn't that look as if the profit to the retailer is much too high? His margin is nearly £1.

WILSON: It certainly looks high, but you must remember that these margins aren't all profit. They're to cover all the expenses, the shop assistant, rents and rates, heating, lighting and all the other costs of a selling organisation. We watch the margins very closely, and we're satisfied that the retailer only pockets about a quarter of that £1.

HOUSEWIFE: Well, take this woollen-style vest I've just bought for my two-year-old boy. I paid 4s for it. I had to buy it two sizes too large because I know it will shrink as soon as I wash it. The shop would only let me have *one* because they said they were so scarce. You know that no child can manage on only one vest?

WILSON: I'm surprised you haven't asked me about nylons.

HOUSEWIFE: Well of course I do like a pair of nylons for best, but I haven't got time to go searching and queuing for them.

WILSON: I've got good news for you here. There should be many more nylons on the market in the new year, because during 1949 the magnificent nylon yarn plant which we're building in Pontypool in South Wales will start going into full-scale production.

HOUSEWIFE: I'm much more interested in things like sheets and towels than nylons. They're so dear and so hard to get.

In the same edition of *Picture Post* is a reader's letter headed, "A Canadian fears his appetite". It reads: "I've never been to England, but now I'm about to realise my childhood dream. I'm

29

looking forward to the beautiful English countryside and the mild climate. Are the rations really as scanty as the local newspapers say? Surely an eighteen-year-old with a small appetite could exist?" It was signed "Reginald M. Andrews, Hans County, Nova Scotia, Canada."

And in the *Sunday Pictorial* there was a quote from Gracie Allen, wife of George Burns. "My husband will never chase another woman. He's too fine, too decent . . . too old."

Well, that was forty years ago. Gracie's no longer with us, but George is over ninety and, according to him, still chasing women.

◆　　◆　　◆

I was invited to the Savage Club and introduced to a man called Mr Battle, who appeared to be something big at EMI. Mr Battle had heard that I was a radio producer and wondered if we couldn't do business together.

Next day I received a telegram from New York saying, "Don't sign with Battle until you've talked to me." It was from someone called Harry Alan Towers. How he found out in New York that I'd been talking to Mr Battle is still a mystery.

Within a week I found myself in Mr Towers's flat in Hallam Street being offered sherry that had been warmed by the fire. I had an amiable conversation with him and his mother, who seemed to have a proprietary interest in this pale young man. We discussed everything but business and when I left I assumed that would be the end of our association.

With John Mills

Two days later he called and asked me to present myself at the Star Sound Studios in Rodmarten Mews near Baker Street. He was starting a new drama series for Radio Luxembourg which he wanted me to produce. It was to be sponsored by Cadbury's, there were twenty-six episodes and he would pay me £100 per show. Well, in those days, you didn't ask questions after an offer like that.

I turned up at the appointed time and was given a script by Harry.

"The cast is waiting for you in the studio," he said.

I walked into the studio and almost dropped the script. The cast were sitting on chairs arranged in a semi-circle for the read-through and in the middle sat John Mills and Jean Simmons! I was going to direct John Mills and Jean Simmons . . . I could hardly wait to get home and tell Barbara I was in charge of stars.

◆　　◆　　◆

She had good news too. There had been a phone call from the office of Laurence Gilliam, Head of BBC Features, who had kindly arranged for both of us to audition with the BBC Drama Department. An appointment had been made, and we were asked to present ourselves to Broadcasting House Reception at 11.00 a.m. on Thursday morning.

Having produced drama for the CBC, I was familiar with auditioning as an actor, and auditioning actors. On those occasions when I'd listened to a dozen or so applicants for the same part I'd noticed that after the first half-dozen the voices began to merge into each other and become virtually indistinguishable. I'd lose my concentration to the point where it would have taken an Orson Welles or a Glynis Johns to make me listen.

Also, a Canadian friend who'd taken a BBC audition had explained that the producers couldn't see the auditionees, only hear them. They might even be on a different floor. "To make any impression on that lot," he said, "you'll have to commit an act of audacity." Barbara and I sat down together and contrived an audition script we hoped would constitute an "act of audacity". It was designed to attract and hold attention, or get us thrown out on our ears.

On the morning of the great day we were shown into a studio by a polite commissionaire and left alone with the microphone. The studio was immense, the ceiling high, and everywhere was the sound of silence.

At that point in time when our judges had presumably been

informed of our presence in the studio, a disembodied voice said through a loudspeaker, "Miss Kelly? Mr Braden? . . . you may begin now."

We let the silence sit there.

"I say, are you there?"

Nothing.

"I thought you said they were ready . . . can you hear me in the studio? Miss Kelly? Mr Braden? I said you may begin now . . . Dammit, there must be some foul-up between here and the studio."

At that point I said quietly to Barbara, "What are you doing here?"

"I've come for an audition."

"So've I. You don't sound English."

"I'm not."

"American?"

"No, Canadian."

"So am I. Toronto?"

"No, Vancouver."

"Me too."

"*There's* a coincidence."

I said, "What are you planning to do, for your audition I mean?"

"Well, I thought of reading Mary's Adoration of the Christ-child from the York Mysteries."

"Sounds like a lot of laughs."

"You don't think it's a good idea?"

"Why don't you try it on me? At least you'll get an honest opinion."

"Okay. Well, here goes."

Slight pause. The banter was in abeyance. Barbara then read the Adoration, simply and with feeling. I say "read". She'd played the part "live" on the CBC every Christmas Day since she was sixteen. It ended:

> Son, as I am simple subject of thine,
> Vouchsafe, sweet Son, I pray to thee,
> That I might take thee in these arms of mine,
> And in this poor weed array thee.
> Thou lovely Lord that last shall aye
> My God, my Lord, my Son so dear
> As Thou to me thy mother chose
> I do beseech Thee of thy Grace,
> For all Mankind that has in mind to worship Thee,
> Thou shall see these souls to save.

Jesu, my Son so free . . .
This boon of thee I crave.

Another pause. Then I said, "You have to be joking."

"No . . . I'm not. What are you planning to offer?"

"Ah. Well, I have this little routine I worked up to establish my versatility, what I do . . . I age from five to eighty-five in thirty seconds."

"How do you do that?"

"I'll show you . . ."

Then I went into my ageing routine which is impossible to explain here, but it had always gone down a treat in Canada. A sort of colloquial parody of the "Seven Ages of Man".

When I'd finished, Barbara sniffed and said, "That's the limpest monologue I've ever heard in my life. You can't be serious!"

. . . and that was the pattern. Each of us did two or three readings scoffed at by the other, and we did a few things together. These included duologues from Shakespeare, Shaw and Thornton Wilder. It must have lasted about twelve minutes. I think we ended with the Queen Anne scene from *Richard III*. Finally Barbara said, "I don't feel we're getting anywhere with this."

I agreed and said, "How do you feel about a cup of coffee?"

"Best suggestion I've heard all morning."

Still talking, we walked out of the studio, closed the door behind us and took the lift to the ground floor.

As we reached the swinging doors of the Reception exit, a commissionaire rushed up and said, "Miss Kelly, Mr Braden? Would you mind waiting a moment?"

About two minutes later a producer approached us and asked if we would mind coming back at 3.30 in the afternoon to do our audition again. Barbara explained that she'd had to miss a rehearsal of *The Male Animal* that morning and didn't feel she could ask the director for the afternoon off as well.

"Ah, yes. That's being directed by Roy Rich, isn't it? He works with us a lot. I'll give him a call and explain. I'm sure he'll understand."

Barbara and I went out to a three-course, five-shilling lunch and wondered what it was all about. Clearly they'd been impressed, but why did they want us to come back and do it again on the same day? At one point Barbara phoned the Arts Theatre and double-checked with Mr Rich that it was all right for her to miss the afternoon rehearsal. Then we just killed time until about 3.20 p.m., walked to Broadcasting House and went in.

We did the audition again, but this time we were asked not to leave the studio, and before we knew it, the place was thronged with people. The Drama Department had phoned every producer in Drama and Light Entertainment and about thirty of them had turned up.

A drama producer called Joel O'Brien booked me to play the part of Lieutenant Mulvaney in his forthcoming production of *While the Sun Shines* by Terence Rattigan; and both of us to take part in a two-hour production of *Green Pastures*, by Marc Connelly.

There was a young light entertainment producer called Ian Messiter who wondered if we could expand the audition to half an hour and put it on the air. We said we couldn't, but would try to think of an alternative idea.

We were taken to Hospitality and given tepid white wine. We met so many producers we couldn't remember all their names. As we walked out of Broadcasting House we decided, with fingers crossed, that our act of audacity had paid off.

The next few weeks were pretty busy. Barbara was rehearsing, I was still directing John Mills in *London Story*. We were involved in radio plays and there were constant calls from Mr Messiter wanting to know when we'd have a half-hour script for him to show the Head of Light Entertainment.

In the evenings we worked at it, and finally came up with an idea called *Leave your name and number*, a situation comedy in which I would play a Canadian actor trying to get work in London, and Barbara would be my agent. We even wrote a song as a theme for the show:

> Leave your name and number
> Say producers by the score
> We'll call you if we need you
> What's your hurry there's the door.
> We leave our name and number,
> But they file it on the floor,
> Tell me why do we keep coming back for more.

In due course we had a script and Ian Messiter sent it to Ronald Waldman, the BBC's Assistant Head of Light Entertainment.

Meantime, *The Male Animal* was about to open. Barbara's recollections of this major event in her life are virtually negligible. She was suffering at the time from a thyroid deficiency and remembers only a feeling of disinterest and weakness. It was her first professional stage appearance and she didn't even understand such terms as "upstage", "downstage", and "prompt corner". To hide her ignorance she learned her lines meticulously, but still claims she had no idea what she was saying or what the play was about. She recalls thinking that Hugh McDermott's perform-ance as the former football hero was well over the top, and that although her own role was a leading part, it seemed to her merely a sounding board for the central role of Tommy Turner (her husband), played by Arthur Hill. On opening night when she should have been in panic, her feeling was one of total apathy. That may be was why she came across as cool and completely in command.

For me it was an exciting opening night. Although the Arts was a theatre club, its reputation was high and all the major critics attended its openings, which took place every four weeks.

The audience reaction was phenomenal, and when the play was over I hurried out to the lobby to try and catch snippets of enthusiastic response, hoping that at least one person would say something like, "Wasn't the girl who played Ellen marvellous?" What I actually heard were lines like, "Where did you park the car?" and "Did you make a reservation for dinner?"

It took me years to learn that that's the sort of thing people always say when they come out of a theatre on opening night.

The reviews for *The Male Animal* were universally favourable.

News Chronicle: ". . . a wonderfully, exquisitely human play. It is also the funniest thing I have seen since the early Marx Brothers. Go and see it. Clamour for it to be brought to the commercial theatre with its perfect cast headed by Arthur Hill, Hugh McDermott and Barbara Kelly." Hugh McDermott, Newton Blick, Barbara Kelly and Jon Farrell) which must remain intact, come what may."

Sunday Express: "How refreshing to see new faces (led by Arthur Hill and Barbara Kelly) so uniformly good."

Kenneth Hurren: ". . . as a warm piece of humorous observation it is a masterpiece. Furthermore it is expertly directed by Roy Rich, and joyously performed by a company (including Arthur Hill,

Daily Express: "Red carpet is hereby rolled out. For me, actress Barbara Kelly made the evening with a fine performance." Leonard Mosley

Within a week the play had been booked into the New Theatre following its four-week run at the Arts. The impresario concerned was the late Henry Sherek, a cigar-smoking man whose girth was such that he had to book two seats on an aeroplane. Mr Sherek explained to the cast, all of whom were being paid £11 a week at the Arts, that although they were moving into a much larger theatre the risk was enormous, and he would have to lower their salaries to £8 a week.

A few days after the opening Barbara and I appeared in Joel O'Brien's production of *Green Pastures*. This play had an enormous cast, and it was fortunate that it was being done on radio because everyone in the cast was supposed to be an American negro.

It would be fair to say that Mr O'Brien all those years ago had

Arthur Hill, Hugh McDermott, Gerry Metcalfe and Barbara Kelly

trouble in finding fifty actors in London who could play American negroes, and there was a great deal of doubling up. It was a Biblical saga and I played both Noah and Moses. Indeed there weren't many North American actors in the country in 1949, and many of them were young men who'd decided to stay on after the war. When the Home Office required them to state their job or profession it was fashionable to say "actor", even if you'd never acted in your life. Entry to Actors' Equity at that time simply consisted of filling in a form.

One of these worthies, whom I shall call Nick, was clearly ill at ease in a radio studio and not too sure what a microphone was. In the scene when Moses comes down from the mountain with the Tablets and announces that the Children of Israel must continue their journey without him because of his imminent death, Mr O'Brien placed me in front of the microphone and required the rest of the cast to form a queue which filed past me, each murmuring, "Goodbye, Moses", to which I, depending on whether I heard a male or female voice, would reply, "Goodbye, son", or "Goodbye, daughter".

Nick was well towards the back of this queue and it occurred to him that it was all sounding rather dull, and perhaps needed an injection of vitality. I had become used to these murmured voices and was thus totally unprepared for the raucous cry of "GEE'BYE, MO-SESSSS!!!!!" How the rest of us got through the rest of this live transmission remains a miracle.

A phone call from Roy Speer of BBC Light Entertainment. He was starting a nine-week summer series to replace the popular *Music Hall*, beginning on July 23rd. It was to be called *Starlight Hour*, and had been presented the year before by Peter Sellers and Benny Hill, Geraldo and his Orchestra, with scripts by Frank Muir, Denis Norden and Sid Colin. This year, none of these was available, so Mr Speer was looking for "new faces" preferably capable of writing their own scripts. Would we be interested in writing and performing a weekly sketch?

We would. Mr Speer arranged an appointment for me with Mr Pat Newman, Head of Light Entertainment Bookings. In his office, Mr Newman looked at me for a long time before he spoke. Then, "Do you know how much Ted Ray makes?"

"No." (I'd never heard of Ted Ray.)

He told me. "Do you know how much *I* make?"

"No."

He told me. "Quite a discrepancy, wouldn't you say?"

"Yes."

"I hope you're not going to be difficult."

"So do I."

"I've been told you did an adequate audition for my colleagues at Broadcasting House, and indeed that you've actually appeared in one or two plays for the Drama Department."

"That's true."

"Also, Ronald Waldman informs me there's some speculation regarding you and Miss Kelly appearing in a programme for *this* department. These roles you played for Drama, were they . . . shall we say . . . supporting parts?"

"No, sir, they were leads."

"American parts, I take it. We're short of American accents since the war."

"Yes, sir, American parts."

"How much have the Drama Department been paying you?"

"Fifteen guineas each per show."

He whistled. "And you don't have an agent?"

"No."

"I can see I'm dealing with a shrewd man."

"No, Mr Newman, it's what they offered."

"DID they? Well, we're a little more generous here in Light Entertainment. I've drawn up a joint contract for you and your wife for the nine programmes. It pays you *twenty-five* guineas each for every show! What do you think of that?"

"It seems very . . . generous."

"I think so. Anything else you'd like?"

It occurred to me that for a "shrewd man" I hadn't done much bargaining. "In Canada," I said, "we always get top billing."

"Do you indeed? Very big Canada, but with a small population. Am I right?"

"Yes, you are."

"And of course you're not *known* here. Not known at all!"

That was true. As a matter of fact, we weren't all that well known in Canada.

He glanced through some papers. "We *do* have a problem. Brian Reece is presenting *Starlight Hour*. Now Brian *is* a star. He's known and loved as 'PC 49' and is appearing at the moment at the Adelphi Theatre in *Tough at the Top*. Are *you* appearing in a West End theatre, Mr Braden?"

"No, but my wife is —"

"— I didn't ask about your wife, I asked about *you!*"

"No, I'm not."

"Exactly. Tell you what I'll do. As you've not been difficult, I'll give you and Miss Kelly top billing after Mr Brian Reece. That can't be bad, now can it?"

"No, Mr Newman."

"Here, I'll just write it in the contract now." Scribble . . . scribble . . . scribble. "There we are. Now take a moment to read it through, then you and Miss Kelly can sign it and return it to me. Take your time."

I thought I'd better go through the motions. It wasn't easy to concentrate because Mr Newman continued to talk about his theatrical background, how difficult some artistes could be, and his active interest in amateur boxing. Suddenly a phrase in the contract stopped me short. I looked at it again.

"Excuse me, Mr Newman. It says here 'to do your act'. What does that mean?"

"Exactly what it says. You and Miss Kelly are being hired to do your act."

"We don't have an act."

"What do you mean you don't 'have an act'!"

"We're going to have to write a sketch for each show."

"To do your act. Once you've written it, that becomes your act!"

"No, sir."

Mr Newman assumed an air of patience. "I'm afraid I don't understand. Are you trying to tell me you wish to be paid extra to write a skit?"

"Nine skits."

"To do your act. That's what it says in your contract. That's what it says in *all* our BBC contracts. Except for writers. We have a different contract for writers because they don't do an *act*! You see?"

"Then I think we should have a writing contract as well as this one."

"So you *are* going to be difficult?"

"I don't mean to be."

"Yes, well, I think I'll just hang on to this contract for now, and have a word with the producer. *Perhaps* I'll see you again, Mr Braden. Good day."

We did meet again and became friends. In my ignorance I had questioned for the first time a basic BBC policy going back to pre-war days when music-hall comedians were indeed hired to "do their act" on radio. In the event Barbara and I were given separate writing contracts for, I think, ten guineas each, to write a sketch.

Pat Newman was as good as his word. The billing for *Starlight Hour* read:

Introduced by **BRIAN REECE** *and featuring*

BERNARD BRADEN and **BARBARA KELLY**

HOWARD MARION-CRAWFORD

ALFRED MARKS

DAPHNE ANDERSON   **MARCIA OWEN**

THE MEN ABOUT TOWN

Peter Yorke and his Concert Orchestra

and a visiting celebrity

Script by The Men About Town, Peter Myers, and Lionel Harris

Production by Roy Speer

TONIGHT AT 8.0

But no writing credit. That went to the Men About Town, Peter Myers and Lionel Harris. There was another regular on the show who contributed script and played small parts. His name was Spike Milligan. He got no credit at all.

Lest all that seem unlikely, let me add a postscript. More than a quarter of a century later, I received a call from a young and talented BBC Radio Light Entertainment producer called John Lloyd. Would I be interested in doing a pilot with Penelope Keith? I said of course I would ... but there was a problem. What problem? Well, Miss Keith was admittedly a television and stage star, but she'd last performed on radio before she'd become famous and her radio fee was set at £75. Mine was £100. Would I do the pilot for £75? I suggested that the problem could equally be solved by raising Miss Keith's fee to £100. The BBC couldn't see it that way. I couldn't see it their way and that seemed an end of it.

Young Mr Lloyd, as puzzled as I, came up with another solution. He had a programme idea in his files which he'd no intention

40

of using on the air, but he could do a pilot of it starring me. We'd simply do two programmes on the same day before the same audience in the Paris Cinema. I'd be paid £100 for the second pilot, and £75 for the one with Miss Keith. This ingenuity was irresistible, and I agreed. Since my programme had a cast of five and involved a musical group, it must have cost the BBC a good deal more than paying Miss Keith an extra £25 but someone's face was saved.

In the event my little mock-up show became a radio series, and the one with Miss Keith, which was called *To the Manor Born*, moved to television and spectacular success. If there's a lesson there, I wish I could fathom it.

What I do know is that in March 1990 young John Lloyd won the BAFTA Desmond Batis award for Service to Television, having produced *Not the Nine O'Clock News*, *Spitting Image* and *Black Adder*.

◆   ◆   ◆

It hadn't occurred to either Barbara or myself that we would need an agent in London, but the combination of my experience with Mr Newman and Henry Sherek's offer to move *The Male Animal* to an important West End theatre in which the cast would work for less money than they had in a smaller club theatre, gave us pause for thought. A Canadian writer called Joe Schull had given us the name of an agent in London, but no address. I asked John Mills if he'd ever heard of a lady called Olive Harding, and he said, "Everyone in the business knows Olive Harding. She's one of the top directors of the Myron Selznick Agency here."

Olive Harding

41

I phoned, and using Joe Schull's name got through to a very pleasant lady who immediately made an appointment to see Barbara and me at her office.

The Selznick office at that time was an imposing suite in St James's Street, and we were shown into Miss Harding's private office and immediately made welcome. She said she'd been trying for several years to sell some of Joe Schull's excellent radio plays to the BBC, but with no luck. Then she asked what we wanted to do. Her feeling was that she could certainly capitalise on Barbara's current appearance in *The Male Animal* which she'd seen, but what did *I* have in mind?

I told her the only thing I had in mind was playing Stanley in *A Streetcar Named Desire*, but that although I'd heard a number of rumours that the play was to be produced in London I'd no idea how to go about offering my services.

Olive said, "It's a good thing you got in touch with me now. They're about to start casting. Larry Olivier's directing, Vivien Leigh is playing Blanche — we represent them both, of course — H.M. Tennent are producing, and they're already looking around for someone to play Stanley. The only names I've heard mentioned are Sam Wanamaker and Richard Burton. Wanamaker's filming *Christ in Concrete* at the moment with Eddy Dmytryk, and Burton, of course, is playing in *The Lady's not for Burning* which is also produced by Tennents, so it's unlikely they'll release him from a successful play that's sure to run for another year. Marlon Brando has offered to come over and do the play for nothing, just for the privilege of working with Olivier, but Larry doesn't seem all that interested. I think he wants it to be *his* production."

So where did that leave *me*?

"I'll put a few feelers out and see how it's going. Meantime, why don't I take the two of you to lunch at the Caprice, where you can be seen?"

Clearly she *was* an important agent, and we were both a little taken aback that she was showing so much interest in two unknown Canadians. Before we left she introduced us to the head of the agency, Cecil Tennant (nothing to do with Tennents). Mr Tennant was just as welcoming, and wished us luck. He was married to the ballet dancer, Irena Baronova. Cecil Tennant is no longer with us, but his daughter Victoria is now a film star.

A few days later we joined Olive for lunch at the Caprice, which in 1949 shared with the Ivy the distinction of being the leading theatrical restaurant in London. Olive pointed out the celebrities sitting at various tables, but unfortunately most of them were totally unknown to us. Whether we were "seen" or not, is a matter of conjecture. Several people came to the table and greeted Olive, but when she introduced us I didn't sense any spark of interest.

When we left Olive promised to phone the moment she had any news on *Streetcar*. I sat by the phone for a few days but, after two weeks, gave it up.

Gilbert Harding phoned one morning and asked me if I could meet him at Paddington Station just before one and accompany him on a journey to Torquay. We'd be back in time for me to pick Barbara up from the theatre. For some reason it was imperative that I see Torquay. The reason of course was that Gilbert always hated being alone, and in the years to come I was to accompany him on many such journeys.

Gilbert Harding

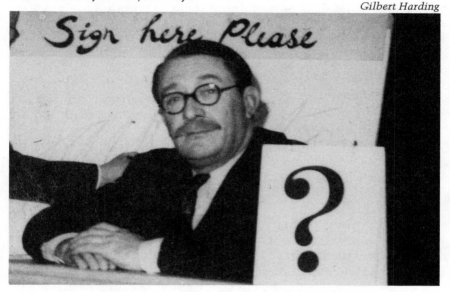

It must be stressed that at this point in time Gilbert was a face totally unknown to the public. He appeared weekly on a radio programme called *Round Britain Quiz*, but that didn't make him recognisable.

Gilbert led me straight to the dining-car where we sat down and were approached by a steward who asked if we'd like something to drink.

Gilbert said, "My friend and I will each have a very large whisky."

The steward apologised and explained that due to the shortage there was no whisky aboard that day.

"In that case we shall each have a very large gin."

The gins were brought and although we'd barely left the station Gilbert began directing my attention to points of interest and the history of each.

A few minutes later a party of four men entered the dining-car, and after they'd been seated the steward brought four tumblers and a bottle of VAT 69 whisky which he placed on the table. As he turned to exit, Gilbert caught his eye and beckoned. The steward joined us and Gilbert said, "Having informed us that there was no whisky aboard, you have now served those gentlemen a *bottle* of the liquid. Explain."

In a hushed voice the steward said, "That is Lord Ammon and his party, sir. They're on an inspection tour."

Lord Ammon had been created an hereditary peer as recently as 1944, and had now been appointed Head of British Railways after its nationalisation. Before I could stop him, Gilbert had got to his feet and proceeded to the other table.

"Which of you gentlemen is Lord Ammon?" he asked.

Lord Ammon identified himself.

"Would you be kind enough to explain to me why it is that my friend and I are unable to obtain a single whisky in this dining-car, while you, our servant, whom we employ to run it for us, are flaunting a bottle of VAT 69?"

Lord Ammon laughed and admitted that it did seem a bit unreasonable. "Perhaps you and your friend would care to join us for a drink," he said.

"Certainly not," said Gilbert. "You're much too recent a peer for me to drink with."

He then turned on his heel and returned to his gin.

A few years later, when everyone was familiar with Gilbert Harding and his lashing tongue, his critics used to accuse him of basing his rudeness on the fact that he was a celebrity. I mention this incident only to point out that Gilbert Harding, when he felt justified, was *always* rude.

One morning a call from Olive Harding: "They're seeing people for *Streetcar*."

"You mean they're holding auditions?"

"No. They're *seeing* people. I've fixed you an appointment at the Globe Theatre for two o'clock with Daphne Rye."

"Daphne Rye?"

"She's Binkie's casting director."

"Who's Binkie?"

Olive laughed. "Binkie is Hugh Beaumont, the Head of H.M. Tennents."

"What's so funny about it?"

She laughed again. "Binkie is the best-known person in the West End theatre, and the most powerful. But everyone refers to him as Binkie, just to prove they're in the know. Hermione Gingold once did a song called 'Who the Hell is Binkie?' and don't ask me —"

"I know who Hermione Gingold is. What do I do?"

"You just go to the stage door of the Globe Theatre, give your name and wait until you're called."

"Thanks, Olive."

"Good luck."

There was a queue at the stage door of the Globe Theatre, and I wasn't invited on to the stage until about 4.30. I'd dressed as much as possible like Stanley, and strolled on in what I fondly thought a perfect impression of his gait. I was chewing gum and acting tough. A feminine voice from the darkened stalls said, "Do you know the play?"

"Yeah, I know the play very well. I know —"

"I see you as Mitch."

"You what! Look, lady, I came here to read Stanley, and I'm not interested in —"

"Next?"

I was motioned off the stage and walked up the stairs to the stage door then out into harsh sunlight.

Once home I phoned Olive in a fury. "The silly cow saw me as Mitch."

"Bernie, darling, Daphne simply recommends, she doesn't select. I'm sure I'll hear from her again."

It never occurred to me that Olive had arranged all this, and had undoubtedly spoken at length to Daphne Rye, recommending me highly. My self-obsession was total.

Several days later . . . another call from Olive. "Tennents have phoned back. They want you to audition."

"Stanley?"

". . . Mitch."

"Oh."

On the appointed day I showed up to take my place in yet another queue. There must have been twenty of us. We were told to take off our jackets and roll up our sleeves.

As I approached within hearing distance of the stage I realised that all the candidates were reading Mitch's proposal scene with an attractive young actress. Closer still I realised that the girl was Mary Laura Wood whom I'd met at a party less than a week before. Another "act of audacity" began to form itself in my mind. It wasn't premeditated, or even thought out. It just happened.

I walked on stage, Mitch number eighteen, clutching my script. Mary Laura gave me a smile of recognition. There is always that moment of confusion allowed for while two people on stage establish their own rapport. In it, I whispered to Mary Laura, "Act one, scene two."

She turned to it and looked up. "It's the wrong part," she whispered.

I told her I knew that.

Daphne Rye's voice suggested it was time we begin. We then embarked on the Napoleonic Code scene with me playing Stanley and Mary Laura gamely reading both Stella and Blanche. After about seven minutes we were stopped. A voice from the darkness interrupted. It said, "This is all very interesting, but it's the wrong part."

I was prepared for the interruption but not for the voice. It was the voice of Sir Laurence Olivier.

My explanation sounded hollow, especially to me. "I'm sorry. I must have turned to the wrong page."

"Would you deign to read the part of Mitch?"

The word "deign" contained three syllables.

"Of course."

I then switched from my impression of Marlon Brando to my impression of Karl Malden, and read Mitch's proposal scene.

"Thank you," said the voice of Sir Laurence Olivier, and as I made to leave, he proceeded to the pit and leaned forward into the light. "Just a moment."

"Sir?"

"Do you strip all right?"

Rehearsals weren't due to start for two months. "Yes, sir, I do."

"We'll be in touch."

Again, I phoned Olive. "I think Olivier liked me. I think he wants me to play Stanley."

"Darling, I do hope you're right."

Blasted woman.

A few days later another call.

"They want to hear you again."

"Stanley?"

". . . Mitch."

"Damn."

No excuse for an act of audacity this time. I dutifully read

Mitch's proposal scene. The famous voice thanked me and I moved towards the wings.

Then . . . "One moment."

"Sir?"

"Would you care to read the Napoleonic Code scene as Stanley. I think you know where it is in the script."

Mary Laura and I grinned at each other.

"Sir!"

The scene was read with gusto. This time we were not interrupted.

"Would you wait there a moment, please?"

I would wait all night.

Now there was a series of agitated whispers from the stalls. Mary Laura took my hand, a friendly gesture for all to see. The whispers became angry, then one voice could be singled out, saying, "But no one's ever *heard* of him."

"I don't care. The man's an actor."

That was the voice of Olivier, and for a moment I didn't care if I got the part or not. But only for a moment.

The voices continued, but unintelligibly. Then, "Thank you, Mr Braden, we'll let you know."

Olive called a week later.

"They want you."

"Stanley?"

". . . Mitch."

"Shit . . . sorry, Olive."

"It's a firm offer."

"Who's playing Stanley?"

"They don't know yet."

"So it could still happen?"

"The contract is to play Mitch. Do you want it or not?"

". . . Okay."

I still had a feeling I'd get to play Stanley.

♦　　♦　　♦

Indeed, I had the cheek to write Sir Laurence a letter saying that since he appeared to have personally liked my reading of the part I'd be grateful if he'd keep me under consideration in the event that no one suitable could be found. He replied with a charming note saying that indeed he'd been impressed with my reading of Stanley, but that it didn't suit the production he had in mind.

Meantime, Richard Burton, in spite of the fact that he was playing in *The Lady's not for Burning*, had insisted on auditioning for Stanley. As an H.M. Tennent contract player he was on £10 a week, and even if he'd got the part that's what he'd have continued to be paid. A friend who was present at that audition told me it was sensational, and that Burton ended an angry scene by picking up a nearby chair and smashing it on the stage. Not only did he not get the part, but Tennents took ten shillings a week out of his pay packet until the chair was paid for.

♦   ♦   ♦

Yet another call from Ian Messiter. Ronald Waldman, Assistant Head of Light Entertainment, had read our script of *Leave your name and number* and would like to see us as soon as possible in his office at Aeolian Hall in New Bond Street. I was slightly nervous because Aeolian Hall was where I'd had my encounter with Mr Newman. We were told to take a lift to the fourth floor. The only other occupant in the lift was a young lady, but that didn't stop me telling Barbara I wasn't all that enthusiastic about our script, and would be much happier doing a situation comedy along the lines of *Ozzie and Harriet*, a then popular programme on NBC Radio in America. When we got out of the lift, the young lady offered to take us to Mr Waldman's office and revealed that she was his secretary.

Mr Waldman told us he'd heard a recording of our audition which had impressed him, and wanted to know some of the things we'd done in Canada. He said he spent a good deal of time in New York, not only listening to radio programmes, but watching their television because he hoped soon to be transferred to television by the BBC, which had not come to terms yet with light entertainment.

While we were outlining our background in Canadian radio with due modesty, the secretary wrote something on a piece of paper and put it in front of Mr Waldman. He glanced at it and then said, "Do you ever watch *Ozzie and Harriet*?" With a grateful look at the secretary I began to enthuse about the show, the way it was written and the way it was produced.

Mr Waldman then said, "I'm a great fan of it as well. In fact I was hoping to introduce something like it into television. At the moment though, I like this script of *Leave your name and number*, and it just happens that we have a hole in our schedules next week. Ian Messiter's very keen, and would like to do it next Thursday at the Paris Cinema with Robert Farnon and his Orchestra. Do you think you could fit it in?"

We thought we could, and left Mr Waldman's office walking on

48

air. There was a message waiting at home from Ian Messiter who wanted to talk about casting. We'd written in a "funny" cleaning lady, an elderly colonel, off which to play our Canadian ignorance, and a somewhat effete radio producer. Naturally we left the casting to Ian, who came up with Miriam Karlin, Norman Shelley and Reginald Purdell.

On the following Thursday we gathered at the Paris Cinema for rehearsal. Miriam Karlin in 1949 was a jolly girl who weighed about twelve stone. (Today she's a svelte eight and a half.)

Miriam Karlin now . . .

and then

Norman Shelley was full of good spirits because on the previous day he'd had the distinction of being the first actor to use the word "fuck" on the Third Programme, in a play by Ben Jonson. Even a BBC drama producer was not prepared to alter the dialogue of Ben Jonson. The only problem was that Mr Shelley had yet to discover anyone who'd heard it. And the fact that there had been no telephone complaints was an indication that very few *had*. Reginald Purdell had no difficulty sounding effete and indeed seemed to revel in it.

After a rehearsal with Robert Farnon and an orchestra that seemed much too large for our little play, the audience was let in, and we recorded the programme. It went on the air that evening, and the reviews exceeded anything we could possibly have imagined.

Samples were:

Evening Standard: "They wrote the very funny script themselves; they played more than twenty different characters, and they wrote the excellent theme song. With one home-made broadcast, the Bradens established themselves as two people who should be back on the air soon."

Daily Herald: "They must have their own weekly programme. They are fresh, bright and new, new new."

Listener: "One clever and highly professional piece of light radio entertainment which must not go unnoted was: *Leave your name and number* with two gifted Canadian top liners in their own script. It was interesting to compare them with Miss Grenfell and Mr Benson. We should like to hear more of Bernard Braden and Barbara Kelly." . . . Phillip Hope-Wallace.

♦   ♦   ♦

Starlight Hour was not due to start until the end of July, and rehearsals for *Streetcar* were delayed to the last week in August, so with Sir Laurence's question "Do you strip all right?" in mind I purchased some weights and began working out every day.

Also, Barbara and I had been invited to join a small privately run tennis club in Edwardes Square. The clubhouse was the former home of Andrew Bonar Law, the only Canadian ever to be Prime Minister of Great Britain, which seemed appropriate, so I spent as much time as possible playing tennis ... until one Sunday afternoon I leapt into the air to attempt one of my famous overhead backhand volleys. It cracked down on to the opposing side, but not as loudly as my knee cracked when I landed on the side of my left foot. By the time I'd limped to the club verandah, the knee had swollen to twice its normal size. Other members phoned for a cab and within minutes Barbara and I were en route to the Casualty Department of St George's Hospital at Hyde Park Corner. To take my mind off the pain I explained to Barbara what a marvellous opportunity this was for us to experience the benefits of the National Health Service, about which I told her I knew a great deal. Indeed, I enthused to such an extent that I almost forgot the pain.

At the hospital, a young man examined the knee and diagnosed a torn cartilage. However, he was not a qualified doctor, so he made an appointment for me to see an eminent orthopaedic surgeon at the hospital the following Wednesday, bandaged the knee, gave me a pair of crutches and sent me on my way. Back in Lower Sloane Street, with *Streetcar* rehearsals in mind, Barbara wondered if Wednesday wasn't a long time to wait for a definite diagnosis. I explained that the point of the NHS was that everyone was treated equally, and at no cost. The orthopaedic surgeon was indeed eminent, with a thriving private practice, and gave up three mornings of his valuable time to see National Health patients every week.

The appointment was for 10.00 a.m. and Barbara reminded me that I had a recording session at noon that day. I assured her I'd have plenty of time to get to the studio.

Carrying my card, I arrived on schedule at the surgery, was given a number and sat on a wooden bench for an hour and a half while the eminent surgeon saw other patients. I then rushed to a pay phone and called Harry Alan Towers to explain that I'd be late for rehearsal. He was most understanding, said he'd take the cast to lunch and delay the recording until 2.30.

Back at Reception the lady said my number had been called and since I hadn't answered, it was assumed I'd left. She wasn't sure the doctor would be able to see me at all. But he did. At one o'clock. A bluff, hearty, confident man, who examined the knee and announced that because of the swelling and contusions it was impossible to make an accurate diagnosis at this stage. He would make an appointment for me to see a physiotherapist next week, and would see me again in a fortnight, when, presumably, the swelling and contusions would have diminished. I murmured that the man in Casualty had suggested a torn cartilage. "No," he said, "that much I can tell you. It's not a cartilage."

The physiotherapist massaged the leg, placed pads on muscles, then applied electric shocks to make them jump. She measured the circumference of the thigh and calf muscles. "I think it's a torn cartilage," she said.

By now I was getting used to the crutches. But the worrying thing was that although there was no pain, the leg was bent into one position. I could neither straighten it, nor bend it back. I could actually drive a car, but could only get around on crutches.

Meantime, *The Male Animal* had moved from the Arts Theatre Club to the New Theatre, and the full play of Henry Sherek's publicity machine went into action. I was not pleased to read the following in the *Evening Standard*: "Bernard Brady [*sic*], husband of Barbara Kelly, leading lady of *The Male Animal*, swung into the New Theatre on crutches to attend an opening night party. He had fallen over the only male animal in the cast, Thurber the cat, and torn a leg muscle."

My next appointment with the doctor took a little longer. The swelling had gone down, and he could now tell me that I'd torn some ligaments. Another appointment with the physiotherapist was in order. He'd see me again in a fortnight.

Meantime, I took part in various plays for the Drama Depart-

Barbara and "Thurber"

52

ment of the BBC and was still directing the John Mills series for Radio Luxembourg. People were taking it for granted that I was permanently crippled because I was always on crutches.

♦ ♦ ♦

The Male Animal by James Thurber and Elliott Nugent. Not all of this play was written by James Thurber, and as with most plays, some parts of it are better than others. Clearly, it follows that what is not so good must have been written by his collaborator . . . the play works into its comic fabric a thread of serious thought. It is strongly yet evenly woven . . . and the weaving must, of course, be Mr Thurber's own. *The Times*

Elliott Nugent flew to London to see *The Male Animal* on June 28th at the New Theatre. He'd been in Ireland looking unsuccessfully for long-lost relatives and decided to see his play before flying back to New York. It had originally been produced there in 1941 but, with a lot of other plays, had closed shortly after the Japanese attack on Pearl Harbor.

I was with Barbara in her dressing room when he came backstage, and told him how much I'd admired his performance in John van Druten's *Voice of the Turtle*. I also particularly remembered a moving scene he'd played with Robert Montgomery in a 1929 film called *So This is College?* He gave me an annoyed look, then said to Barbara, "You made me cry when you said the line about 'the Shropshire Lad'. I always hoped to hear it said that way."

Barbara thanked him.

He looked at us both again, and said, "Hey, d'you know a place we can get a decent meal in this town at this hour?"

We said we did.

"Right. Let me pay my respects to the rest of the cast and we're off."

At the Albany Club it quickly became apparent that Elliott was less interested in a decent meal than a few double whiskies on the rocks and getting a few things off his chest. He pulled a sheaf of reviews from his breast pocket, and began to leaf through them, reading the headlines aloud. "Listen to this," he said: " 'Still an addict of Thurber . . . Thurber comes to London . . . The Thurber scene . . . Cream of Thurber . . . Thurber comedy . . . A Thurber joke . . . The Thurber touch . . .' What the hell am *I*, dirt?"

One of us murmured something about James Thurber being England's favourite American humorist.

"I know, I know. He took over from Mark Twain as *Punch*'s hero. But Thurber never wrote a play in his life, goddammit. I've written twelve. I starred in Booth Tarkington's *Seventeen* when I was a kid. I'm a writer, actor and director. I directed one of Harold Lloyd's films and five of Bob Hope's. *The Great Gatsby*'s playing in the West End right now with Alan Ladd. Guess who directed it?"

"You did."

"Goddamm right I did."

He toyed with his steak and ordered another drink.

"Jesus, it's like I didn't exist. You know the one that really gets me? It's that bit about the 'Thurber Touch'."

He pulled out yet another review and shoved it at us. "Look at this, look at this!"

We had, many times. It described a scene in *The Male Animal* where an ageing football hero decides to demonstrate one of his great plays from yesteryear. He uses a teacup as the football and, holding it aloft, backs towards the French windows ready to throw his forward pass. At that moment Tommy, the jealous hero, passes by the windows, lifts the cup out of his hands and disappears. The reviewer had singled out this incident as best defining "the Thurber touch".

"You know what happened?" said Elliott. "I'll tell you. It wasn't even in the goddammed play. I played Tommy in the New York production and I wasn't in that scene. So during rehearsals I used to walk back and forth behind the set learning my lines. One day I happened to glance up and see this teacup staring me in the face, so I just picked it out of the guy's hand and kept on walking. Then I heard this maniacal laughter and it was Thurber rolling around in the aisles screaming, 'Leave it in, leave it in!' The one moment picked out by this bastard as the Thurber touch was mine, and it was an accident at that."

By now Elliott, what with his pardonable resentment at being ignored by the London critics and the amount he'd had to drink, was becoming disorientated. He looked first at Barbara, then at me, and clearly hadn't the faintest idea who we were. He looked around the room, and obviously didn't know where he was. To our embarrassment he began to cry . . . silently. Great tears rolled down his cheeks as he sat in these foreign surroundings, where no one knew who Elliott Nugent was.

At that moment we heard a voice cry, "Elliott!"

Unsteadily his eyes went to the sound which had come from a man standing in the centre of the dance floor.

"Sam," cried Elliott. "Sam Zimbalist!"

Carefully, he got to his feet and wove his way towards the familiar face. Mr Zimbalist must have had a few because he was weaving too.

"Elliott!"

"Sam!"

Both crying unashamedly they fell into each other's arms and began to dance ponderously together as the customers applauded and the band played on.

Barbara and I paid the bill and slipped quietly out of the club. We never saw Elliott again.

Many years later I told this story to Leueen McGrath, the widow of George Kaufman and a friend of both Elliott Nugent and James Thurber.

"Poor Elliott," she said, "but the critic was right. That *was* the Thurber Touch."

"What was?"

"Saying 'Leave it in.'"

◆   ◆   ◆

On July 1st, I drove to Liverpool to meet our two eldest children, Chris and Kelly, who'd come seven thousand miles with their

Kelly, Nita and Chris

maternal grandmother to spend the summer with us and see their mother in *The Male Animal*. Barbara's mother also lived in Vancouver, and the baby Kim was staying with my father. Henry Sherek, who I was coming to think of as the Abominable Showman, sent a photographer to take some shots when I met the boat. All he got were pictures of two sobbing children wondering why their father was on crutches. I was beginning to wonder too, and to take it pretty seriously. The physiotherapist had told me I'd lost two inches round my thigh and that she was still convinced it was a cartilage.

At my next appointment with the specialist, he looked at my card, then at me. "Are you the chap on the radio?" he said.

I admitted it.

Kelly, Chris and Barbara

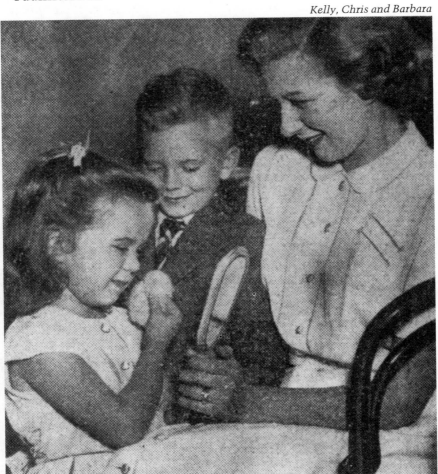

56

"Saw your wife in *The Male Animal*. Marvellous performance!"

I agreed.

"This knee of yours. Why didn't you come and see me privately?"

"Because I believe in the National Health Service."

"Highly laudable. Well, I'll tell you the situation. You've torn a cartilage, and it will have to come out."

"That's what everyone else said."

"Yes, but I wanted to be sure."

I then confessed my worries about rehearsals for *Streetcar* which were getting closer all the time.

"Right. I'll book you a room here tonight, and remove the cartilage in the morning. Have you on your feet in no time at all."

So "the chap on the radio with a wife in a West End play" would now jump the queue.

"No, thank you," I said.

I went home and phoned John Mills who gave me the name of a surgeon he knew, a Mr Gray. Mr Gray booked me into the London Clinic and removed the cartilage.

On the day I left the clinic I went down in the lift with the man who'd failed to diagnose the trouble. He was sharing a joke with another doctor about a cosmetic operation he'd just performed, naming the lady and his fee.

I never did get the full bend back in that leg so was unable ever again to do my favourite party trick in which I held a cane horizontally in front of me and jumped over it. A sad loss to my repertoire.

♦   ♦   ♦

The children and Barbara's mother stayed with us for more than a month. We were able to rent the basement flat at 34 Lower Sloane Street and installed them there with a temporary nanny, a delightful girl called Joan Cole. They were shown all the sights of London, saw Barbara's play and were highly entertained.

I hired a car and we took trips to the country. They were particularly interested in the fact that I could still drive a car with my left leg locked into a bent position. Much of what we showed them was lost on Chris and Kelly, I suppose because it was a bit of a culture shock at the ages of six and four.

Certainly they were intrigued by Madame Tussaud's, and Kelly had an interesting conversation (from her point of view) with the commissionaire at the head of the stairs, who turned out to be a dummy.

Since Barbara and I were both heavily involved in work most of the time, Barbara's mother showed them round places which she remembered from the First World War. Too often she couldn't find those places because the Blitz had wiped them out during the Second World War.

I do recall the occasional night out with Barbara's mother. Nita had been an ambulance driver in the First World War, married an Irish soldier, and emigrated to Canada in 1919. This was the first time she'd been back to London, and she was enjoying it to the full. She was one of those London ladies who hadn't lost her accent in thirty years and still spoke in, I imagine, the manner of well-brought-up girls of her time. "Girls" for example, she still pronounced as "gels".

One night we took her to the Caprice for dinner. We'd told her it was the "in" theatrical restaurant, and as we were shown to our table she lagged behind, staring at all the customers in the hope of seeing a famous face. We were slightly embarrassed by this because by now we imagined that people were recognising *us*. When she was finally persuaded to sit down at a banquette, she looked immediately to her right and found she was sitting just beside . . . GREER GARSON! Well, we had to order for her. She just sat there with her eyes riveted on Miss Garson, who was trying to hold a conversation with her husband, a Mr Fogelson. Inevitably she became aware of eyes boring into her, glanced at Nita, then immediately away again. To no avail. The eyes remained fixed on her countenance. Suddenly she turned and stared straight back at Nita. What she got was a beaming smile and a coy wave from a distance of six inches. Mr and Mrs Fogelson asked to be moved to another table.

♦   ♦   ♦

Sound Magazine, September, 1949 – "*Starlight Hour* will be off soon to make way for *Autumn Music Hall* but through its talented cast at least, especially in Bernard Braden and Barbara Kelly, it has a distinct and distinctive charm. Do the powers that be not feel it?"

Daily Worker, 23rd September, 1949 – "Brightest broadcast of the week was the first of the new series *Murder under the counter* by Bernard Braden in the Light Programme."

Daily Express, 7th September, 1949 –"Braden has been here only a short four or five months, but is already starring in two radio shows. In the second he presents a character of his own invention, 'Uncle Gabby', who is a wicked old charmer. To be the originator of a new London cry in four months is impressive to say the least, yet Uncle's 'Hull o o o there' seems to be the song of the dawn in my neighbourhood."

Starlight Hour was an immediate success and gave Barbara and me even more publicity. In our weekly playlet Barbara played herself, and I played a garrulous old man, Uncle Gabby, who pretended to be deaf and always entered with a raucous "HELLOOOO there!" Sample dialogue:

GABBY: HELLOOOOOO there.
BARBARA: Uncle Gabby, why are you late?
GABBY: Eh?
BARBARA: Why are you late?
GABBY: What d'you say?
BARBARA: Oh, never mind.
GABBY: I bet you wanna know why I'm late, Barbara.

. . . And then into a long and improbable monologue as to why he *was* late, usually involving an unexpected encounter with his friend Rishigan Fishigan from Sissigan, Michigan, or Roy Dejectedly, late of the Ohio State Home for the Shy.

At one point it looked as if we'd have to skip a couple of programmes because of my stay in the London Clinic, but no. Producer Roy Speer brought microphones into my room at the clinic and we recorded two of the episodes there. Hard to believe in this day and age, but this made the front page of the *Evening Standard* with a two-column picture.

Recording "Starlight Hour" at the London Clinic

Once out of the clinic I rented a bicycle and rode madly around Pimlico trying to build up my wasted leg. Rehearsals for *Streetcar* were about to begin.

In spite of all the exercise I'd taken, or possibly because of it, I was still limping badly on the first morning of rehearsal. The incisions weren't fully healed and had a tendency to bleed if I rode my bicycle too fast or too long. I took a cab to the stage door of the Globe Theatre and stashed my two canes in a cubicle, then made my way slowly down the stairs to the stage area. Since Mitch was involved in a good deal of physical activity during the play there was a strong possibility that my first day of rehearsal would be my last.

Happily, Sir Laurence had decided on a whole week of "readings". The cast sat in a semi-circle on the stage. We faced another semi-circle of chairs, the one in the middle occupied by Sir Laurence, the others by various people whose duties seemed to consist of solemnly passing messages to the director from the wings. He would either nod and tear them up, or scribble a reply, and we would wait while it in turn was passed by five hands to right or left until it disappeared.

My first reaction on seeing Vivien Leigh was one of stunned disbelief. I'd thought her beautiful on screen, but was totally unprepared for the personal impact. She was wearing a simple black jersey dress, the figure was superb, but the symmetry of the face beyond belief. I'd never seen anything so perfect. As I gaped, Renée Asherson complimented her on her dress.

"I'm glad you like it," said Vivien, "you're going to see a lot of it in the next few weeks."

Apart from sneaking sidelong glances at this vision during the first readthrough, my feelings were relatively secure . . . even smug. Given a week of readings there was a good chance my limp wouldn't be found out, and as a radio actor, I was used to "giving a performance" on paper. From time to time I gave Bonar Colleano, who was playing Stanley, a look of loathing.

Although I hadn't met him before, I'd been present at an incident which caused me to take a dislike to him. I'd been sitting in a BBC producer's office when Colleano walked in unannounced, with an enormous Dobermann dog, and clutching a script he'd obviously been given to read. He tore the script in half, then in quarters, and dropped it on the floor.

"That's what I think of your script," he said, at which point the dog cocked a leg and peed on it.

As he walked out Colleano said, "The dog's a good critic too."

So I was delighted to hear Colleano give an appalling reading of

Stanley. With the exception of Vivien, who'd taken an intensive course in the Southern American accent for *Gone with the Wind*, and a black American girl, all the others had trouble with the accent. Renée was taking tuition, Theodore Bikel was an Israeli, Lyn Evans was Welsh, and the others English, but I was particularly pleased with Bonar's apparent ineptitude. Sir Laurence gave no notes, but dismissed us for the day on the grounds that he was considering some changes in the script, including cuts. He asked me to stay behind. For one blissful moment I thought he was going to ask me to take over from Bonar. The others left the stage, including Vivien, and we were left alone. I waited.

"There's blood on your left sock," he said.

"There is?" I was all surprise.

"Yes. It wasn't there when we started."

The jig was up. One of the incisions had started bleeding and had seeped through the bandage down my leg. It was time to tell Sir Laurence the truth.

He listened impassively, then smiled and said, "Four weeks before we open in Manchester. I think you can make it. We can change certain things. For example, when you lift Blanche to show how strong you are, instead of lifting her up ballet-style, you can lift her up sideways and take all the weight on your right foot. Meantime, keep flexing that quadricep."

He walked off. I sat there for a few minutes flexing my quadricep, then walked up the stairs hardly limping at all. What I didn't know was that he'd had the same operation the year before in Australia and missed only two performances of *Richard III*.

Readings of the play continued throughout the week, punctuated by interruptions by the Boys' Brigade on either side of Sir Laurence passing notes and replies to and from the wings. I don't remember any of these gentlemen ever speaking. In scenes where I wasn't involved, I took to betting with myself as to which side the next note would come from, and in which direction the reply would be passed. Sir Laurence was aware of the incongruity of the situation. One morning an envelope appeared and was solemnly passed from hand to hand until it reached him, by which time we'd stopped reading. There was a silence while he studied the envelope for some time. Then he looked up at us and said, "Laurence Olivier, c/o *The Sunday Graphic* . . . oh well, they know they can always get me there."

Gradually I became aware that there was a purpose to these

readings. Our distinguished director was systematically altering the script and, on occasion, cutting it. I found this disturbing because nobody was really giving a performance, most of the Southern accents were abominable, and until they were right, many of the nuances of the lines would be lost.

I couldn't discuss it in the breaks because I didn't know any of the cast, with the exception of Lyn Evans, the Welshman, who made no pretence of understanding his *part* let alone the play. Also, it was none of my business.

The only person who argued from time to time was Vivien.

"Puss," she'd say, "are you absolutely sure you want to cut that line?"

"Puss," he'd reply, "absolutely."

And on we'd go. I wondered if Tennessee Williams had agreed to let Sir Laurence make these changes. He hadn't.

There's a point in the play where Blanche (Vivien) asks Stella (Renée) how she can bear to live with an oaf like Stanley.

Stella replies, "There are things that happen between a man and woman in the dark that sort of make everything else seem unimportant."

One day Renée read the line, and Sir Laurence said, "I'm afraid that will have to go."

"Larry," said Vivien, "you must be joking!"

"But I'm not, Puss, I'm not."

"Not only is it the most important line in the play, it's the point of the play!"

"A London audience will laugh, and we can't afford a laugh here."

For the next five minutes, they went at it hammer and tongs with neither giving way. Then Sir Laurence, realising that the cast was being treated to what had become a family row between the theatre's best-known husband and wife, called a halt.

"We must get on with the rehearsal, Puss. We'll hold this in abeyance and discuss it later."

For the rest of the play Vivien gave a very sulky reading.

Next morning we were all on tenter-hooks, awaiting the crucial moment.

It came, and Renée read the line. As the reading continued, Lyn leaned into my ear and whispered, "There *are* things that happen between a man and woman in the dark that sort of make everything else seem unimportant."

Perhaps he understood the play better than I thought.

In the second week, we took to the stage, and I was terrified. The slight limp apart, I'd never appeared professionally on stage

62

before and to be directed by Sir Laurence Olivier and play love scenes with Vivien Leigh was not my idea of an easy initiation.

♦   ♦   ♦

Radio Times: "9.30. 'Johnny Washington Esquire.' The adventures of a gentleman of leisure by Francis Durbridge. (1) 'The Perfect Alibi' . . . Johnny Washington – Bernard Braden, Inspector Marlow – Ivan Samson, Harry – David Kossoff, Ricky – Ian Sadler, Virginia – Margery Mars, Dave – Raf de la Torre, First Man – Andrew Faulds, Second Man – Malcolm Hayes, Waiter – Alastair Duncan."

Daily Herald, 12th August, 1949 – "I said Donald Peers would be a wow, and I said the Piddingtons would sweep the country. Now I say if you listen to J. Washington Esq. you'll hear the first of a long, long series of man-about-town adventures which will become the grown-ups' Dick Barton."

Streetcar was to open in Manchester, and having signed to play Johnny Washington Esquire by Francis Durbridge for the BBC, I was frantically recording the programmes in advance.

It was about the adventures of an American safecracker. One of the episodes required Johnny to masquerade as an upper-class Englishman, and the producer, Martyn C. Webster, took me aside: "Would you like me to get someone in to do it for you?"

Martyn C. Webster

Allowing for exceptions, there are few things so embarrassing to an English audience as a North American actor attempting an English accent. For North Americans the same holds true of English actors trying to sound American.

For many years I thought of myself as one of the exceptions. During my years with the CBC I had played Shakespeare and Shaw without criticism. At the CBC there was a London East End actor called Larry Burford, a middle-aged man who was invariably cast as a Cockney, which of course he was. But at the beginning of every readthrough Larry would say to the producer: "D'you want it Limey or strite Canadian?" We used to laugh at Larry, but it never occurred to me to think that I couldn't play "Limey".

While in Vancouver, I played the role of Paul Temple, and after one performance I received a phone call from a visiting composer, Arthur Benjamin, because "It was so warming to hear a genuine English voice so far away from home." I was flattered at the time, but now think the fact of being so far away from home had robbed Mr Benjamin of his critical ear . . . particularly since his original home was Australia.

I told Mr Webster I'd like to have a bash at Johnny masquerading as an Englishman before he made a decision, so he told the rest of the cast to take a break and repaired to the control room. Shortly his voice came through the loudspeaker: "Let's try a rehearsal." Drawing heavily on my impression of Ronald Colman, I read the page of script and waited for a reaction. When Martyn opened his microphone, he was laughing.

"No good?" I asked.

"It was fine," he said, "just fine. Let's record it."

So we did. The cast was brought back, none of them thought it was me, and we proceeded with rehearsals. After the show Martyn and I went to the Bolivar, a BBC club, for a drink. I said, "You were laughing after that rehearsal, what went wrong?"

"Nothing, dear fellow. It was perfectly satisfactory."

"Come on, Martyn, why were you laughing?"

"Do relax," said Martyn. "It was English through and through. I recognised three public schools, and two chaps I've never been able to quite place."

I went back to playing straight Canadian.

♦　　♦　　♦

Except, of course, when playing Mitch in *A Streetcar Named Desire*.

The plot of the play can be described simply, but inadequately.

Vivien as Blanche Dubois, with Mitc.

Blanche Dubois, having taken a streetcar called "Desire" gets off at a street named "Elysian Fields" where she plans to visit her sister, Stella Kowalski. She is distressed to learn that Elysian Fields is in a slum between the railway tracks and the river in New Orleans. Stella lives in two rooms and is pregnant by a husband whom Williams describes as a man who "sizes up women at a glance, with sexual classification, crude images flashing into his mind, and determining the way he smiles at them".

From the beginning of the play, Blanche is clearly fighting for her sanity and has fled to Stella as a last resort. The husband, Stanley, sizes her up at a glance as simply an easy lay, totally insensitive to the fact that she's obviously on the verge of a nervous breakdown. He therefore resents her genteel airs and the fact that Stella, who *does* understand Blanche's problem, supports her sister against her husband.

Stanley's friend Mitch, a simple man, who lives with his mother and worries about her health, is fascinated by Blanche and invites her out to dinner. Knowing that Mitch may be her last chance to regain a degree of respectability, Blanche cultivates him and reveals not all of her past, in the hope of eliciting a proposal of marriage. She tells him that, as a young girl, she fell in love with and married a young man whom she discovered at the wedding reception in the embrace of another man. Mitch proposes and Blanche accepts.

Meanwhile, Stanley has been checking up on Blanche's more recent past, and acquires enough circumstantial evidence to satisfy him that Blanche has been a prostitute. He informs Mitch, then confronts Blanche and Stella with his evidence in so callous and brutal a manner as to bring on the birth of Stella's baby.

Returning late from the hospital, drunkenly proud of his father-hood, he confronts Blanche yet again. She pretends she's had a telegram from a millionaire boyfriend inviting her to join him. Stanley calls her bluff and when she threatens him with a broken bottle, disarms her. Then, with the words "you and me have had this date from the beginning", he rapes her.

In the final scene, Blanche, having been persuaded by Stella that she's being picked up by a friend, suddenly realises that the two people at the door are a doctor and nurse, and that she is being committed to an asylum. She attempts to escape and is thrown roughly to the floor by the nurse. The doctor, recognising a

66

touching vulnerability, orders her release, helps her up, and offers his arm. As Blanche takes it, she looks up at him trustingly, and murmurs, "Whoever you are, I have always depended on the kindness of strangers."

As she exits, the play ends with "The woman upstairs" comforting Stella while Stanley and his friends, including Mitch, resume their poker game.

What none of us in the cast knew was that during the period of our rehearsals and the run of the play, Vivien Leigh was fighting for *her* sanity.

◆　　◆　　◆

As rehearsals progressed I became convinced of three things:

1. that Olivier was a brilliant director,
2. that he didn't understand the play, and
3. that Vivien did.

But there was a more important problem. Vivien Leigh was not an actress, and knew it. She also knew that the person who understood her limitations best was her husband, the director. So . . . when he gave her a direction she knew was wrong for the play, she couldn't be certain if he was giving that direction simply because he didn't understand, or to find a way around her own inadequacies.

He was like a magician, Olivier. One morning I was sitting in the stalls watching him direct Bonar Colleano and Renée Asherson in a scene that involved a deal of flurried movement. They couldn't seem to get it, although Renée was naturally graceful and Bonar a trained athlete and acrobat. Eventually Olivier mounted the stage to demonstrate what he wanted them to do. First he was Bonar, then he was Renée. It seemed incredibly simple as he did it, but somehow they couldn't seem to reproduce it together. I thought them very stupid.

Later that day I was rehearsing a scene with Vivien in which I was required to lift her from the floor, turn her round to a wall and lift the shade off a lamp so that Blanche could be seen in a bare light. Finally Olivier came on the stage to show me how to do it. He did it three times in succession, and it was like watching quicksilver. I could no more have done it than fly, but I realised that to anyone sitting in the stalls it must have looked incredibly simple. I achieved a semblance of it eventually, but it was never in a class with what he did.

There was one elaborate fight scene in the play involving all the

67

men in the cast, and Olivier devoted an entire day to choreographing it. As outlined by Tennessee Williams it was all over in a few seconds, but Olivier made it last about two minutes. Split-second timing, spectacular falls, furniture overturned, faked blows with sound effects, grunts and groans, ending with Stanley being knocked out and dragged into the bathroom where the shower was turned on to cool him off. To the audience it had the quality of genuine danger for the actors, and it must have looked as though at least one performer had been genuinely hurt. Well into the run of the play, we used to rehearse it regularly because there was always the possibility that someone *could* have been injured. Indeed, it happened once. But that couldn't have been blamed on Olivier.

He was incredible on detail . . . and helpful. Bonar Colleano had ordered some specially made tee-shirts with padded shoulders, the short arms loose, and coming almost to the elbow. He showed one of these to Olivier, explaining that they were designed to make him look bulkier. Olivier laughed.

"You know," he said, "this reminds me of when I was doing *Wuthering Heights*. I thought my arms too thin . . . and they were. So I designed a shirt with dolman sleeves, loose at the bottom, and ending halfway down the forearm. William Wyler tried to talk me

Bonar Colleano as Stanley

out of it. He said, 'Wear ordinary sleeves, down to the wrist if you like, but if you wear this I promise you'll regret it.' "

"What's that got to do with *this* shirt?" Bonar asked.

"You say you want to look bulkier. Why? You're slim, but you're all muscle and sinew. You radiate physical energy. Why not make the most of what you are? Wear a tight tee-shirt with short sleeves that really cut into your biceps. That way you'll *feel* your muscles and be aware of your strength. It will help your performance."

"What did *you* do? In *Wuthering Heights*, I mean."

"I didn't take the director's advice, and now I can't bear to watch that film. All I can see is my forearms sticking out of those sleeves like matchsticks."

Bonar grunted. "Okay. I'll try it your way." He didn't regret it.

Barbara was still not enjoying her run in *The Male Animal*, and feeling very much the amateur among professionals.

One night she was playing a scene with Hugh McDermott which was supposed to be interrupted by the arrival of another actor. The doorbell was rung at the proper time by the Assistant Stage Manager and McDermott opened the door only to discover there was no one there. The actor concerned was asleep in his dressing room three floors up. Only Barbara and McDermott could see that he was facing an empty doorway.

Barbara thought to herself, "Now I'm going to see how a real pro behaves when faced with an impossible situation. This should be really interesting."

McDermott turned to her and said, "It's the Dean of Philosophy. He wants to see me outside." He then went through the door and closed it behind him, leaving her alone on stage. Barbara stood centre stage facing the door and could hear footsteps running up the three flights of stairs to waken the actor, then footsteps running *down* three flights of stairs. The onus was on her to fill the time.

"What did you do?" I asked her.

"I walked over to a coffee table, picked up a magazine, sat down on the settee and pretended to read it."

What seemed an eternity to her was a matter of seconds to the audience and nobody noticed anything had gone wrong. By the time McDermott re-entered the room with the other actor, Barbara found she was totally relaxed and quite enjoyed the rest of the performance.

The other occasion that served to loosen her up was at a matinée, when she arrived, as she thought, in plenty of time to change and apply her make-up, only to discover that her watch had stopped, and she was in fact due on stage within ten seconds. She made her entrance in the clothes she was wearing, and in street make-up, and was surprised to discover that since, again, the audience didn't notice anything wrong, she was able to play the scene with a new sense of confidence.

♦ ♦ ♦

Now, in early September, it was time for me to leave for Manchester where there would be several more weeks of rehearsal before *Streetcar* would open at the Opera House. Shortly before we left there was a personal word for me from Sir Laurence.

He said, "I'm afraid the moustache will have to go. D'you mind shaving it off?"

Did I mind! I'd grown that moustache ten years ago before I'd even met my wife. She'd never seen me without it. Neither had my children. Did I mind!

"Of course not," I said.

The next morning I stood and looked at myself in the mirror. The family was assembling for breakfast. Quickly I grabbed the razor and shaved off the moustache. If I'd stripped off my clothes I couldn't have felt more naked than I did as I sat down at the table. Everyone behaved as if nothing had happened.

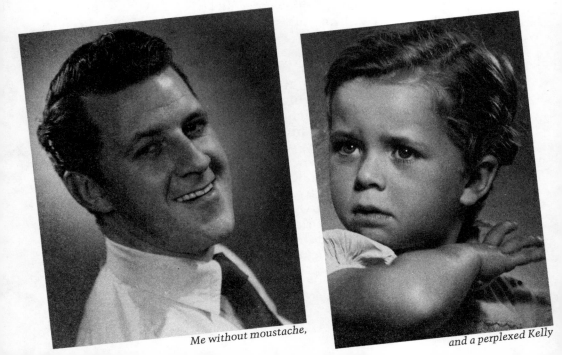

Me without moustache,   *and a perplexed Kelly*

"Pass the sugar, please." ... "Not too much Chris, it's rationed." ... "Can we go riding today?" ... "We'll see." ...

Barbara, her mother, six-year-old Chris and four-year-old Kelly all behaved exactly as usual. Finally Kelly put down her spoon, rested her chin in both hands and stared at me for a very long time. Then she said, "I don't understand you this morning. I just don't understand you at all."

That's when Barbara noticed, and started to laugh.

♦   ♦   ♦

It may have amused her, but I found it hugely embarrassing, not just during rehearsals but for most of the run of the play. The pictures taken of the production by Angus McBean made me look self-conscious and it was at least four or five months before my face began to look natural to me in a mirror.

I said a fond farewell to the children before leaving for Manchester, and shortly afterwards they started their long journey back to Vancouver.

♦   ♦   ♦

The set had been built, and I became increasingly concerned at the direction the play was taking. On the one hand, Olivier was changing the script and cutting more lines every day on the grounds that they were too tasteless for British audiences. On the other hand, he would suddenly insert new bits of business that struck me as being totally tasteless. At the beginning of the play there was a flurry of movement amongst characters on the stage designed simply to create an atmosphere before the entrance of Blanche. Upstage was a gauze backcloth the width of the set which functioned as the back walls of the two rooms in the apartment, but when lit from behind showed the street outside. A prostitute leaned against a lamp-post downstage and from behind came a newsboy who winked as he passed her and delivered a paper to the front door. On a whim, Olivier suggested that she rip his flies as he went by. This was rehearsed for half an hour, but the following day it was removed from the business.

Apart from being a neophyte, I had another problem. My contract didn't arrive at the Myron Selznick Agency until after we were in Manchester and when Olive sent it to me it contained several clauses I'd never agreed to, and others I'd asked for which were not included. I'd asked for featured billing, which was not mentioned. I'd asked for the contract to be limited to six months

71

(we were still thinking of returning to Canada before too long), but the contract said, "for the run of the play". Worst of all, and to me somewhat insulting, was a clause that had never been discussed. I was required to *understudy* the part of Stanley.

I phoned Olive in high dudgeon and she said, "Darling, I'm sure it's a mistake. Binkie's in Manchester with you. He's staying at the same hotel as you. Why don't you just have a word with him? I'm sure you can straighten it out in five minutes between you."

Every morning before rehearsal I phoned Binkie Beaumont's suite, only to be told he wasn't available. He stayed unavailable until it was time for me to go to the theatre. Every evening I tried him again when I got back to the hotel. Same difficulty. Sometimes the elusive Mr Beaumont was on another line, sometimes he was out, and on one occasion he'd had to dash back to London for an important meeting.

Meantime, rehearsals continued, and I continued to worry, particularly about the accents.

Lyn Evans played Steve, the man who lived upstairs and played poker with the rest of us, throwing in jokes written by Williams in a Southern dialect. One of these was about an old lady on her way to mass who, afraid of being late, began to run, tripped and fell down. Picking herself up she arrived in front of the church, dishevelled and breathless, stopped a passing policeman and

Lyn Evans

asked, "Is mass out yet?" Williams spelled it, "Is myass out yet?" because the Southern pronunciation was crucial to the joke. The policeman replied, "I don't know, lady, but your hat's on crooked."

Normally, Lyn would be the first to get a joke, but because he was taught all the words phonetically, he never really understood any of his lines. Indeed, six months into the run of the play he came off stage shaking his head and muttering, and when I asked him what the problem was he said, "Damn it, I can never figure out why the audience laughs at that line."

The opening of the play was fast approaching, and still no contact with Mr Beaumont. One day, a notice was posted on the bulletin board announcing an understudy rehearsal the following morning at ten o'clock. There was no opportunity for me to have a private word with Sir Laurence, so I just didn't turn up for the rehearsal. I had no intention of understudying Stanley.

In the afternoon Olivier walked up to me and said, "You weren't at the understudy rehearsal today."

"No."

"When we finish here this afternoon, perhaps I could have a word with you in your dressing room."

"Yes, sir."

Later, I waited in my dressing room for ten or fifteen minutes, until there was a knock on the door.

"Come in."

Sir Laurence entered and sat down. "You didn't come to the understudy rehearsal, and you didn't tell us you wouldn't be there."

"No, sir."

"Well, I'm afraid your contract calls for you to attend."

"I haven't signed my contract."

"Oh. Do you mind telling me why?"

"Partly because I never agreed to understudy Stanley, and I don't want to do it."

"But you gave an excellent reading of Stanley."

"And you told me in a letter that my concept of the character wouldn't fit in with your production."

"Well?"

"Well, if I had to go on as Stanley some night, it still wouldn't fit in with your production, would it?"

As I said it, the sheer insolence of the remark hit me like a blow from a sledgehammer. If he'd fired me on the spot I wouldn't have been surprised, or have blamed him. All that happened is that the Olivier eyes became laser beams and I could feel myself shrivel.

They conveyed an understanding of my rudeness and a disapproval like nothing I'd ever experienced except in a headmaster's office. Then the beams lessened and the eyes became normal again.

"You said you hadn't signed your contract. Does this mean you don't intend to open in the play?"

"No, sir. As soon as I can meet Mr Beaumont I'm sure we can straighten it out."

"And if you can't find Mr Beaumont?"

"I'll still open in the play."

"I see. Would you be kind enough to attend understudy rehearsals until I can find a replacement?"

"Yes, sir."

"Thank you. Good night."

I sat there for a few minutes and shook.

Events during the next few days ensured that there would be no more understudy rehearsals until after the play opened.

♦　　♦　　♦

Unbeknownst to any of us, Irene Selznick, who had produced the play in New York, was present in Manchester where she'd been discouraged from attending rehearsals. Mrs Selznick was no ordinary lady. She was the daughter of Louis B. Mayer, the Head of MGM, and the former wife of the most famous of the independent producers, David O. Selznick. Mrs Selznick had slipped quietly into a rehearsal and had been appalled by what she'd seen.

She insisted on a meeting with Sir Laurence where she expressed her unhappiness scene by scene and word by word. The cuts were the least of her worries, in spite of the fact that Williams had sent a telegram to the Tennent office saying: "Deeply distressed over proposed cuts in script since all material already cut has proven essential to character development, and quality of play."

In her autobiography, *A Private View*, she describes her meeting with Olivier and Vivien (who insisted on being present) as "a bruising experience for one and all".

♦　　♦　　♦

During the next few days many of the cuts were restored, and the entire ambience of the play seemed to change, as our director concentrated on the characterisations of all the actors, including Vivien. So much so that when Mrs Selznick slipped into another

74

rehearsal, she cabled Tennessee Williams: "Much better. Many changes. If only a few more . . . however most vital ones accomplished."

I, of course, knew nothing of this at the time.

♦　　♦　　♦

Opening night at the Royal Opera House, Manchester. Perhaps because Barbara couldn't be there, I've no recollection of it. Only of the party afterwards in the dining room of the Midland Hotel. There was a long table and I was seated between Vivien and Irene Selznick. Mrs Selznick had sent me a telegram saying: "I think you have a great capacity for *Streetcar* and success." I thanked her, and she said, "Are you happy in the part?"

I told her. At length. I ate the food and drank the wine without noticing it. I told her about seeing the 500th performance in New York, about my reaction to Brando, about my admiration for Olivier and Vivien, about my auditions and about my reservations − reservations, hell − about my horror of the cuts, the changes, the lack of understanding of the play. But mostly I told her about my anger at not being cast as Stanley. I knew I'd given a better reading than Colleano, and Sir Laurence knew it too. Why then, had he not *cast* me as Stanley and why had I been submitted to the indignity of being asked to understudy the role? I let my personal rancour outweigh my concern about the play itself. I used her as an outlet for my anger, with no sensitivity as to what might be her own feelings about the production.

Mrs Selznick made no mention of her own problems, which

Irene Selznick

were far greater than mine. She didn't tell me that her contract with Binkie Beaumont called for the English production to follow the style of her own New York production, and under no circumstances were any cuts to be made in the text. She simply said quietly, "Let me tell you something. Sir Laurence made it very clear to us that he wanted this to be *his* production. Now then. Tennessee and I were present at your second audition. When you read Mitch he leaned across to me and said, 'He's seen the New York production a hundred times.' When he heard you read Stanley he said, 'I was wrong. He's never missed a performance.'"

Now, why had it never occurred to me that someone who'd seen the New York production might also see this one, and would realise that I was merely giving an impression of another actor's performance? I began to sink lower in my chair.

"You understand," Mrs Selznick went on, "that if Sir Laurence had discovered you'd based your reading on Brando, he'd have blamed Tennessee and me. So we vetoed you as Stanley . . . but we did want you to play Mitch."

This remarkable woman had listened sympathetically to my self-centred complaints, eased my mind, and reminded me that I'd earned no divine right to the role of Stanley. I was suitably chastened.

♦　　♦　　♦

Up to this point in the chronicle, I wasted a lot of time checking out with friends and colleagues who are still around my memories of forty years ago. Theirs differed substantially. Mrs Selznick, for example, now insists that Tennessee Williams was not present at my audition, which, if I'd accepted her version would have killed a very good story.

I finally decided to eschew other people's memories after taking a friend to lunch and asking him what *he* remembered about *Streetcar*. He said, "My main recollection is you telling me about a telephone call you made as Mitch during the play from a phone fixed to the upstage flat of the set. You said that Bonar used to stand behind the flat while you were making the call and fill in the gaps with lewd remarks about which you could do nothing because you had to stick with the Tennessee Williams script."

I turned white but he didn't notice.

"That story stayed with me to such an extent that if I go to see a play today and the curtain rises on a set which includes a telephone on the upstage flat, I have to be carried out of the theatre laughing before the play begins."

I hurried home and re-read the play from beginning to end. I was right. At no point during the play did I make a telephone call upstage or anywhere else.

It was at that point I decided to depend on my own memory for this book. Hence the dedication.

◆　　◆　　◆

From the dining room on that opening night some of our party moved to the Oliviers' suite at the Midland Hotel. Famous faces had made the trip from London, and they were all crowded into this enormous room with a buffet laden with most of the foodstuffs still rationed in England. Gradually they thinned out, until only those actually associated with the play were still there. All the food was gone, and Vivien the first to notice.

"Puss," she said to her husband, "ring down to Room Service and order some chicken sandwiches and champagne."

Obediently Sir Laurence picked up the phone. "This is Sir Laurence Olivier," he murmured. "I wonder if we could have some chicken sandwiches and possibly a bottle or two of champagne."

He listened a moment, then hung up, and turned to Vivien with a shrug. "Sorry, Puss. Room Service is closed. After all, it is 2.30 in the morning."

Before Vivien could respond, the phone was jerked off the hook by Bonar Colleano, who demanded to be connected with Room Service.

"Listen," he said, "Colleano here. If you don't have three dozen chicken sandwiches and a dozen bottles of champagne in the Olivier suite in five minutes, I'm going to come down there and personally destroy this dump, brick by brick."

It arrived, and quickly. For me, the rest of the party is a haze. I must have had my share of the champagne, because the following morning I was *not* ready for the phone to ring in my room.

"Yah?"

"Binkie here."

"Wha'?"

"Binkie Beaumont. I understand you've been trying to get in touch with me?"

"Yeah, all week."

"I'm down in the breakfast room. Why don't you join me?"

The word "breakfast" almost made me throw up, but this was important. The hitherto elusive Mr Beaumont was now seeking *me* out. An opportunity not to be missed.

"I'll be down in five minutes."

Binkie

There he sat, the imperturbable Binkie, tucking into kippers and powdered eggs.

"Good morning, Mr Braden, you were very good last night. So are the reviews. What will you have?"

"Just black coffee, please."

"Coffee it is. Now then, I gather from Olive Harding there's some slight misunderstanding about your contract."

"Well, it's more than a misunderstanding."

"Do tell me."

"First, it's in my contract to understudy Stanley, and I never agreed to that."

"I believe you've sorted that one out with Larry."

"Yes, but I asked for billing, which I haven't been given and a six-month get-out clause. The contract is for the run of the play."

Mr Beaumont took a mouthful of kipper, chewed, and swallowed it. "What do you propose to do about it?"

"It's quite simple. I haven't signed the contract, and I'm not going to until the wording's altered."

"I see. Now, it's my understanding that under our agreement with Equity if a player opens on a first night he shall be considered to have signed his contract, and all clauses in the contract as set out by us must be adhered to."

"Pardon?"

"You needn't take my word for it. I'm sure your agent will bear me out . . . and so will your union."

So that was why Mr Beaumont had been so unobtainable all week, and so accessible now.

"I'll have to discuss this with my agent."

"Of course you will. Now as to the billing, I'm afraid that's not possible at the moment. Miss Leigh and Mr Colleano are well-known names in the West End as indeed is Miss Asherson. I understand you're getting some sort of reputation in radio, and it may be at some future date that could be useful to us, in which case we might well put your name up on the billboards."

"Mr Beaumont, I have commitments in Canada."

"Well, should you elect to flee the country, I don't think we'd be in a position to extradite you. Short of that, I shall expect you to honour your contract with me, which is for the entire run of the play in the West End of London. I'm hoping for two or three years. Ah, here's your coffee. Will you excuse me?"

And he was gone. A quick phone call to Olive confirmed he was right on all counts. It was to be the last run-of-the-play contract I *never* signed, and the only time I never had a get-out clause agreed before a play opened.

Because all the men had to be in reasonable physical shape for *Streetcar*, Sir Laurence had decreed that we work out with weights every evening before the show, and for some reason the weights were kept in my dressing room. Colleano gathered us all together before the second night in Manchester and put forward an idea.

"Listen," he said, "you guys all know that Olivier is a nut on

make-up. How long does it take to put the stuff on? Half an hour? Well, I don't know about the rest of you, but I'm not wearing any tonight. Just a bit of Nujol smeared on the face to make it look sweaty, and that'll come off with Kleenex."

"But as you said," Theo Bikel told him, "make-up is important to Olivier. He's bound to notice."

"The hell he is. He's got his wife in two follow spots throughout the play, and we're working mostly in the dark. I'm laying odds he won't notice."

We all went along with Bonar that evening, and he was right. Sir Laurence gave copious notes during the two weeks in Manchester, but never once did he refer to our lack of make-up, and none of us wore it during the entire run of the play.

He also called rehearsals nearly every day, and it seemed to me that most of them were for the purpose of further enhancing Vivien's performance at Colleano's expense. He was being asked to modify almost everything he did.

There is a scene when Blanche's sister, Stella, arranges a small birthday dinner for Blanche, attended only by herself, Blanche and Stanley. It's a pathetic little scene, made more so by the fact that Blanche can't resist teasing Stanley who finally erupts in what he believes to be righteous anger, stands up and sweeps everything off the table, including the cake and candles.

Olivier called a rehearsal of this scene and suggested that Stanley stay seated as he sweeps the table clear. (This was the same scene in which Richard Burton during his audition had, inadvertently, smashed the chair.)

Vivien was quick to object. "It's not possible," she said. "Nobody in those circumstances would stay seated. It's unnatural, Larry. Anybody who was going to do something like that would stand up to do it!"

Olivier was adamant. I was starting to feel sorry for Colleano.

On the other hand, many of Olivier's notes to the other actors were pertinent, and sometimes chillingly succinct. I mentioned earlier the fight scene he'd choreographed and the fact that one mistake on the part of any actor involved could cause injury. One night in Manchester Olivier called all the participants in the fight together on stage after the show and said, "I sat in the sixth row of the stalls tonight, and after that particular scene a man sitting behind me said to the lady he was with, 'Not a very good fight'." He then walked off the stage and left us to think it over. Needless to say we rehearsed it several times before we left.

One morning when no rehearsal had been called I got a phone call from Colleano.

"Hey kid, d'you play golf?"

Throughout rehearsals I don't think we'd exchanged a word. And now I was "kid". I was also about eight years older than Colleano.

"Yeah, a little."

"Right. We've been invited to have a game at Hoylake. Meet me in the lobby at ten o'clock."

He hung up.

At Hoylake we got the full VIP treatment. Nothing to do with *Streetcar*. Colleano was a film star and an American. Bobby Jones, the famous American amateur golfer, had won the British Open Championship on this course in 1927. It completed his Grand Slam of American Amateur, American Open, British Amateur and British Open in a single year . . . a feat never to be duplicated.

While Colleano regaled the members who'd invited him, I wandered over to a framed scorecard . . . Bobby Jones in the final round of the 1927 Open, and was joined by an elderly club member.

"You know about Jones?"

"A little."

"Bit of a fraud it was."

"How's that?"

"Well, there was this Irishman shot a twenty-nine on the outward nine in the morning. Looked bad for Jones, so the American press chappies got the Irishman into a bar and plied him with whisky throughout the lunch break. He shot a forty-seven in the afternoon and Jones got his Grand Slam. That's what I mean by a bit of a fraud."

Colleano beckoned. "Come on, kid, we're due on the tee. Let's go to the pro shop and get some clubs."

By the time we got to the tee it was surrounded by club members and guests anxious to see how Colleano played golf. After a bit of good-natured raillery he pointed his driver at me and said, "You go first."

I'd never played golf to a gallery before. Nervously I addressed the ball, stepped back, took a practice swing, then addressed again. Slow back swing, hold it, remember to turn the hips as you come through, keep the eyes down. My ball flew straight and true for a hundred yards, then veered fifty yards to the right and plopped unerringly into a bunker. There was a general murmur of polite condolence.

Now Colleano teed up his ball, stepped back and turned to face the green. He shaded his eyes with one hand, then grasped the club, addressed the ball, waggled his ass once or twice, and let fly. Two hundred and fifty yards straight down the fairway. Wild applause from the gallery. He acknowledged it with a mixture of modesty and "Well, what did you expect?" and moved to pick up his bag. The gallery retired to the clubhouse.

I played a safe shot out of the trap and topped my third so it rolled just a few feet past his first shot. He put out a cigarette and said, "What club would you play from here?"

"You're asking *me*?"

"Yeah. I'm a poor judge of distance."

"Well . . . I'd say a three iron should get you on the green."

He picked out the club, addressed the ball, and whiffed it by about three inches. Tried again. This time he drove the head of the club into the fairway about a foot behind the ball. Again. The club hit the ground behind the ball and pushed it straight up in the air about fifty feet. It landed a few yards in front of him. With no change of expression he picked up his bag and carried it forward. Looked at me.

"Still the same club, you reckon?"

I nodded. He took an almighty swipe that sent the ball forward about ten feet, well short of the divot.

Now he started to laugh. Chuckling at first, then gradually into guffaws. Clutching at his stomach he fell to the ground and rolled over and over, still laughing. Finally he sat up, wiping tears from his eyes, and gradually the laughter subsided.

"I don't get it," I said. "What's so funny?"

"What's funny is that I've never played before."

"What?"

"Never even been on a golf course. I've only ever seen golf played by the pros in newsreels."

"Then how do you explain that drive off the tee?"

"I told you. I've only watched the best. Also . . ."

"Yeah?"

His face became serious. "I had an audience."

"So what do we do now?"

"I'm sick of golf. Why don't we walk slowly round the course, mark our cards on each hole according to what we *should* have scored, then go back and brag a little at the bar."

I shrugged. "Okay."

"Oh. There's one more thing."

"What's that?"

"I get to win."

He grinned. I was starting to like Colleano.

◆　　◆　　◆

Early in the second week of the Manchester run I had my first intimation of "something strange about Vivien".

The only time we ever spent together alone, off-stage, was a two-minute period before the curtain went up on the second act, which began with the two of us walking up a ramp to "the street", and by some miracle achieved by set designer Joe Mielziner, crossing the stage, then re-crossing it to arrive at the front door of the apartment at which she was staying.

When I say two minutes, it could have varied by thirty seconds either way, but certainly both of us were always in position in plenty of time before the curtain went up. We'd engage in conversation about what had happened during the day. Sometimes she'd be Lady Olivier, and sometimes she'd be Vivien, depending largely on how the first act had gone. As Vivien she'd be friendly, and curious about the activities of other members of the cast. As Lady Olivier she'd be aloof and formal. One night, definitely as Vivien, she confided that she and Larry were having dinner that evening after the show with David O. Selznick and his new wife, Jennifer Jones, as well as the former Mrs Selznick, Irene.

She said, "I think I'm going to play Blanche in the film of *Streetcar*, and I'm going to suggest to David that you should play Mitch, because I think you're so good in the role."

While I was trying to stammer my thanks the curtain rose and we embarked on the scene.

The following night as we stood together before the same scene she made small talk and I decided that I was certainly not going to ask her what David Selznick had said. During the next four nights when we were alone the subject never came up, and I made a point of not raising it. On the Saturday night I realised we were at the end of our Manchester run, and I wouldn't see Vivien again until the following week in London, so I swallowed my pride and asked her if she'd mentioned me to Mr Selznick. Smoothing an invisible crease from her skirt on which she appeared to be concentrating, she said casually, "Oh . . . yes, I did mention you to David as a possibility for Mitch in the film."

After a fairly long pause, and hating myself, I said, "What was his reaction?"

There was another long pause, then just as the curtain rose, she said, "Oh . . . he said . . . 'a bit Shirley Temple, I thought'."

Then she linked her arm in mine and we started walking up the ramp to begin the scene. The timing was impeccable, and the subject was never raised again. It was the first of many similar encounters I was to have with Vivien, or Lady Olivier. She had this endearing quality of expressing admiration and affection

84

until the result she wanted was achieved, then she'd favour you with a head butt.

In the event, Vivien did star in the film of *A Streetcar Named Desire* and won an Academy Award for her performance. The puzzling thing was that David O. Selznick had nothing whatever to do with the production.

♦   ♦   ♦

In 1949, and indeed through most of the fifties, it was customary for new plays to tour anything up to fifteen weeks before coming into London. If the London run was reasonably successful the play would tour again for possibly eighteen to twenty weeks in other cities. There were more than forty number one touring dates at the time.

Because Sir Laurence was committed to a new season at the St James's Theatre under his personal management, it had been decided to limit the tour of *Streetcar* to just the two weeks in Manchester.

Mancunians were not surprised. They considered themselves the ultimate sophisticates as theatre-goers, backed by the prestige of the then *Manchester Guardian*. The ladies wore long dresses, and the men dinner jackets, not just on the first night, but during every night of the run. After the show the stall and dress circle ticket-holders would congregate in the main dining room of the Midland Hotel which was "the place" to eat. There was also the possibility of encountering members of the cast dining there, possibly even Sir Laurence and Lady Olivier.

Those of us who *did* eat in the Midland dining room were regularly accosted by men in dinner jackets saying, "We liked it, and you know what they always say ... 'If they like it in Manchester, they'll like it any place.'"

What they didn't know was that – at least in 1949 – it was generally felt by West End managements that if they liked it in Manchester, the play was in trouble, and would probably need script changes and a great deal of rehearsal to get it right for London.

After two or three nights of constantly interrupted meals given over to these back-handed compliments by Mancunians, Colleano suggested we find somewhere else to eat, and he and I took to going to a downstairs club called Nick's where there were no dinner jackets to be seen, and the food was infinitely better than at the Midland, because it was obtained on the black market. One night towards the end of the two-week run we were seated at the bar prior to eating when down the staircase came three couples, all the ladies in long dresses, and all the men in dinner jackets. One of the men walked up to Colleano and said, "We liked it, and you know what they always say . . . 'If they like it in Manchester, they'll like it any place.'"

Colleano said, "Do you know what I always say? 'If you like Manchester, you'll like any place.'" Well . . . the dinner jacket threw a punch, and before I knew it, I was heavily involved in the first fist fight I'd had since high school. As usual in these cases, most of the punches were clumsily thrown, and it wasn't long before Nick himself moved in to break it up. What surprised me was that when it was over, Nick threw the Mancunians out and showed us into dinner. Nick was a showbiz fan.

◆　　◆　　◆

The Opera House was fully booked for the entire Manchester run and then it was time to return to London for the main event.

We started rehearsing again on Monday 10th at the Aldwych Theatre, and when we came out in the afternoon I for one was surprised to see at the side of the theatre a group of people sitting on little folding chairs. The gallery queue had been started at 6.30 that morning by a woman civil servant, and would continue to grow until Wednesday evening when the gallery doors opened. Every bookable seat had been taken for the rest of the year. Ticket agency deals amounting to £50,000 were whispered about in awe. This may not sound a lot in these days of Andrew Lloyd Webber musicals, but you must keep in mind that the top price for a theatre ticket in London at that time was 12s 6d (62½p).

Aware as I was of the importance of Sir Laurence and Vivien I had not been prepared for the incredible publicity attending the arrival of *A Streetcar Named Desire*. Rehearsals intensified. One of the key factors in *Streetcar* was meant to be the all-pervading heat that should be apparent on the stage. Olivier kept reminding us all that we had to be aware constantly to fight the enervating humidity. But he still wasn't satisfied with the effect and had steam jets built into the area where Blanche took baths. These rose above the partition on stage and sometimes steamed up the set to such an extent that we really were fighting lassitude. On the Wednesday after the dress rehearsal Sir Laurence came to my dressing room and slumped down in a chair.

"I want to talk to you."

My arrogance had gone. I expected to be fired.

"I want to ask you a favour," he said. "I suspect that you

86

understand this play better than most members of the cast, but I wonder how much you understand of London audiences. I never wanted to be involved in the play, but when Vivien was determined to do it, I felt I had to direct it. London's never seen a play like this, and I was surprised we got it past the Lord Chamberlain, even with the changes we had to make. To the critics and the audiences it will be a foreign play, not an American play, a foreign play. If the critics lead the audiences in the wrong direction, the wrong people will come to see it, for the wrong reasons. In my experience there comes a point in every play when one section of the audience takes over the rest psychologically. I don't mean a group of people sitting together, they can be spread all over the house, but they somehow impose themselves on the rest of the audience.

"I think it happens in the scene at the end of the first act before you come on at the end to take Blanche out to dinner. The first scene of act two is entirely between you and Blanche and, depending on how the audience is behaving up to that point, that scene represents the only opportunity to control them. But unless you watch the previous scene from the beginning you won't know how to control them. So this is the favour. I'd like you to stand in the wings throughout the entire last scene of the first act, and just sense the audience reaction.

"If they've behaved like a normal audience you can play the next scene as we rehearsed it. If they've read wrong meanings into what's happened before and are getting out of hand, then I'd suggest you cut all the comedy out of the next scene, take it right down, and do everything in your power to get sympathy for Blanche. If you do that, we just might get the audience back in the right frame of mind. Will you do that?"

I said I would, because I understood for the first time exactly what he'd been trying to do in rehearsals. All the things I'd totally disagreed with. I understood it, but I still didn't believe the audiences could possibly react as he expected them to. In the event he proved to be absolutely right.

He put a hand on my shoulder, said, "Good night and good luck", and left wearily.

Again I sat alone in my dressing room for a while going through in my mind what he'd said, and finally realised he'd paid me a great compliment in suggesting that I might be able to alter the course of events within the play.

◆   ◆   ◆

Sidney Charteris wrote in the magazine *Sound*:

> On the opening night a strong force of police stretched their sinews to keep open a narrow lane in the vast gawping crowd outside through which ticket-holders struggled their slow way into the theatre. And when they were in, and the doors closed behind them, a crowd remained with the noses of the front rank pressed grotesquely against the glass panels until the play was over. Then came the maddest fight of the night – the audience striving to get out through a solid mass of sightseers, walled by a line of waiting cars. Such was the setting for the West End première of *A Streetcar Named Desire* and the biggest example of London lunacy in my theatrical experience.

Inside the theatre we knew none of this. As usual with a first night, the curtain was late up, probably due to the very scene outside the theatre described by Charteris, but first-night audiences are notorious for their lack of reaction to any play. On this occasion their mood wasn't helped by the fact that Vivien Leigh had had all the ashtrays removed from the seats, and most of us on stage smoked continuously. In any case, it was a numbing experience, this lack of reaction, especially after the over-reaction of audiences in Manchester. The one-time critic of the *Evening Standard*, Sir Beverley Baxter, once said that in his twenty-five years of attending first nights in the West End theatre he didn't think the make-up of the audience had changed by more than five per cent. By the end of the play I don't think any of us had the faintest idea what the reaction was going to be at the final curtain.

In those days the gallery was a big factor. It was dominated by an inveterate first-nighter, a woman, known in the business as Madame Defarges. According to legend, when the curtain fell, everyone in the gallery looked to her for a thumbs-up or thumbs-down, and reacted accordingly.

The entire cast formed a line across the stage, and the curtain rose as we faced the audience. I stood holding hands between Vivien and Renée Asherson. Above the applause and shouts could be heard from the gallery the chanting of a single word. Vivien said to me, "What are they saying, what are they saying?" I told her I couldn't make it out. But I could. They were chanting "ASHERSON, ASHERSON".

Meantime, the curtain was going up and down like a demented yo-yo. This resulted the following day in newspapers reporting that there'd been anything from nine to sixteen curtain calls.

Suddenly Olivier appeared like a streak of lightning through the pass door and ordered the curtain lowered. It was not raised again.

To the best of my knowledge it was the last performance of the play Olivier ever saw.

♦   ♦   ♦

Colleano had insisted that the first-night party be at his place. Well . . . when I say "his place" it was actually a mansion in Regent's Park which had been rented by Colleano's new partner, an American gentleman, who'd formed a company to make feature films. I think Bonar saw the first-night party as an opportunity also to launch a new company. Certainly there were a number of people there who had nothing to do with the production of *Streetcar*.

The Oliviers were held up in Vivien's dressing room entertaining a host of well-wishers, and didn't actually arrive until after 1.30.

Meantime, the morning papers had arrived and they were something to behold. The reviews took second place to the scramble outside the theatre, illustrated with innumerable pictures. One paper said:

> . . . Crowded ticket queuers demonstrated angrily outside the Aldwych Theatre today. The crowd departed the queue a hundred and fifty yards long when the box office opened at 10.00 a.m. and ninety gallery tickets were issued. Then about a hundred people who had not been able to get tickets protested that some of those in front of them had been issued with two tickets. A fight started amongst some of the queuers, and for some time Drury Lane was blocked to traffic.

There were shots of distinguished first-nighters, including film stars and politicians. The reviews themselves, when we got to them, fulfilled all of Sir Laurence's fears about the critics misleading the public.

The Daily Graphic: "The audience last night saw the play as a thoroughly unpleasant, grim, vicious American tragedy shot through with sentiment, American-style. There are scenes among the most harrowing ever seen on the London stage. There were twelve curtain calls."

The Daily Herald: ". . . the play is one of unrelieved sordidness and the squalid New Orleans setting is inhabited by vicious, boorish, quarrelsome people."

The Times: ". . . The purpose of this play is to reveal a prostitute's past in her present. In her pathetic attempts to revive her childhood memories her fading features are exposed to the merciless light of an unshaded bulb, and when she is raped her fumbling reason gives way altogether. She is led away to an asylum . . . the play is perilously near to soliloquy with rare interludes of action. Miss Leigh drifts to ruin on a tide of words."

Daily Express: ". . . Whoever said this is a great play? It is sordid, sexual. In this hell a brutish, bragging young Pole lives with his adoring young wife. The wife's sister comes to see them. She is trying to keep secret the fact that her life's been one long, immoral failure. This sordid story is geared to bring out as much sexual detail as is permissible on the stage.

The Daily Mirror: ". . . if you like to see a pregnant woman beaten up, if you like seeing a demented girl's arms being twisted behind her back by an iron-faced nurse, if you like seeing a crude American immigrant raping his sister-in-law while his wife is having a baby, if you like these things, you will like this latest American neurotic drama."

And so on and so on. Only the *Daily Telegraph* had a kind word.

". . . *A Streetcar Named Desire* is a moving drama from America. If the enthusiasm was not as overwhelming as on some first nights, it was because the house was numbed by the pitiful final curtain when the frustrated faded butterfly of a woman was taken off to a mental home."

Richard Findlater *The Tribune*: ". . . Vivien Leigh, in the role of Blanche, gives a remarkably skilful and sustained piece of acting. She sinks herself in the part, and she draws out Blanche's pathetic affectations, her intimations of lost innocence, her fundamental gentleness, the imminent hysteria; in such contrasted scenes as that of the birthday party and the soliciting of the young caller, she is admirable. But she fails, for the most part, to move. One admires her skill and resolution, but these are not enough.

Bonar Colleano's performance is a remarkable, controlled portrait, savagely real, but never caricatured. The brutality always seems a natural part of a natural man, except where the dramatist stresses it beyond any actor's powers. In a very different key, Bernard Braden's portrait is as remarkable: it is he, and not Miss Leigh, that strikes home to our hearts, with the suggestion of a deeper inner dignity and simplicity."

The acting came in for some criticism, but it was the play they were after, and they went straight for the throat.

♦ ♦ ♦

As is usual in these circumstances, everyone blamed the critics instead of the show, and the party was conducted as if we had a smash hit on our hands which, of course, we did. But I sensed that most of the people concerned would drop the false bonhomie the moment they left. I went miserably home to an empty flat, because Barbara had opened two nights earlier at the Theatre Royal, Brighton in *The Male Animal*.

During the rest of the week, and the one that followed, the publicity continued unabated, as did the damning reviews.

The Tribune: "... almost entirely lacking in dramatic insight."

The Evening Standard: "... nothing is left out that would help ensure a pleasant evening in the theatre for those who find excitement in lust and brutality."

The Evening News: "... a powerful, violent and disagreeable piece."

Sound: "... the play is sordid, sickeningly sentimental, has scarcely a single decent impulse, or a streak of humanity, and is entirely devoid of humour."

The Catholic Herald: "... lust, lunacy and the dreams that rise from sloth are the ingredients in this recipe for entertainment."

Punch: "... Mr Williams employs all manner of specious tricks to suggest that what is little more than exhibitionism is a work of art. If this is a great play, as New York appears to think, I am Ivan the Terrible."

The Observer: "... we are supposed to be moved out purged and fortified by a major modern tragedy, whereas all we have heard and seen is a messy little anecdote that somehow took the fancy of New York and must therefore be fashionable in London."

Picture Post: "... a play without consummation."

(This did not stop the *Standard* from proudly announcing that it had secured the rights to publish "the most controversial play of modern times" which would begin as a serial in the *Evening Standard* the following Monday.)

The attendant publicity followed well-worn lines. The *Daily Herald* reported that Lady Ravensdale had asked the Public Morality Council, "Could nothing have been done to stop putting on this play?" As the daughter of Marquess Curzon she had friends in high places, and her query was taken up with feature articles in the *New Statesman*, the *Daily Herald* (of course), the *Standard* and the *Catholic Herald*. The *New Statesman* pointed out that if you'd read the Sunday papers you would now be aware of phrases like: "a garbage heap", "crude bellowings of sex", "the reptile house at the zoo" and "talk like cesspools". It then added, "Mr Williams will either develop more positive values, or decline into the most successful playwright of our day."

Princess Alice and her husband the Earl of Athlone did not attend a special charity performance of *Streetcar*, because they did not approve of the play's subject matter.

The *Daily Mail* reported the inevitable vicar getting in on the act. ". . . the Priest Vicar of Southwark in the cathedral magazine asks: 'Is there no statesman in high places to speak out from other than political or economic matters and tell the United States to keep its sewage?'"

The *Daily Express*, having heard that Vivien had been offered the part of Blanche in the proposed film advised: "Say 'No' Vivien! No to the film of *A Streetcar Named Desire*. What *Streetcar* has to offer can't be put in a film. No censor would pass it."

And perhaps inevitably, the *Daily Tribune* reported that ". . . a twenty-two-year-old bank clerk died in a gas-filled room after seeing the play *A Streetcar Named Desire*."

Most damning of all was that virtually every review of the play referred to Blanche as "a prostitute", which she wasn't, and made a point of featuring the "rape" scene. The result was that a large proportion of people who came to see the play came only to see Vivien Leigh raped on stage. During the course of the run she received in the post an average of fifteen condoms a week.

At lunch one day, I asked Binkie Beaumont why he thought the majority of critics had reviewed the play so badly. Binkie said, "Critics, quite justifiably, like to think they make a contribution to the theatre and that to some extent they influence who will, or will not, pay to see the show. On this occasion we usurped that prerogative. The combination of Vivien Leigh, Sir Laurence Olivier, and the reputation of Tennessee Williams created, well before the event, a sure-fire hit. I think the critics knew that, and did their best to counteract it, but it was hopeless. In damning the play all they did was contribute to a box office success. The same applies to the ridiculous publicity. You can't buy a seat for this production before Christmas, and Lady Ravensdale helped contribute to the demand."

Another factor that Binkie didn't refer to wasn't so easily explained. For this production and for the Arthur Miller play preceding it, *Death of a Salesman*, Binkie had created Tennent Productions, a non-profit company (and therefore exempt from taxation), and had enlisted the Arts Council in backing both shows as contributing to culture. This meant that both productions paid no tax, while independent productions of the works of Shakespeare *did* pay tax. The result was a prolonged debate in the House of Lords and then in the House of Commons where, of all people, Sir Stafford Cripps (known as Christ and Carrots) was, as the Minister concerned, required to defend both the Labour government and the Arts Council for this obvious paradox.

◆   ◆   ◆

Meantime, we continued to play to full houses, and I continued to produce *London Story* with John Mills. Johnny was a delight to work with, and we saw a lot of each other. One day at lunch he asked me out of the blue if I'd ever directed a film. I said I hadn't and he asked if I'd be interested in trying it.

Well, of course, I'd be interested, but I was totally without experience. Johnny said he thought that didn't matter. The technical side of filming was in good hands, but he felt England was short of directors who could work with actors. He and his wife Mary Hayley Bell had just purchased the screen rights of a book, and as he outlined the plot I realised I'd read it. It was called *Little Boy Lost* and had been written by Marghanita Laski. Johnny said, "Good. If you're familiar with it, why not have a go at turning it into a screenplay?" I jumped at the suggestion and from then on, all my spare time was devoted to that project.

By now the tour of *The Male Animal* had finished and Barbara and I found ourselves invited to parties all over London. We met famous people who seemed to think we were famous too. It soon became clear that their interest was centred solely on *Streetcar*. Questions were thrown at me from all sides, mainly about Vivien and the atmosphere backstage, and how we all felt about working in such a play. It usually emerged that none of the people had seen the play, and few of them intended to.

It was a pleasant change, then, to be invited one evening to the home of Laurence Gilliam and his wife where there was only one other guest, a young man called Peter Ustinov. It turned out to be my first "Peter Ustinov" evening. For a few minutes I attempted to trade stories with him, but a few glances at my wife made it clear that she'd heard all my stories before, and would prefer that I shut up and listen to Mr Ustinov.

Peter had just returned from Rome where he'd played Nero in *Quo Vadis*. It was his first American film and initially he'd been fascinated by the director, Mervyn Le Roy. Le Roy was a dyed-in-the-wool Californian and never tired of extolling the virtues of that state.

93

Peter Ustinov

"Peter," he said one day, "I've just had a new house built in one of the canyons and I really miss it. This house has a dining room built like the back of a Spanish galleon and it overlooks the canyon, and sometimes when you're sitting there having dinner you can look out over the canyon and it's like . . . you're going away."

He was also very pro the Cold War and anti-Communist. One morning he accosted Ustinov and said, "That's the stuff to give the bastards, eh Peter?"

Peter wanted to know what stuff and what bastards.

"You mean you didn't read the *Herald Tribune* this morning? Litvinov arrived in New York yesterday by boat, and the long-shoremen wouldn't unload his bags. That's the stuff to give the bastards, eh?"

Peter suggested that in a civilised country like England the dockers would have unloaded Litvinov's bags first so they could start trouble on a proper level, but he sensed that Mr Le Roy either didn't understand or approve, so he decided to make some mischief. He discovered an extra on the set, a man built rather along the lines of the late Sydney Greenstreet, and dressed him in a white linen suit with a straw hat. The next morning he introduced this gentleman to Mervyn Le Roy as a friend of his who happened to be the Russian Air Attaché in Rome. Le Roy recoiled in horror and all he could think of to say was, "How do you like the sets?"

At this point Peter was prepared to reveal the joke, but found he'd underestimated his extra who said, "At home, we have beegar."

"What do you think of the costumes? We're taking them with us when we go, you know."

"At home they would be more colourful and richer."

Le Roy called Peter aside. "What did you say this guy was? Russian what?"

"The Russian Air Attaché for Rome."

"What's he doing on the set?"

"I invited him. He's a friend of mine."

Le Roy whispered into his ear and said, "Peter . . . you're playing with fire."

Peter said, "Isn't that what I'm supposed to do in this film?"

By now Ustinov had convinced himself that Le Roy was representative of all Americans, so he thought he knew how to treat the producer, Sam Zimbalist, who arrived on the set several weeks after shooting started. Now Zimbalist was a former actor, who'd started with the left-wing Group Theatre in New York where, because of his bulk, he always played the bloated capitalist, with little to do but listen to the fiery orations of those playing union members. Since the Group Theatre was strapped for funds the only props they could afford were cigars for the bloated capitalist to smoke. Listening to his fellow actors night after night, Zimbalist began to think, "What's wrong with sitting behind a desk, and smoking cigars while all these other guys are beating their chests?" So he went to Hollywood and became a producer.

"Peter," said Mervyn Le Roy, "this is Mr Zimbalist, the producer of the picture."

"How do you do, Mr Zimbalist. Are you by any chance related to —"

"No. I'm not related to the violinist. What's your racial origin, Mr Ustinov?"

"Well . . . I had one grandmother who was born in Odessa."

"Hasn't everybody?"

95

It was at this point that Ustinov realised Le Roy was not necessarily representative of all Americans.

In his autobiography *Dear Me*, Ustinov refers to the making of *Quo Vadis* as making him feel that he'd widened his horizons irrevocably. He says: "No one who spends close to five months in Rome, that glut of overripe peaches in a dish of hills, can ever be quite the same." Indeed he tells many anecdotes about the making of the film and his experiences with Mervyn Le Roy.

I think it's a tribute to Peter's ability as a story-teller that I, on the basis of spending one evening with him shortly after his return to London, have been able to add to those anecdotes rather than repeat the ones he used in the book.

Moreover, with all that time has done to his rich memory, he appears to have left out the tag of one of the stories he *does* tell. It's about the occasion in the Colosseum when former boxer Buddy Baer as Ursus was supposed to wrestle and kill a bull by breaking its neck. ("As Nero, naturally I had the best seat in the house.") For various reasons a chloroformed cow was used instead of a bull, and Peter explains that every time Buddy Baer twisted its neck and stood in triumph with his foot on its carcass, the cow looked up at him and mooed pathetically. What he doesn't mention, but did that evening, was that after one particular take the public address system through which comments were passed to a mass of extras was heard to emit the memorable words: "Mr Le Roy can still see de udder."

Twenty years after this evening, I found myself in conversation with Rebecca West, and asked her who was her favourite raconteur. Without hesitation she answered, "Sasha Ustinov."

"Don't you mean Peter?"

"No," she said, "Sasha. He was Peter's father."

A few months after our evening together Peter made his first trip to New York to help promote the opening of *Quo Vadis*. It was new territory and when he got into his first New York cab, he wondered if he'd be able to understand the cab driver or the cab driver *him*. As he opened his mouth to state his destination, the driver said, "Quo vadis, Mr Ustinov?"

On the Monday of the last week in October, I was taken to lunch at the Caprice, and as I was leaving was stopped by the mountainous figure of Henry Sherek, who introduced me to his lunch companion, Harold Hobson, theatre critic of the *Sunday Times*. Mr Hobson said, "What are you doing in that terrible play?" His review had not been kind. Some of my anger with the critics welled up, and I began to harass Mr Hobson for his lack of understanding. Henry Sherek interrupted me long enough to offer me a seat and order me a cup of coffee. I hardly noticed. For the next fifteen to twenty minutes I gave Mr Hobson the benefit of my opinion, explained that Blanche was not a prostitute, that we were all proud to be taking part in a moving play etc. etc. Mr Hobson was taken aback, Henry Sherek was embarrassed, and I left anticipating that my theatrical career in London might be shorter than I'd imagined.

On Sunday, November 3rd I was staggered to read in the *Sunday Times* the following, under Mr Hobson's byline:

A Streetcar Named Desire
Aldwych

When this play opened, the pressure of other productions prevented my dealing with it adequately. The condemnation of this play does grave harm, not least by suggesting to the salacious that it is the sort of thing they will enjoy, while discouraging serious theatre-goers from seeing it. It might keep the right audiences away from the Aldwych and pack the wrong ones in. *Streetcar* has been spoken of as "a nasty and a vulgar play", yet it is strictly and even puritanically moral. It is the story of a woman, not otherwise questionable, whose sexual nature, against the strivings of better things in her, is rendered so uncontrollable by circumstances, that she ends in madness ... without compromise of principles or concession to sentimentality, Mr Williams, looking into Blanche with inflexible judgement, but also with human pity, legitimately finds in her story many moments of touching beauty ... at the end of the third scene of the opening act, Harold Mitchell, the best of her blustering, filthy-tempered, brother-in-law's poker-playing friends, offers to light her cigarette. It is the

Mitch with Blanche

tiniest thing in the world, the commonest courtesy; it is also the first kindness shown to Blanche since the curtain rises, and she almost breaks down. Anyone who can watch this episode unmoved must be as insensitive as he is imperceptive . . .

I saw the play again on Wednesday afternoon, and found it almost unbearably poignant. I said a month ago that this performance casts out pity with terror. I was wrong. The terror is there, and the struggle with the woman medical attendant chills the spine. But the pity is overwhelming. Out of a score of brilliant details in Miss Leigh's performance, I will mention only one. Her pathetic nervous brightening at the merest suggestion of a compliment is heart-rending. I do not know which to admire the more, the power, the emotion of this performance, or the courage that enables Miss Leigh to go on giving it with undimmed lustre amidst these foolish suggestions that her play is a public indecency.

When Tennessee Williams died in February 1983, the *Sunday Times* invited their doyen of theatre critics to comment. Sir Harold Hobson wrote of the "sensational" *A Streetcar Named Desire* at the Aldwych in 1949. He said:

This story of a girl of good family reduced by rape to destitution, degradation and madness in New Orleans galvanised the British public which reacted with screams of hysteria. It was denounced as an evil thing, and Vivien Leigh, who played the debauched Blanche Dubois was vilified as an evil woman . . . the British stage was never the same again. The days of "boy meets girl", "boy falls in love with girl", "boy marries girl" were over.

I wasn't the only member of the *Streetcar* cast to be invited to parties. Anyone who had anything to do with the production was on everyone's invitation list. Since liquor was rationed, most parties in those days were bottle parties, but *Streetcar* people were often told they didn't need to bring a bottle. One member of the cast, Theodore Bikel, who played one of the poker players, was an Israeli actor who sang and played the guitar. Kenneth Tynan used to say that if you went to a party you waited outside the door and if you heard Theo's guitar, you went to another party. In fairness, Bikel became a popular folk guitarist and singer in the United States later, and played the lead on Broadway opposite Julie Andrews in *The Sound of Music*.

Bikel's role in *Streetcar* can only be described as minor, and the seating of the poker table was such that he usually had his back to the audience. Within weeks of the opening he began to tell the other male members of the cast about the number of fan letters he was getting from young ladies anxious to make his acquaintance. Bonar and I found this difficult to believe, but we were constantly bombarded with stories of his latest conquest, and amorous weekends spent with his fans. It was typical of Colleano that he decided to put Theo to the test.

Bonar arranged for his current girlfriend, Christine Norden, to write a letter allegedly from a girl who wished to meet Theo, and, if he agreed, to pick him up after the Saturday night performance in her chauffeur-driven limousine and take him home for a late supper. Needless to say, this letter was brandished about to the other male members of the cast as proof that Theo was not exaggerating. On the night in question, Bonar arranged for a chauffeur-driven car to arrive at the stage door at the appropriate time. In the back seat sat Christine Norden's attractive younger sister, aged fifteen. Meantime Bonar had arranged for another chauffeur-driven car, containing most of the cast including myself, to arrive at Christine's flat about ten minutes in advance of the expected arrival of Theo and his "fan".

The flat had a divided living room with doors and partition. Bonar had a talent for improvisation, and while we were en route he persuaded our driver to enter the flat five minutes after Theo's arrival, and pretend to be the young lady's husband. The driver demurred, but £10 changed his mind.

So . . . when Theo and the young lady arrived, about eight of us were seated in the dark on the other side of the partition. Christine's sister, doing everything in her power to appear sophisticated, offered Theo a drink and put on a Doris Day LP while she retired to the bedroom to "slip into something more comfortable". Through a slit in the door we could see Theo who, keeping one finger firmly on the telephone rest to make sure it wasn't actually connected, pretended to dial five calls and conducted five one-way conversations in five different languages. When the girl returned in her negligée and just as Theo was making his move towards her, the front door suddenly burst open and the driver appeared, pretending to be an outraged husband. It was a thoroughly convincing scene because (a) there had been no opportunity to tell the girl of this extra dimension to the plan, and (b) the driver was understandably nervous and therefore totally believable. He seemed genuinely upset as, of course, did the girl. At a point when we heard Theo say, "She never told me she was married", Bonar flung open the doors and we burst in on the scene.

Theo's first reaction was to say, "I knew all about it from the beginning, and just played along to amuse you."

Bonar said, "Theo, you were where you were supposed to be when you were supposed to be, and you've been caught red-handed."

At this point Theo looked around at us all and said, "Why don't we have a party? I'll go home and get my guitar."

◆　　◆　　◆

It was about this time that our lease ran out in Lower Sloane Street, and Barbara set about finding another place to live. Eventually she found us a ground-floor flat in a place called Chatsworth Court in Pembroke Road, close to our tennis club in Edwardes Square.

By now, the weather wasn't too good for tennis, but our new home boasted a squash court, so we purchased racquets and a ball and one day ventured on to the court for our first game of squash. After a few minutes we seemed to be getting the hang of it. Indeed I was getting quite confident, and as I stood behind Barbara waiting for her to make her next shot her back swing caught me square on the nose. Automatically I stepped quickly to her left just in time to catch the follow through in exactly the same place. Slowly I sank to the floor holding both hands over my nose and feeling it swell as I did. My pain was not eased by the fact that Barbara had also collapsed to the floor and was rolling about in paroxysms of laughter. By the time we got back to the flat the nose was twice its normal size and there were black circles under both my eyes. Barbara put a cold cloth over the evidence and phoned a doctor. He arrived and after a brief examination pronounced the nose broken and said if I came to his surgery within the next day or two he would set it.

There remained one small problem. I had to go on stage that night and appear to be a possible suitor for Vivien's affections. It never occurred to me not to show up. I borrowed some make-up from Barbara, and sitting in my dressing room did my best to mask the damage, but clearly it was going to show. It seemed only fair to go to Vivien's dressing room and knock on her door. When I entered, she took one look and said, "What happened to you?"

I mumbled something about playing squash and the fact that the damage had been done by my wife. Vivien sat me in front of her mirror and improved on my make-up job to the point where

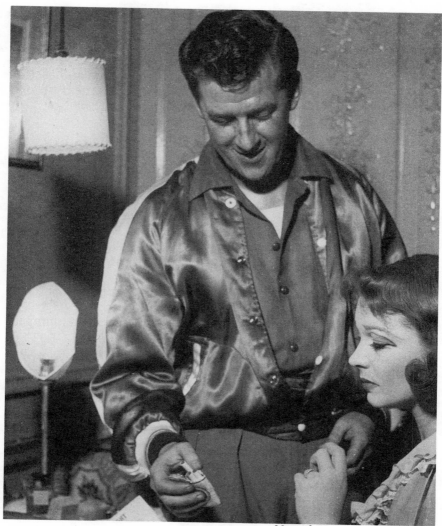

Me with Vivien in dressing-room

she decided I could probably get away with it, without attracting laughs in the wrong places.

As I was leaving, she said, "Your wife did that to you?"

"Yes."

"And were you playing squash at the time?"

It did help to lighten the atmosphere. In the event, I never got around to having the nose re-set, and it still shows.

♦ ♦ ♦

One afternoon I came home to Chatsworth Court to find all the blinds drawn outside our ground-floor flat. It was unusual, but I assumed Barbara had gone out and simply decided to draw the blinds. I used my key to get in and found the place in darkness, the curtains drawn as well. After calling Barbara's name and getting no reply I turned on some lights and moved towards the bedroom. When I opened the door and turned on the light there she was, lying in bed under the covers.

"What's the matter?"

She pointed to her wardrobe. "Look in there," she said. Inside was a truly stunning frock, but all the other hangers were empty.

"What's happened?"

"Well . . . I just decided to go shopping and saw that dress in a window in Kensington High Street, and I bought it."

"So?"

"It cost £95."

I whistled. In 1950 £95 was a lot of money. She seemed about to cry so I said quickly, "So what?"

"I brought it home before I realised it was pounds and not dollars, then I realised what I'd done."

"It's a beautiful dress, darling, but why are all the other hangers empty?"

"Because I shouldn't have bought it . . . so I grabbed all my other clothes and sold them at a barrow in North End Road."

"That wasn't very bright. You can't wear that dress every —"

"*You're* not very bright! Don't you understand? It has nothing to do with the clothes. I didn't feel guilty about buying the dress. I feel guilty about the children. They should be here with us . . . or we should be with them."

She was right . . . and I *should* have understood. From then on I tried to. It wasn't that difficult. I missed them too.

My "run-of-the-play" clause in *Streetcar* was giving me cause for concern. Here we were, Barbara and I, seven thousand miles from home and our children. The original idea had been to spend a year in England and then return home, hopefully to start a film industry, but if that wasn't on, to take up, as near as possible, where we'd left off in Canada. If *Streetcar* ran for a couple of years we'd be putting a strain on our professional connections and, more particularly, on my father, who'd taken on the burden of being responsible for the three children, even though there was a couple to look after them.

He wrote regularly, and was at some pains not to ask if and when we were coming back. It's only in the light of re-reading his letters that I now realise how great a burden it was, and how scrupulously he avoided asking the question. His wife of thirty-five years had died only the year before, and a house full of children, far from being a compensation, must have been in some ways an aggravation.

His letters were frequent and optimistic, but reading between the lines, as I can do now, there was an infinite loneliness of which I was blissfully unaware at the time. Also, he was terminally ill.

He phoned us on Christmas Day 1949, having sent us a turkey, to report on the progress of the children, and offer season's greetings. Chris and Kelly were each given their turn, and one-year-old Kim was held up to the phone to listen to her parents say "Merry Christmas". At some point, an extension phone was lifted and I heard the housekeeper say, "Your father is not well. He is very ill." Then his voice rasped through angrily, "Put down that phone, Mrs Fulton." He then proceeded to tell me he had a slight cold, and expected to recover quickly. I took his word for it. Christmas is a busy time for preachers. There are extra weddings, christenings and people to visit. It was *easier* to take his word for it.

Barbara and I spent a quiet Christmas interrupted only by performances of *Streetcar* and Barbara's first television play, *The Long Christmas Dinner* by Thornton Wilder, which was broadcast live on Tuesday, December 27th.

It certainly didn't occur to me that a proposed new radio series for the BBC would complicate matters. The BBC was constantly introducing new programmes and few of them ran longer than six or seven weeks.

In this case the instigator was a BBC producer called Pat Dixon who was known as the "stormy petrel" of Aeolian Hall (headquarters of Light Entertainment). Pat kept an unfurled Confederate flag in his office to underline his independence of the BBC hierarchy, and regular attempts to promote him into a safe desk job were met with scorn. When he disapproved of a memo from above, the sound of his anger could be heard in Bond Street, and it was said that executives would hide in the men's room rather than face him.

In late 1949 he conceived the idea of a breakfast programme that would make people laugh, and set about making it happen. Pat always started with writers and in this case he wanted Frank Muir and Denis Norden. Frank and Denis were together because

103

someone else in the BBC had thought up another programme to star Joy Nichols, an effervescent Australian girl. Naturally Joy would need support and the chosen pair was Dick Bentley and Jimmy Edwards. Dick had his own writer in the person of Denis Norden, and Jimmy had Frank Muir. Put them all together and the result was *Take it From Here*, one of the most successful radio shows the BBC had ever produced.

Pat felt – he told me later – that Frank and Denis weren't being fully extended, that they were restricted by the format of *Take it From Here*, and needed to be given their heads. Frank and Denis were interested in the money, but not too sure they wanted to stick their necks out writing what was to be, by 1949 standards, a mild form of anarchy.

Still, given certain conditions, they agreed to write the show. That settled, Pat said, "Now . . . who shall we get to play the lead?"

Frank and Denis suggested me. We'd met at the home of the late Richard Findlater and his then wife, Romany Bain. Also, they'd heard the pilot show of *Leave your name and number* and thought it had possibilities.

I think there was another reason. During the war British comedy writers had been exposed to the American Forces Network and had heard for the first time on radio the likes of Jack Benny, Bob Hope, Fred Allen and Groucho Marx. My Canadian accent offered an opportunity for Frank and Denis to write in an

Pat Dixon

American style, while retaining their own individuality. In the event, the only problem was mine. It took me several weeks to stop doing an imitation of Groucho and find a character of my own.

Typically, Pat Dixon hadn't heard of me. "Where can I catch him?" he asked.

In due course he attended a performance of *Streetcar* and promptly hired me. What there was in my performance as Mitch that made him think I could front a comedy show, I'll never understand. Perhaps it was his trust in Frank and Denis.

♦   ♦   ♦

On Saturday, January 14th, 1950 an announcement appeared on the bulletin board backstage of the Aldwych Theatre, heralding the 100th performance of *A Streetcar Named Desire*, and the entire cast was invited to join Miss Leigh for a glass of champagne after the evening performance to celebrate the occasion in her dressing room.

Well . . . not quite the entire cast. The technical crew was not included, nor indeed were the two distinguished musicians Kenny Baker and Norman Stenfalt. *They* were invited to partake of several cases of beer *under* the stage, behind the pit. They did not partake, but repaired to various pubs in the neighbourhood and celebrated as they saw fit. The cases of beer were not opened.

The rest of us assembled in due course in twos and threes in what was admittedly a small area, albeit a suite of two rooms. There was indeed champagne, served by Robert Helpmann who'd been invited as a weekend guest to the Oliviers' country home, Notley Abbey, and therefore pressed into service.

Helpmann took the opportunity to tell me of his *first* visit to Notley Abbey. He'd been given directions, but as with most of us they somehow went wrong. Notley Abbey was in the vicinity of a village called Thame, and after an hour or so enquiring of directions, Helpmann decided to forget Notley Abbey and concentrate on Thame. Arriving at some hamlet at an hour well past midnight, Helpmann saw a policeman and, anxious not to prolong the conversation, stopped his car, pointed ahead and asked, "Thame?" . . . The policeman looked at his watch and said, "Faive and twenty past one, sir."

What emerged fairly soon was that there was not a *lot* of champagne. The idea seemed to be that we should just have one drink and leave. This was made particularly clear to the only imported American in our cast, a lady called Bruce West, who'd

105

been brought from New York specifically for the show. She played a minute part, but with total authenticity.

Sensing Vivien's desire to "get this thing over with as quickly as possible" Bruce paused at the door as she left, leaned sensually against the door jamb and said, "When I did *The Pirate* with the Lunts in New York, on the 100th performance it was $100 bills for each and every member of the cast." On that note she left.

The rest of us were not too far behind.

♦ ♦ ♦

A few days later we all sat down in Pat Dixon's office for the first readthrough of the first programme of *Breakfast with Braden*. Singers Pearl Carr and Benny Lee, bandleader Nat Temple, arranger Malcolm Lockyer and announcer Ronald Fletcher . . . with Pat in the chair. Only three or four times in my life have I sat through a readthrough that had the smell of success and a sense of excitement from the beginning. This was one. Muir and Norden had evolved characters for all of us. My opening line was, "Hello, my name is Bernard Braden and I'm not an Englishman trying to sound like an American. I'm a Canadian trying to sound like an American . . . and this is not a flash suit I'm wearing it's my pyjamas." Typically, Frank and Denis had incorporated Pat's "Who shall we get to play the lead?" in my opening monologue . . . "Some of you might like to know how a show like this gets on the air. Well, it's quite simple. The planners are sitting around a table playing bridge, when one of them says, 'Look, we simply must find a title for this new programme.' Eventually someone

Breakfast cast

says, 'How about, *Breakfast with Braden*' and someone else says, 'Great, but who shall we get to play the lead?' Would you believe they spent three months looking for a guy called 'Breakfast' before they got round to me?"

But the monologue was merely an introduction. I knew that Pearl Carr and Benny Lee were singers, I hadn't realised how brilliant they were at reading lines. Muir and Norden had given them good lines . . . but more than that . . . a persona that blended with each of the others. It was typically painstaking of Frank and Denis that they conceived relationships between all these people. To Benny and Pearl I was "Mr Braden", while I called them "Benny and Pearl". I called Ronald Fletcher, "*Mr* Fletcher", he called me "Braden". To him, Nat Temple was "Temple", Benny Lee was "Lee" and Pearl was "Miss Carr". Nat Temple called Ronald Fletcher "Fletch boy" and he called me "Bern". Thanks to our writers, we all knew where we stood with each other from the beginning.

One of the conditions imposed by Frank and Denis was that there would be no writing credits. In attempting to meet Pat's request that the show would be unlike any other on radio, they'd conceived the idea of a script that didn't sound as if it had been written, and they felt that my approach, North American in style, lent itself to the idea. Accordingly, the script was full of interruptions, non sequiturs and tangents. I might begin the programme with some exercises which would start with, "First, place one foot on the mantelpiece, then —" I'd be interrupted by the sound effect of a door opening and a man saying, "Sorry, wrong studio," after which the door would close. I would then embark on another

Denis Norden and Frank Muir

train of thought, leading up to something like, "There was this pig that found itself –" at which point Benny Lee would enter and say, "Good morning, Mr Braden. Sorry I'm late." I'd ask him why he was late, and he'd say, "My wife had trouble making the tea." I'd suggest that wasn't a very good excuse, and Benny would say, "It's not very easy making tea when you've got one foot on the mantelpiece."

Then we'd change the subject until I was reminded that it was time for Pearl to sing a song. After the song, I would immediately say, "I was going to tell you about this pig, wasn't I?"

By using this technique, and skilfully writing lines that sounded like ad libs, Frank and Denis hoped to convince the radio audience that the show was totally unrehearsed and had not been written. Theoretically, we were just saying whatever came into our heads.

Pearl and Benny

Charlie Katz

After the readthrough no lines were changed and there was no more rehearsal. Pearl and Benny had already rehearsed their numbers with the orchestra, so we went straight into the studio and recorded the show! This was based on another theory of Pat Dixon's. The band, having never heard the lines before, functioned as the studio audience. One of them, Charlie Katz, had so distinctive and infectious a laugh that eventually he was written into the show, and it was revealed that in addition to there being a Mrs Katz, there were also several kittens. One more Dixon rule. Whatever went wrong, however badly, we had to get ourselves out of it. There would be no stopping the recording.

I've discussed that first show with everyone concerned since, and each had the same initial feeling of taking part in something special. Pat's sense of spontaneity had a lot to do with it. So did Frank Muir and Denis Norden.

Barbara sat in the control room for that first show. On our way home she said, "I think you've got a winner there."

The first *Breakfast with Braden* was billed to go out on Saturday morning, January 21st. It didn't. Something intervened.

♦ ♦ ♦

At the theatre a few nights after the recording I was called to the stage door after the first act to take a telephone call. The voice was instantly recognisable. Dr Riggs, who'd been our family doctor since 1923.

"Bernard?"

"Yes, Dr Riggs."

"It's Dr Riggs."

"I know."

"Somebody gave me this number in case I wanted you urgently."

"What is it?"

"I'm calling from Vancouver."

"Yes."

"If you want to see your father alive, you'd better get here as quickly as possible."

"Oh . . . thank you."

"Goodbye."

He hung up. This wasn't rudeness. It was probably the first transatlantic call he'd ever made, and Dr Riggs was a frugal man. What he didn't know was that I must now go on stage and play a long scene with Vivien. No time to set anything in motion.

Throughout that scene I thought only of my father whom I'd come to believe would never die. When you've been in a play for some months, it's possible to think of something other than the play, but not advisable. About fifteen minutes into the scene I realised I was being unfair to Vivien and to the audience. I must pull myself together and concentrate on the play. I made a conscious effort and immediately forgot my lines. Suddenly I was on the wrong side of the stage, and Vivien was looking at me with a very puzzled expression. I went back to thinking of my father and finished the scene – indeed the play – without difficulty.

No point in telling anyone that night. The following morning I phoned Binkie and relayed Dr Riggs's message. He was immediately sympathetic, but said he must check with Sir Laurence. Did I have any idea how long I'd be gone? I said I didn't. Within minutes he called back to tell me that both Sir Laurence and Vivien had agreed that I must fly to Vancouver on the first possible plane and that all three of them would use their influence to facilitate it. Meantime, Sir Laurence was unavailable to rehearse my understudy, so would I be kind enough to take an understudy rehearsal that afternoon?

I'm not sure to this day if Sir Laurence was unavailable. It may just have been a way to keep me busy and thinking of something else while I waited for the plane. Barbara said she'd stay home to take any messages that might come from Vancouver or the H.M. Tennent office. She also started packing my bag. At the theatre, Vivien and the rest of the cast turned up for rehearsal, but mostly we concentrated on the two-handers between Vivien and Theo Bikel, who would be playing Mitch. Concerned though I was, I can't deny there was something exciting in directing a rehearsal with Vivien Leigh and I became totally engrossed. Vivien must have been aware that in my enthusiasm I was directing *her* as much as I was Theo. I've no idea how much time passed before Sir Laurence appeared. He whispered that a flight had been booked that evening and that I should leave now to pick up my suitcase. He was prepared to take the rest of the rehearsal. Slightly miffed, I approached the stage and spoke confidentially to Vivien. Was there anything particular she'd like me to say to the understudy?

"You might recommend a good cologne."

I realised she was simply telling me to get my mind on something else, and it snapped me out of it.

"And," said Vivien, "I want you back as soon as possible, but not before you're ready to come."

Barbara gave me an understanding farewell, some letters she'd written for the children and a letter that had just arrived . . . from my father.

The flight gave me plenty of time to think about Dad. It was the pre-jet era, with landings at Goose Bay, Montreal, Toronto, Winnipeg, Calgary and finally, after thirty-six hours, Vancouver. There'd been other hold-ups too, because it was winter in Canada, and even Vancouver was covered in snow. There had been time of course for me to read and re-read my father's letter.

Dear Bernard,

This is not a very nice letter to write. It somewhat looks as though the curtain is falling and is not likely to come up for another scene. I have been apprehensive of this for some time – hence my curiosity to know your plans, and my hope that the year you arranged with me to be away – would be all.

After physical and X-ray exams they found a luscious malignant cancer in the lower bowel. It stands like this now – I go into hospital on Tuesday, they will make an exploratory and if it has not spread will go after it. Otherwise, we will just sit and wait.

Funny – but apart from the inconvenience to you and the Church, nothing bothers me a lot. Chances are about 20% in my favour. We will gamble on that.

Love to you and Barbara.   Dad.

I was met by several elders of my father's congregation, and taken by car to Vancouver General Hospital. A bit groggy from lack of sleep, I tried to concentrate as Dr Riggs explained that Dad had been in a coma for several days, but they'd given him a massive shot of adrenalin and he should be able to recognise me, however briefly.

The problem was that I hardly recognised *him*. He was skeleton thin, the thick dark hair of his head was sparse and white. A nurse said, "Dr Braden, your son is here."

"Hello," he said, and opened his one eye. It was fiercely aware. "On the way here I made them stop at the bank and close out my safety deposit box. You'll find the contents at the house."

"How are you?"

"Ready to die. I'm glad you came."

"So am I."

"That's not what I mean. You're the only person I can tell. You see, I don't believe any more."

"Believe?"

"In God. I've known it for several years, but I couldn't tell anyone. Will you get that nurse out of here?"

She heard, and was gone.

"I'm not rambling. If I had any faith I lost it when your mother died. What I believe in now is your children, especially the baby. Look after them."

"I will."

"And Barbara. You were very lucky to find her."

"I know."

"And even luckier that she didn't choose someone else. Never forget that."

"I won't."

He sighed. "We were both lucky. I'm tired now. I want to sleep" . . . the eye closed. It opened again. "There were $10,000 in that deposit box. Count it." The eye closed again.

I waited for a moment then called the nurse. She said, "I think the adrenalin's worn off."

She followed me into the corridor. "I was standing in the room with another nurse," she said, "day before yesterday, and I said, 'I don't think he'll last till his son gets here.' She was about to agree, when we heard this voice from the bed say, 'I'll be here.'"

The surgeon was waiting on the ground floor. "There was nothing to be done," he said. "We opened him up, but there was nothing we could do. I've never had a patient in that condition who hadn't already been in hospital for six months."

I was stopped at Reception. The girl said, "When your father

112

came in, we asked him to fill out the usual form. He signed it and said, 'Someone else can fill in the rest when they take me out.' "

Mert Gordon dropped me off at the parsonage. "You'll find the contents of your father's safety deposit box in his study."

"Thank you."

"I'll bet he asked you to count it."

"He did."

Mert gave a short laugh and was gone.

Inside I was greeted by Sally Fulton, the housekeeper.

"They just phoned from the hospital," she said. "Your father's dead."

♦　　♦　　♦

In the circumstances, I'd have liked to spend the next few days with my children, but the death of my father was a matter of some importance in Vancouver, and for me there were attendant responsibilities. His picture and obituary were on the front pages of every paper, and he was the subject of lead editorials. Telegrams and letters began flooding in, not just from British Columbia, but from all over Canada. I was back in the world of my childhood, and now it was London that seemed very far away.

The Board of Trustees of his Church relieved me of such things as funeral arrangements, because it was to be a civic funeral, but the phone rang incessantly, and this was no time to take it off the hook. As a pastor of a church with a thousand families, he'd made a lot of friends in twenty-five years and it was understandable that they wanted to remember him personally.

One call came from a man on Vancouver Island who was particularly anxious to come to the funeral, but only if he could have a last look at his old friend. Now the concept of a wasted body lying in an open coffin for people to see was abhorrent to me, so I told the gentleman I'd have to phone him back. I then called Dr Riggs for advice. He agreed with me, said he considered it a barbaric custom, but asked me to weigh his opinion and mine against that of, not only this one friend, but of many others who would expect to view the body, some of whom had known my father longer than I had. Accordingly the official announcement of the funeral stated that: "Remains will lie in state from 1.30–2.30 p.m."

One thing that pleased me about the obituaries was that nearly all of them mentioned his humour: "Reverend Dr E. D. Braden, beloved minister who was never caught without a smile or a jest, died today in General Hospital." Many years later when I was

113

introduced to Bob Hope for the first time, he said, "Braden. It's an unusual name. The only other Braden I ever met was in Vancouver. I was speaking at the Annual Meeting of the Rotary Club there and it struck me as strange that the outgoing President ran all the race-tracks in the city, and the incoming President was a preacher, name of Braden. In my speech I used it as an example of the influence of Rotary on the community. Then this man stood up and said, 'There is nothing unusual about a clergyman following a race-course owner into this job. Sam Randall and I have always had a perfect understanding. I stay away from the races, and he stays away from church.' I never forgot that."

It was extraordinary how the most important people in the city gathered round. Top businessmen, the Mayor, the Head of the Anglican Church, and the leading Catholic priest. All phoned me to offer help. The city's top accountant was to handle finances, and the foremost lawyer was to probate the will. And all this for a man who had never earned more than $66 a week in his life.

Not quite true. In 1935 at the depth of the Depression he'd been appointed a member of a three-man Royal Commission to investigate the plight of the out-of-work men in the province who'd been placed in what were called "Relief Camps" in Northern British Columbia. This lasted for three months and he was paid at the rate of $33 a day. All this money he gave back to the Church but finally agreed to accept a new typewriter. Now, fifteen years later, he was still using that same typewriter, and he reminded me in his will that it belonged to the Church. Six months after his death his place was taken by another clergyman who, when the Trustees had sorted out the requirements, was provided with an assistant minister and a secretary.

A year before his death my father had been accorded an honour that to the best of my knowledge remains unique. He'd bought his first Model T Ford in 1918 and traded it in on a new one every two years, always through the same dealer, Vancouver Motors.

One day in 1948 he was working in his study when a Vancouver Motors' salesman walked in and said, "May I borrow the keys to your car, Dr Braden?" They were thrown to him and he disappeared. Two hours later my father looked out the front door to find the car hadn't been returned, but a brand-new one was in its place. He phoned Vancouver Motors and the manager said, "We've been working it out, Dr Braden, and given the number of cars you've bought from us since 1918 we reckon you now qualify for a fleet rate, so for the rest of your life we're providing you with a new car every two years."

The funeral was held in his own church and it was recorded that "crowds overflowed into the porches, and many listened over loudspeakers in the Guild Room behind the church". The cleric who delivered the address said, "He had to be persuaded to go into hospital. Last year he cancelled a holiday at the last minute because he could not bring himself to leave sick parishioners. But with all his intensity there was still his glorious humour with which he underlined the fundamental issues of life." In one of the mourners' cars outside the church when, again according to the paper, "many persons both old and young were in tears", there was a moment which he would have fully understood and chuckled at. It always takes time for a funeral cortège to get under way, and while we were waiting, my Uncle Tommy was suddenly reminded of an amusing incident, and said, "Do you remember that time on the picnic when your dad . . ." He then retold the anecdote and all of us in the car burst out laughing. Then we noticed the shocked faces peering in at us and, realising they could not possibly understand, we recomposed our demeanour suitably. City police escorted more than fifty cars which followed the hearse to Ocean View Burial Park in Burnaby where my father was lowered into the ground beside my mother.

Father and Parishioners

Now, at last, there was time to renew my acquaintance with the children, the youngest of whom hadn't the faintest idea who I was. It was also time to consider the future seriously.

Mr and Mrs Fulton had emigrated from Scotland to Canada. Mrs Fulton had become our housekeeper in Toronto while her husband worked at another job. After thinking it over they'd agreed to come with us to Vancouver, and look after the children in the parsonage, while we spent our "year" in London. When we left there was no question in anyone's mind but that we were coming back. Now I was bound by my "run-of-the-play" contract in *Streetcar* and both Barbara and I were receiving other offers in London. I'd had many telegrams from Canadian Broadcasting executives on the death of my father, but none of them extended to offering work in Canada.

The parsonage, of course, belonged to the Church, as did all the furniture, and, while we knew that the Board of Trustees would be generous with time, eventually the Fultons and the children would have to move out to make way for the new incumbent.

After a long phone call to Barbara in London we agreed that the only alternative was to move there and take the children with us. But what about our moral responsibility to Mr and Mrs Fulton? Barbara made a suggestion.

Late that evening after the children were in bed I put the suggestion to the Fultons that they consider re-emigrating to Britain, providing we could find a place for all of us to live. They asked for time to think it over, and I certainly didn't blame them.

I suspect they had long arguments, but that in the end their affection for the children, and particularly Mrs Fulton's having been in a sense a mother to Kim, the youngest, for nearly a year was the deciding factor. They agreed to come with us.

Now I had to tell the children, but that proved to be the least of my difficulties. The two elder were at an age to be flexible, and Kim was in no position to make up her own mind.

It took me nearly two weeks to deal with matters in Vancouver and by the time I left plans were under way for a new community centre to be named after my father, and a radio series had been planned in which he would be the subject of the first programme under the title *Builders of British Columbia*. There were four commercial radio stations in Vancouver and, given the commercial rivalry between them, I was particularly pleased that the reaction to this first broadcast on Station CJOR was such that it was repeated on all three of the other stations.

In all I received more than three thousand letters and telegrams, many from people I didn't know. One of these was from a lady who wrote:

Your father and I went to the same country school and we were friends. One summer Saturday, I was walking with him behind a plough and a horse. I talked and he ploughed. We must have been about twelve years old. Suddenly through some trees on the edge of the field, I caught a glimpse of something moving and glinting brightly in the sun. I took his arm and stopped him. "Look," I said. He looked and said, "That will be the bicycle my father promised me. It's being delivered today." Then he shook the reins of the horse and resumed ploughing. I asked him if he wasn't going to examine the bike. He said, "No. If I do that now I'll get too excited. This field's got to be finished today, and I've got to plough a straight furrow."

I kept that letter in my wallet until the wallet was stolen in the south of France. I don't think it was the sentiment of the letter that intrigued me so much as the fact that it came from someone who'd known my father and what he'd looked like when he was twelve years old.

Now it was time to fly back to London. I stopped off in Toronto briefly to say hello to some friends, and noted yet again that no one seemed wildly enthusiastic about my returning.

From Toronto I flew to Montreal, which theoretically should have been the last stop before London. Prevailing winds were such that normally the flight could be made non-stop. In those days passports were actually checked on the plane for some reason and I became aware during the flight that members of the cabin crew were looking at me askance. At first I thought I was being over-sensitive, but then one of the stewards knocked on the cockpit door, and members of the flying crew came out individually and looked at *me*. Then there was an announcement that we would, after all, land at Goose Bay. When we got there I, alone of all the passengers, was asked to disembark and taken to a shack that housed immigration.

The officer took my passport, studied it carefully, and asked me if I was sure I was me. I said I was pretty sure, at which point the captain of the plane was ushered in. It emerged that, by coincidence, this particular crew, while I was in Vancouver, had all attended a performance of *A Streetcar Named Desire* and had seen Theodore Bikel in the role of Mitch. For some reason the programme hadn't been changed and Mitch was apparently played by Bernard Braden. Hence the mystery. It was cleared up

117

with a single phone call, and I was offered free champagne on the remainder of the flight.

We landed in London on a Saturday morning, on February 11th, which would have been my father's birthday. The headline in the paper I was given announced that the beloved comedian Sydney Field had died. At the time he was playing the lead in *Harvey* at the Prince of Wales Theatre.

Back at Chatsworth Court, Barbara and I talked about what had gone on during the past two weeks, then I decided to catch up on some sleep. First, though, Barbara felt I should phone H.M. Tennent's office and let them know I was back. I hadn't thought about the play since I left, but I'd have the entire weekend to go through it again . . . indeed Vivien had found the role of Blanche so exhausting that she'd cancelled Monday night performances, so I'd have till Tuesday.

I duly made the call and went to bed. Five minutes later came a call from the Tennent office. Miss Leigh had been informed of my return during the matinée and would be most grateful if I'd come in and do the Saturday evening performance. There wasn't really much I could say. She'd been kindness itself, and I was under contract to perform every night.

As usual, I followed Sir Laurence's advice and carefully watched the scene he'd wanted me to see from the wings. In due course I made my little entrance carrying a bunch of roses. Vivien said, "Ah, my Rosenkavalier", accepted the flowers and she added, "Bow to me." I gave my shy little bow and the curtain fell to prolonged applause. Vivien hugged me and said, "That's the first time we've had applause on that scene since you left."

We never . . . ever . . . got it again.

♦   ♦   ♦

The following day, Barbara and I spent most of our time considering the implications of moving the family to London. It was agreed that she look for suitable accommodation and that, given a good hefty mortgage, we'd probably be better off buying than renting. We liked the area where we were, and someone at the tennis club had told her that there were a number of houses for sale in Edwardes Square. Apparently, during the Blitz, someone had picked up most of the houses in the Square at £500 each, and was now in the process of selling them off. They were superb Queen Anne houses, but now they cost the exorbitant amount of

118

£10,000 each, and in the event, it turned out that they were too small for our requirements.

I was still a bit wary of purchasing rather than renting because, although we'd been lucky so far, we might suddenly find ourselves without work of any kind.

It was at this point that Barbara brought out the cuttings from newspapers that had arrived during my absence in Canada. I'd totally forgotten that the first transmission of *Breakfast with Braden* had gone out during my absence. Barbara handed me the cuttings and went into the other room.

Manchester Guardian: "Until last Saturday, I would have unhesitatingly placed *Take it From Here* as the one radio show of the radio week not to be missed. Now, after listening to the latest Bernard Braden breakfast show, I am not so sure."

Daily Mail: "Last Saturday, unheralded, Bernard Braden broke into the lean morning period with the unpretentious but highly amusing *Breakfast with Braden*. Now if the BBC are smart he should get his chance. If the BBC are smart."

Evening Post: "Tucked away at 8.15 a.m. on a Saturday morning is a programme called *Breakfast with Braden*. This is going to be the successor of *Take it From Here*. It is bright, breezy, homely, impishly sprightly and shakes the listener into a chuckling wakefulness that sets him right for the day."

Evening Despatch: "I stumbled across a programme with Bernard Braden last Saturday morning because I wanted to check the time. Why did none of you tell me about it? He's funny and he's original, and what on earth is he doing on a programme at that time in the morning when he should have a peak hour timing? The only joke I can remember was: 'Have you an unconscious desire to leave your wife? Or have you a desire to leave your wife unconscious?' If you're conscious at 8.15 on Saturday mornings, try *Breakfast with Braden*."

Sunday Graphic: "Some weeks ago I pleaded for a change of broadcast time for *Breakfast with Braden*. Recently the BBC decided that this show should have a repeat broadcast – at a time, I presumed, when more could listen. Now I find they have implemented their decision. *Breakfast with Braden* goes out to a new audience on Wednesdays at 7.15 a.m. I give up."

Western Mail: "You will concede, I'm sure, that a comic that can make you rock with laughter at an hour when most of us cannot look a kipper in the face must be a bigger national benefactor than the Ministry of Food."

Evening Gazette: "Do you *Breakfast with Braden* at 8.15 on Saturday mornings? If this is too early for you to enjoy the delightful light conversation of Canadian Bernard Braden, I have good news for you. I hear he's to start a new series with his wife in April."

Evening News: ". . . I am not amused by early morning broadcasts, yet Mr Braden's American commentator eulogising 'The Towers of London' interfered seriously with breakfast ritual. Tourist visitors were exhorted to look for the tablet to that famous vocalist Florence Nightingale who sang in several of London's Squares."

Daily Mirror: "Any show that can make me laugh at 8.15 in the morning is funny. I rate Canadian Bernard Braden with his remarkably good team mates, as the best thing in comedy since *Take it From Here*. The Home Service is crying out for comedy and here is radio's number two buried at breakfast time."

Kinematograph Weekly: "According to radio comedian Bernard Braden, he has just completed a picture, *The Fourth Man*, which takes place entirely in a zither with Anton Karas supplying the music by knocking his head against a sewer."

Sunday Empire News: "8.20 in the morning finds me particularly unresponsive, especially to anybody trying to be funny, but there's a chap on the radio who's got me listening regularly. Name of Bernard Braden. Remarkable young man. Remarkable programme."

While I was mulling over these reviews in a kind of stunned silence, Barbara walked back into the room and said, "What are you worried about? The BBC have asked for a series of *Leave your name and number*, you're still doing the Johnny Mills show for Cadbury, and your second series with Gracie Fields starts on April 2nd. *Streetcar* looks as if it's set to run until at least the end of the year. Oh . . . I forgot to mention that Olive Harding phoned to say that the Assistant Head of Radio Drama called and said they want to do Joe Schull's play *The Concert* with us in the leads. And what about that film Johnny's asked you to direct?"

Which reminded me. I'd taken the book of *Little Boy Lost* with me, and had virtually finished the first treatment on the plane. It was about a GI who'd discovered after returning to America that he'd fathered a child in Paris, and that its mother had died. He'd then returned to Paris to try to find his son. I'd worked out an opening title sequence in which the shadows of the five-year-old boy and his father were projected against a brick wall. They were elongated shadows, but the boy was dwarfed by his father and they kept missing each other.

Now I could hardly wait to try it out on Johnny. At our next recording session I took the treatment along with me, but before I could get it out of my briefcase Johnny said, "I'm sorry to tell you this, Bernie, but while you were away I got an offer for the rights of *Little Boy Lost*, and it was such good money I couldn't turn it down. I sold it to Bing Crosby."

The film was made in 1953. It was written and directed by George Seaton and starred Bing Crosby and Claude Dauphin. Leslie Halliwell in his film guide describes it as "a rather dull tearjerker".

With respect to everyone concerned, I still like to think Johnny and I could have made it into something more successful, but we'll never know because it was the last time I was ever invited to direct a feature film.

◆　　◆　　◆

Another cutting had turned up in the batch Barbara had provided which also gave me a great deal of pleasure. It was a review of *A Streetcar Named Desire* by Richard Findlater and it began:

I went to see the *Streetcar* last week for the first time. Now, in retrospect, how ridiculously insular seem the press attacks against the play last autumn, one of those curious outbreaks of puritanism that afflict the British journalist when confronted with characters speaking the truth . . . this is good theatre and it is to be judged as theatre, not as a sermon or a literary exercise.

One simple flaw in the play, it seems, is the Lord Chamberlain's responsibility – and what a mealy-mouthed hypocrisy it is to be sure. At a crucial point in the play Blanche describes her unsuccessful marriage, the reason, it is intimated, for her present nymphomania. Soon after her marriage, she says, she went into a room and discovered her husband with "someone else". The audience, naturally enough, concludes that this was another woman, but in Mr Williams's original text, Blanche reveals it was an older man. This was deleted because we do not mention such things on a London stage – though making

121

fun of "pansy" manners is a staple of contemporary comedy. Later in the play, much later, the audience is considerably surprised and puzzled when Stella, Blanche's sister, describes the first husband as "a degenerate". The original term was "homosexual". This seems to me a striking example of the crassness and crudity of British play censorship. To equate "homosexuality" with "degeneracy" is at once absurd and offensive. And by these cuts, the balance of Mr Williams's play has been severely affected.

What particularly pleased me about this review was the revelation that these changes had stemmed from the Lord Chamberlain's office. I'd been blaming them on Sir Laurence.

♦ ♦ ♦

In that month of February, President Truman had officially ordered work to begin on the hydrogen bomb. He said the work would continue until a satisfactory plan for international control could be achieved . . . on February 4th Dr Klaus Fuchs, a leading British atomic scientist, was arrested on two charges of passing on atomic information which might help the enemy. It was against this background that the Labour government decided to call a general election on February 24th.

For Barbara and me it was a matter of some interest to find how general elections were conducted in this country. During all our lives in Canada politics had been dominated by two political parties, the Conservatives and the Liberals. The Conservatives followed roughly the line of the Tory Party in Britain, but the Liberals could in no sense be likened to the British Labour Party. Labour had been in power for nearly five years and were now laying the success of their policies on the line.

But what were those policies, and indeed what were the Tories putting up against them? We were used to not understanding our own Canadian politicians, but with Labour and Conservatives being so far apart we thought the issues would be clearer here.

They weren't. What we gathered from the newspapers was that the government was saying that Labour had brought full employment which would stay if a Labour government was returned. Production was rising, and would continue to rise under the next Labour government. The quickest way to get prices down was to get wages up. The emphasis would be on improving the lot of ordinary people at the expense of what they called "people who were not useful". Labour would keep its promises.

The Tories planned reduced taxation to offset wages that were

122

becoming too high. Prosperous industries that used to pay taxes had been nationalised and the public was having to pay far more to shoulder the losses caused by nationalisation. By stopping nationalisation and creating confidence abroad, a Tory government would be able to fight rising costs. There was the suggestion that the Americans were suspicious of Labour, and much was made of the popularity of Winston Churchill in the United States, coupled with the idea that with him as Prime Minister, we would also get more co-operation from the British Commonwealth and from Europe.

During the run-up to the election, the most highly publicised incident came when Churchill promised that under a Tory government, the amount of petrol available to car owners would be substantially increased and Aneurin Bevan promptly accused him of offering this as a bribe for votes.

Most of the campaigning seemed to consist of accusations and counter-accusations ... the same as in Canada. We turned to what I've always believed the most sensible opinions – and still do – letters from ordinary people to the papers.

In the *Daily Mirror*, for example, there was a letter from a man who was going to vote Labour but added:

I'm not at all impressed by plans for blocks of super flats which will be completed in 1954 (unless there's another crisis). I want a home – two rooms and a kitchen, I want it now, and I can't accept the excuses given as to why I'm not getting it. Just put a kitchen to every two rooms and a lot of us will be satisfied. My wife is thirty-five and wants a baby and there are many more like us.

Writing in the *Daily Mail*, a hotel manager said:

Legislation is directed against luxury and towards austerity. On the other hand there is a desperate need for dollars. If we're going to attract tourists to spend those dollars, our hotels must be comfortable and to some extent presentable. My hotel had its rear blown out by a doodle-bug, and I've only recently got a permit application through for renovation. I then had to queue for a company that would undertake to do the job. I can't help thinking these things should move a little faster.

In another Labour paper, a lady wrote:

We in Britain, whether we like it or not, are faced with the absolute necessity of a planned economy. We can no longer exact tribute from

123

our former Empire in return for the privilege of being ruled by us, and in ourselves we are a very little country. I joined the Labour Party because I saw that very handwriting on the wall. The Conservatives can criticise the government for lack of colour or inexperience, but they cannot criticise the basic policy, since it is the only possible policy under the circumstances.

In the *Telegraph*:

We in England have always considered ourselves artisans, craftsmen, not just at manufacturing things, but in any job we take on. Young people who take jobs now don't count on staying. They're union men, and they think entirely in terms of hours and wages. The point is that emergencies arise every day which can't be solved in terms of time and money. They require decency and loyalty. Our younger men have loyalty only to their unions.

In the *Daily Herald*:

Under the present government, I think youngsters are going to be judged on their capabilities, not their bank accounts. My younger brother wants to be a doctor. Under the National Health Scheme, if he's got the capability, he'll get the chance. There'll be work and a good living for him without having to buy a practice or setting up in some fashionable section of London where people pay money to have their tonsils looked at. If this government can weather the economic strain that would be faced by any other British government now, we're going to find England the best run, best educated country in the world, bar none.

In the *Daily Express*:

I'm studying to be an artist. That leaves me two alternatives. If I take a job with a commercial firm, I may ensure my worth as a commodity at the expense of my art. If I choose to carry on experimenting, in the hope of discovering something new and interesting, I run the risk of being classed as someone engaged in unnecessary work. I might conceivably be chucked into another job. On the other hand, what's the point in becoming successful? Income tax is utterly destructive as far as ambition is concerned. When you push a tax to the point where part of a man's income is as good as confiscated, you're not levying tax, you're imposing a penalty, and that should be done by a court of law, not a tax inspector. I mean it's got to the point where the less work one does, the less tax one pays. Then it follows that if it's a case of giving up beer, tobacco or work, the three great tax producers, work is by far the easiest to do without.

Barbara and I decided it was just as well we didn't have a vote. What really bothered us was the fact that because we had got lucky so fast, we were living in some kind of no-man's-land where, although we were subject to rationing, we were being taken to restaurants and clubs that didn't seem to be. If you had the money, you could eat caviare and pâté de foie gras. They didn't seem to be rationed. Was it that the Labour government wasn't aware of this double economy, or was it that they just didn't have the time or the people to police it?

We moved among the privileged, and seemed to be privileged ourselves.

On election night we were invited to an exclusive club behind Piccadilly Circus, as guests of Bonar Colleano. It was a close election, and results were slow in arriving. There was no television, so every once in a while someone would nip out and have a look at the lighted scoreboard in the Circus. People in the club were drinking and talking and waiting for hour after hour. The atmosphere was getting duller by the minute. Well, that wasn't the life for Colleano, even on election night. So to keep himself interested, he stepped behind the bar and served drinks for the best part of an hour. When he sensed that even his assumed Italian accent and making a point of serving the wrong drinks to the wrong people wasn't relieving the tedium, he organised an impromptu concert.

He found a girl who could sing, discovered Denny Vaughan drinking lemonade behind a pillar and ensconced him firmly on the piano seat, and recruited two or three other reluctant entertainers. After everyone else had done his bit, Colleano put on a twenty-minute act, in the course of which he ruined a perfectly good suit, cut his hand on a broken wine glass, and entertained everyone hugely.

It took nerve for a popular entertainer to go out on a limb with an unrehearsed show that offered no financial reward, no critical acclaim and which the audience didn't really want to see in the first place. By the time Colleano was finished, the atmosphere in the club had changed from one of bored lethargy to one of stimulated gaiety and satisfaction. Most people seemed to have forgotten which party they wanted to win.

After the largest voting turnout of the century, the result was virtually stalemate with Labour leading the Tories by about ten

125

seats, in the certain knowledge that another election would have to be faced in the near future.

♦   ♦   ♦

A few weeks into the run of *Breakfast with Braden* Frank Muir and Denis Norden realised that they really *had* taken on more writing chores than they could comfortably handle, and said so. This news coincided with a letter from an old friend of mine, Eric Nicol.

Eric and I had worked together in Vancouver, and in one of his plays I'd been given what I still consider the ultimate line in marriage proposals: "If I came to you stark naked and said, 'This is all I am, this is all I have, and this will only diminish with the years, the bargain would still be yours.'"

Eric's letter came from Paris, where he was at the Sorbonne

Eric Nicol

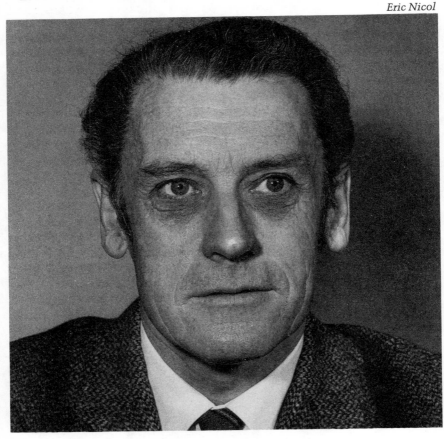

126

writing a PhD thesis on Giraudoux, and living at Maison Cana-
dien on a grant of $20 a month. Maison Canadien he described as
"the sort of place where they lower the net on the ping pong table
New Year's Eve so people can dance". The reason for the letter,
though, was serious. Eric had been writing his thesis as an excuse
to translate the plays of Giraudoux so that he could arrange for
their production in the West End and on Broadway. So engrossed
was he in this task that he'd failed to notice the successful
production of several of these plays in the West End and on
Broadway.

A meeting was arranged with Frank and Denis along with Pat
Dixon, as a result of which it was agreed that Eric would be
presented to the BBC Contracts Department as an eminent comedy writer, now living in Paris, who just *might* be persuaded to
come to London if the price was right. The case was put forward
by Pat Dixon with his usual innocent guile, and before writing a
single word, Eric was suddenly making more money than he'd
ever seen in his life.

Fortunately, he formed a mutual admiration society with Frank
and Denis, although they worked separately.

Eric added two dimensions to the show. First, he was familiar
with my own idiom and speech patterns and second, he couldn't
believe our announcer Ronald Fletcher. From the beginning,
Fletcher had accepted his stint on the show as an assignment and
seemed totally disinterested in and, indeed, unaware of the jokes.
Frank and Denis had largely contented themselves with giving
Ronnie some fairly un-BBC lines to say, usually as the last line of
the show, e.g. "Isn't it amazing that cats have two holes in their
fur exactly where their eyes are?"

Eric was fascinated with his deadpan delivery.

"D'you suppose," he asked me, "that he behaves like that at
home?"

I said, "Why don't you ask him?"

Eric invited Ronnie out for a cup of coffee and reported back.

"He went to Shrewsbury and Cambridge, played golf at Cambridge, and was runner-up in the French Amateur Championship.
His father left him some money with which he started a business
that was unsuccessful, partly because he was an inveterate
gambler. That's when he applied for a job with the BBC. He
continued to gamble, and was into his bookmaker for several
thousand pounds, at which point the bookmaker agreed to write
off the debt on condition that Mr Fletcher never backed another
horse. That night he went to the dog track. Last December he lost
all his Christmas money just before the big day . . . he has a wife

and children, and asked his bank manager for a loan. The manager asked him for collateral, and he offered his BBC salary. When he told him what that was the manager said, 'Would a pound be all right?' None of this went down too well with his wife who has recently advertised in *The Times* for a lighthouse in which to live. All this with a straight face, Bernie!"

"So?"

Eric provided Ronnie with a mother who would not be able to hold her head up again until he was released from this dreadful chore of announcing *Breakfast with Braden* . . . "What will the Suffragan Bishop say?"

I was a colonial boor, Nat Temple just a boor, Benny Lee an ignoramus, and Miss Carr? Well, Ronnie had a slight crush on Miss Carr, who, according to the Norden and Muir script, had a crush on me. After a few weeks of this the real Ronald Fletcher began to take an interest in the show, found some of the lines funny, and revealed himself as a compulsive giggler.

The problem with Eric was that he was prone to sexual innuendo, although it was some time before anyone in the BBC noticed it, other than Pat Dixon who encouraged it. Eventually I was summoned to the office of Michael Standing, then Head of BBC Light Entertainment. Appearing before Mr Standing should have been Pat's job but he'd convinced me that Mr Standing would take a less arbitrary attitude with me.

Mr Standing sat at his desk and pointed to a section of dialogue from the previous week's script, already broadcast.

"Does that mean what I think it means?"

"Well, sir, I think it means whatever you take it to mean. There would seem to be more than one interpretation possible."

Mr Standing rose to his full height, which was considerable. He walked to his office window overlooking Bond Street and gazed out. He was wearing blue trousers, a blue shirt and tie, even blue shoes.

"Mr Braden," he said firmly, "in my capacity as Head of Light Entertainment in the BBC I want you to understand that I will not wear blue material."

Now, *you* must understand that in 1950 *I* did not understand the words "wear" and "blue" in the context in which he was using them. I simply burst out laughing and fled the room.

Back in Pat Dixon's office I finally overcame my hysterics long enough to tell him what had happened. Pat picked up his phone, got on to Mr Standing and tried to explain. Mr Standing was kind enough to understand and forgive, but still insisted he would not wear blue material. Pat assigned *me* to convey the bad news to

Eric, who listened carefully and then said, "Bernie, when I'm working through a sketch I write in a straight line. If I have to work around the line, at that moment the sketch won't be funny. If you and Pat can write around it and still make it funny, I won't be offended."

We did our best . . . *not* to "write around" any oftener than we had to, eg., during one of Uncle Gabby's monologues Eric had him reminiscing about his days in the Yukon. "Those was tough times up there in those days," he wrote. "No women available. No, sir. About the only form of animal life was sheep. The most popular song that year in the Yukon was 'It Had To Be Ewe' . . ." Pat simply changed the spelling in the script from "ewe" to "you", and the censor passed it, leaving the listeners to draw their own conclusions.

It took me some time to realise that BBC producers, by choice, didn't understand anything about technicalities. This was left to the technicians. They were considered to be two breeds of people. One supplied creativity, and the other the means to transmit it. I'd been brought up in an entirely different school. In fact, I'd started in radio as an engineer. When a complicated sound effect was written into our script and the sound technician said, "It can't be done", it was all I could do to stop myself running up and showing how it *could* be done. At one point I suggested to Pat that we might get more variety into the programme technically if instead of using only "ribbon" microphones, we could put the singers on a "cardioid".

Pat said, "What's a cardioid?"

I explained that it was a microphone which could be used in three ways. That it could function as a ribbon microphone which allowed two performers to be heard one on either side, or by simply using a screwdriver it could be adjusted to have a wide field on one side and no sound coming out of the other, or by another adjustment with the screwdriver, it could be made omni-directional.

Pat said he'd look into it, and the next week reported that the BBC did *have* several cardioids, but they were all assigned to drama, and not considered suitable for light entertainment. I said I didn't think that seemed reasonable, so Pat made an appointment for me to see the BBC's Head of Sound, a technical gentleman, whose office was even more impressive than that of Mr Standing. His opening line was, "I understand you don't like our ribbon microphone?"

"It's not that, sir. I just feel that by using a cardioid as well we can add to the production values of the show."

129

"You think the cardioid is superior to the ribbon microphone?"

"No, sir. In fact, I think we'll lose a degree of technical quality by using the cardioid, but the actual quality of sound is sometimes not as important as the variety of sound."

Well, we got our cardioid, but we were very lucky to have any microphones at all. Pat had neglected to tell me that this gentleman had invented the ribbon microphone.

◆　　　◆　　　◆

Lyn Evans, playing Steve in *Streetcar*, continued to keep us amused when, as usually happens, a play becomes a chore rather than something you look forward to every night. One evening Lyn missed his call when the curtain was supposed to go up with the four poker players assembled on stage. Rushing down the stairs, he appeared from the wings and calmly stepped over a parapet to take his place at the table. When the Stage Manager mentioned yet again that the parapet represented a wall, Lyn said, "Bloody rubbish. What's the point of going through a door and making a right turn when all you have to do is walk straight to the table, just by lifting one leg over a six-inch-high parapet?" In fairness, I

Bonar, Lyn, me and Theo

think most of the audience would have agreed with him. At one Saturday matinée we were going through a routine at the poker table when Lyn seriously lost his way, not for the first time. It's a cardinal rule in the theatre that if you're playing a game like poker you deliberately don't play the game. You listen to the other actors' lines and say yours.

In this instance, Colleano, as Stanley, was supposed to hold a flush, and everyone else threw in their hands. That way the play could continue. By some freak coincidence Lyn had drawn four aces and he flatly refused to throw his hand in. It took a great deal of persuasion, including a hefty kick on the shins, to get him to continue with the play.

His best moment, though, came in an evening performance, again at the poker table. Steve, the character he played, was an inveterate story-teller, and one of his stories was told while he was dealing the cards. As he dealt he was supposed to say, "This ole farmer's out back of his house, throwin' corn to the chickens, when all at once he hears a loud cackle and this young hen comes lickety split round the side of the house with the rooster right behind her and gainin' on her fast. But when the rooster catches sight of the farmer throwin' the corn, he puts on the brakes, and lets the hen get away and starts peckin' corn. And the ole farmer says, 'Lord God, I hope's I never gits *that* hongry.' "

I can only paraphrase what Lyn actually said, but it sounded like, "This old farmer is throwin' corn to the chickens when this rooster comes round the side of the house . . . no, it's a chicken that comes round the side of the house . . . and the old farmer's chasin' it and gainin' . . . no, that's not right. This rooster is throwin' corn to the chickens, when the old farmer starts peckin' the corn and the hen . . . oh, fuck it!" It was indicative of the quality of our audience that night that Lyn got a big laugh, and nobody complained at the box office.

◆　　◆　　◆

Barbara and I found ourselves spending a lot of time in the company of Colleano. Sometimes with his wife, sometimes with girlfriends, but more often than not on his own, which surprised us a little. He was in his mid-twenties at the time and very much a man about town. Except for the American accent most people thought he was Italian. His complexion was dark, his hair black, and his eyes had a flashing Latin quality. Night-club violinists who serenaded from table to table usually tipped Bonar a wink when they played "Santa Lucia". In point of fact he was Irish. The family name was Sullivan and Bonar had been born in Australia. He rarely talked about his childhood, but one night at our place after a few drinks, he began to do just that.

Like so many people born into show business, he'd had to pick up his education on the run, as it were.

The Flying Colleanos were one of the most famous circus acts of all times. His Uncle Maurice had been the first performer to do a triple somersault on the slack wire, and Bonar himself was earning $250 at the age of six walking a tightrope in New York's Madison Square Gardens.

At the Chicago World's Fair in 1933 a huge grandstand had been built at the edge of Lake Michigan to accommodate the aquatic events. Someone had conceived the brilliant idea of opening the first evening's performance by putting young Bonar on a surfboard behind a power boat which, on cue, was to travel at full speed into the lighted area, towing Bonar with one hand holding the rope and the other waving an American flag. The boat started with a jerk, and when the surfboard appeared there was nobody on it. Also, someone had forgotten to ask Bonar if he could swim. By the time they found him he'd nearly drowned. The showbiz answer to that was to spend the rest of the next day teaching him to swim.

Half the time he never knew what country he was in. On one occasion the Flying Colleanos disembarked at Cherbourg and took the train to Paris where Bonar's parents could hardly wait to go out for the evening and renew old acquaintances in Montmartre. Bonar was put to bed, aged six, in the hotel room, and left alone. He woke up hungry, and knew enough to pick up the phone and ask for room service. Unfortunately he didn't understand French, in fact he didn't know there was any language other than English. Panic set in and a few minutes later a small boy in pyjamas was picked up in the street by the local gendarmes and was still sobbing several hours later when his parents came to collect him.

It was an aspect of Colleano we hadn't encountered before and went a long way to explaining the brashness of his personality which most people took at face value.

◆　◆　◆

On March 10th Gracie Fields arrived to commence recording our second series for Radio Luxembourg. The first series of twenty-six programmes had been recorded in 1949 at the rate of one a day. Because Gracie was booked to carry out a concert tour in Canada beginning on April 1st, she'd informed the producers of our series

With Gracie Fields

that she'd make six months' broadcasts of *The Gracie Fields Show* in two weeks.

I needed one day off a week to record *Breakfast with Braden* so in twelve days we had to do twenty-six shows.

I'd never been a fan of Gracie Fields. I knew that she had a reputation for being "the queen of the guffaw and the lump in the throat", but until our first rehearsal, I'd never experienced either the guffaw or the lump in the throat. Gracie's method, which was well ahead of her era, was to record the rehearsal. She'd listen to the playback of the rehearsal, and if she approved, that recorded rehearsal became part of the show. Her finale for the first show was the Albert Hay Mallote version of "The Lord's Prayer". On the first rehearsal/recording with Billy Ternent's Orchestra, she sang her way through to: ". . . for thine is the Kingdom and the Power and the Glory for ever and *ever* . . . Amen." The second "ever" involved a very high note, and on it, Gracie's voice cracked wide open. Without a breath pause, she turned to the orchestra and said, "All together now!" From that moment I became a fan.

At this period in her career Gracie was conscious that she was an important entertainer, and tended to dress the part. Her grey hair was beautifully coiffed, and she draped herself in mid-calf-length mink coats, with matching hats. Somehow it made her look like Mrs Winston Churchill.

One day she and I were returning from lunch to Rodmarten Mews where the studio was, by way of Bond Street, and this distinguished-looking lady was window shopping. After twenty minutes of this stop/start journey, I noticed that we were due to rehearse/record within ten minutes, and mentioned it to Gracie. There were people watching her under the impression that she *was* Mrs Churchill, and they were then treated to the sight and sound of Gracie Fields turning to the street, and summoning a cab by placing two fingers to her mouth and emitting a raucous whistle, which applied the brakes to half a dozen cabs. This was the Gracie that I came to know and love.

That same evening I was, of course, appearing on stage in *Streetcar*. Within the few minutes before curtain-up there was always a brief gossip conducted by Vivien from the chaise-longue that was part of the set. One night she singled me out for attention because she'd read somewhere that I was doing a series with Gracie Fields on Radio Luxembourg. Did I think Gracie would be interested in seeing *Streetcar*? House seats could be arranged and charged to the management. When would I be seeing Gracie? Would I be kind enough to invite her? Any night . . . any night at all. Vivien would arrange it to suit Gracie.

At the end of the show Vivien returned to the subject. I promised to speak to Gracie.

Later, I asked one of the other women in the cast just why Vivien Leigh was so interested in impressing Gracie Fields, of all people? Each was a star, but in such different ways.

The actress said, "Oh, that's easy. Vivien's first screen role was a small part in a film starring Gracie Fields."

At our next recording session I chose a moment to mention Vivien's invitation to Gracie.

"Ee, love," she said, "I don't think it's my cup of tea, do you?"

I didn't, but I also didn't fancy the idea of telling Vivien that, for whatever reason, Gracie wasn't accepting the invitation. Somehow I managed to persuade Miss Fields to come to the Aldwych Theatre on a specific Saturday night accompanied by a friend.

Vivien expressed herself delighted, the tickets were arranged and delivered by me.

I've mentioned that although the house was sold out every night, it was often full of the wrong people. Especially at the second show on Saturday nights. On the evening that Gracie was there we were faced with a particularly unruly group and controlling them was not easy.

After the show, back in my dressing room I found Gracie seated at the mirror, scribbling a note.

"I'm writing to Vivien," she said. "I was right, love. It wasn't my cup of tea. I thought you were all lovely, and that's what I'm saying in this note. Would you be kind enough to deliver it for me?"

"You mean you're not going round to see her?"

"I couldn't, love. I just couldn't."

I changed, then took the note to Vivien's dressing room and lifted my hand to knock on the door. I couldn't, I just couldn't. Cravenly, I knelt down and slipped the envelope under the door.

What I didn't know was that Vivien had laid on lobster and champagne for Gracie Fields.

Because we didn't play on Mondays, there was a long weekend in which to forget both Vivien and Gracie, and I was pretty good at that. On the Tuesday evening before curtain-up Vivien was vivacious and friendly, recounting stories of what had happened at the weekend at Notley Abbey. It wasn't till we were standing together before the last scene in the second act that, as I went to take her hand, she pulled it away. Then as the curtain rose, and we started walking up the ramp that represented the street she said quietly, "I don't think much of your friend's manners."

I didn't know what the hell she was talking about. What friend? There wasn't time to ask her; we were into the scene.

The scene was played entirely between Blanche and Mitch, and ended with Mitch proposing marriage. Now, I think Vivien spoke and timed that line deliberately to throw me and she meant, at the end of the act, to tell me off for slipping the note under the door on Saturday night instead of facing her.

As it happened, the scene played better that night than it ever had before. The audience seemed to understand all the nuances and Vivien rose to it. She played for subtlety. The audience reacted superbly and Vivien, I think, forgot about Gracie and lost herself in the scene.

I didn't. I just kept wondering what she'd meant. It never occurred to me to connect "my friend" and Gracie. I meant to

135

have it out with Vivien as soon as the curtain fell. The fact that the scene was going well cut no ice with me.

Act two of *Streetcar* ends as follows:

MITCH: (*drawing her slowly into his arms*): You need some-
           body, and I need somebody too. Could it be . . . you
           and me, Blanche?
(*She stares at him vacantly for a moment, then with a soft cry, huddles in his embrace. She makes a sobbing effort to speak, but the words won't come. He kisses her forehead and her eyes and finally her lips. Her breath is drawn and released in long grateful sobs.*)
BLANCHE: Sometimes, there's God . . . so quickly!

As the curtain fell to a storm of applause, Vivien did something that happened only very occasionally. She gave me a little bump and a grind.

I, still thinking of my "bad-mannered friend" said, "What the hell was *that* about?" . . . and Vivien, thinking that I meant the bump and grind, stepped back and smacked me smartly in the face, then disappeared into her dressing room. It was too late to explain. The subject of Gracie Fields was never mentioned between us again.

♦　　♦　　♦

If being involved in *Streetcar* had caused us to be invited to parties, the cult following that came with *Breakfast with Braden* increased our popularity, particularly with expatriate Americans.

One of the first "celebrity" parties to which we were invited was hosted by Larry Adler at his St John's Wood home. The guest of honour that night was Lena Horne and there came inevitably a moment when she was asked to sing. Her musical director at the time was her then husband, Lennie Hayton, and when Miss Horne agreed to perform, he, naturally, took his place at the piano. It was a crowded party, and when Miss Horne began to sing people were still talking in groups. I made a point of facing Miss Horne because I was anxious to hear her. There was a man facing me who kept on talking during the performance about *Breakfast with Braden* and seemed to take it as a personal offence that she continued to sing while he was speaking. He began to talk more loudly, and, at a point when Lena Horne paused for effect at a crucial moment in "Summertime" the man facing me said,

"She's not really very good, is she?" All eyes turned to me, the person facing the performer.

For the rest of the evening I made myself as scarce as possible and tried, in particular, to avoid the man who'd made the gaffe. Eventually he made his way through to where I thought I was safely hiding and introduced himself as Eric Ambler, the well-known writer. He insisted on taking my telephone number, and I thought that would be an end of it. In fact, I thought it was the last party I would ever be invited to.

A few weeks later came an invitation to dinner at the home of Mr and Mrs Eric Ambler. I was of a mind not to accept it, but Barbara insisted it would be rude to refuse and so on a Sunday in late March we found ourselves at a dinner party where we were the only couple not in evening dress. It wasn't a good beginning. The saving grace for me was that among the guests was the actress Kay Walsh whom I'd long admired.

In due course the ladies left the table and the men passed round the port. The moment our host said, "Shall we join the ladies?" I made a point of being the first back to the drawing room, and made a beeline for Kay Walsh. Now when I admire someone, I always make a point of thinking up something that I think will be provocative, make the person realise that I have special knowledge of her particular qualities. I knew that Kay Walsh had been married to David Lean, had co-written the script of *Great Expectations* with him, and had played Nancy in the film *Oliver Twist*. It had to be something less obvious if I wanted to make an impression.

Eric Ambler, a proper host, was already with us asking what we'd like to drink. As he moved away to the cocktail cabinet, I said to Miss Walsh, "I've always been an admirer of your work, but I particularly enjoyed your performance in an otherwise undistinguished film called *October Man*."

She moved away a little and as I followed her she nodded her head in Ambler's direction and said, "It's the only film he ever produced."

In a sense, I felt that Eric and I were now even. Fortunately, we remained friends.

♦   ♦   ♦

Olive Harding had been incredibly kind and helpful to Barbara and me, so we were particularly pleased that we were able to sell a Canadian play to the Drama Department of the BBC, written by

Joseph Schull, the man who had given us a letter of introduction to Olive.

The Concert was a play we'd already done on the Canadian Broadcasting Corporation, and it created a sensation when it appeared on the BBC Light Programme in the spring of 1950. It told the story of a nurse, blinded in the war, struggling to regain her independence by resisting her parents, who wanted to look after her, and living alone in a flat in Montreal. A chance meeting led to a growing friendship with a Dr Richard Jennings, and as the relationship grew, she invited him to attend a symphony concert with her parents. He turned down the invitation, and when she next knocked on his door in the same block of flats, he had a friend answer the door and tell her that Dr Jennings had moved away. When the friend accused him of unnecessary brutality he said, "To her I am Dr Jennings, a friend, but to her parents and everyone else at that concert I would be a buck nigger."

The play was uniformly well-reviewed, although we received a rather odd letter from a distinguished consultant, who maintained that we'd cheated by having me play the part of a negro. Everyone knew, he said, that a negro's voice is immediately identifiable, and that had we cast a negro, the game would have been given away from the beginning. I don't know if the distinguished consultant is still alive, but I wonder if he could now listen to, say, newsreader Trevor McDonald with his eyes closed and identify him as a negro, or for that matter, any number of distinguished black actors we now see and hear regularly on television.

One reviewer said:

This play, written for Canadian radio by Joseph Schull, stands clearly above the endless notes, discordant and otherwise, that have issued from the BBC's hurdy-gurdy since the beginning of the year. Even the critical ear listening with the closest attention never gained an inkling of whence the play was leading and when the ending came it really was a surprise. It gave the impression of being written, played and produced with the very deepest sincerity in a cause that is much in the air today. I have purposely refrained from revealing the story of this outstanding example of radio drama at a more popular hour, for those who missed the Wednesday production.

Barbara garnered most of the acting reviews, with Joyce Grenfell writing in the *Listener*: "Her interpretation of Anne verged on the sublime."

138

She was immediately invited to read *The White Oaks of Jalna* on the BBC's *Book at Bedtime*.

♦   ♦   ♦

Breakfast with Braden was gathering more publicity than even those of us involved in it thought it deserved. A review in the *Daily Express* said:

> I have praised this show before, but it's only by being a constant irritant – like R. C. Sherriff's strawberry pip under the plate, that one can finally get the BBC to listen. The sketch about the BBC Director of the Unspoken Word – in charge of "pauses, commas, and coughs" – was pure malice and pure joy. Braden – who writes the show – is as cosy as carpet slippers, as astringent as a good mouthwash, at least as witty as his nearest rival and very human.

One phrase in that review was starting to cause me trouble. The suggestion that I wrote the show resulted from the fact that Frank and Denis didn't want a credit and since he only wrote part of the show, Eric didn't feel he could take one.

In fact my astringency and wit were totally the creation of the three writers, but people who assumed I wrote it tended to steer clear of me. One night I found myself at a dinner party seated next to Terry-Thomas, then pioneering television comedy with his

Terry-Thomas

popular show *How Do You View?* When Terry turned in my direction he went white and said, "I particularly asked not to be seated next to you, I don't like being insulted." I assured him this wasn't my intention and that, indeed, I would be fascinated to learn about television from him because I was hoping to get into that field myself. Terry relaxed and explained that the fascinating thing about television for him was that viewers, unlike radio listeners, appeared to be under the impression that he could see *them* as well as they could see *him*. He said, "Only the other day I was walking along Kensington High Street when I was stopped by a woman in the street who said, 'Mr Thomas, how do you like our new curtains?'" It was a profound observation and I never forgot it.

Terry made another point about television which seems obvious now but I hadn't realised it at the time. He said, "If you're doing a comedy series on television, your personality will carry you through the first six shows. After that, it's the writing that counts."

The fact remained that I was getting a reputation for wit I didn't deserve, and I did spend a lot of time in the show insulting my colleagues:

The theory that a good tune would always survive a bad performance has just been blasted by Nat Temple and his Orchestra, playing "Don't Blame Me". Who else?

Temple's band only do these sessions because they're no longer steady enough to walk the kerb.

For those of you who've just come into the room and found that a loved one has shot himself, that was Benny Lee singing "Liza". Mind you, it isn't easy to give the listeners what they want. Benny Lee's head, for instance. Comes off easily enough, but how are you going to divide it fairly amongst a thousand people?

That was "PS I Love You" sung by Pearl Carr, and we can only hope that PS was listening, because no one else would recognise the tune.

That was Ronald Fletcher, the BBC announcer. Mr Fletcher had himself put on the day shift because unless he can get away early to the news cinema, he has to sit beside almost any girl at all.

Frank and Denis always ended the programme with a final line from Ronald Fletcher. I don't know if they deliberately made a rod for their backs, but they certainly managed to keep up a high standard over several years. Older people still come up to me and quote them, laughing heartily the while. Examples include:

The programme you have just heard will be reprinted in the *Listener* over the editor's dead body . . .

Mr Nat Temple appeared by courtesy of the Greenwich Magistrate's Court . . .

Mr Benny Lee can be heard in concert this week in the Penicillin Room of the Streatham Cash Chemists . . .

This programme has been recorded by the Pacific Service of the BBC, and may be heard in Northern Australia on January 17th at 8.00 p.m. old time. BOAC takes you there and brings you back . . .

And so another *Breakfast with Braden* shows how much better things look on paper . . .

It is an offence to have a wireless on too loud these still summer evenings. It can annoy your neighbour. An even better way is to throw a dead cat on his lawn . . .

Sir Malcolm Sargent will conduct the Promenade Concerts at the Royal Albert Hall this season. He's done rather well for himself, hasn't he? . . .

Bernard Braden's latest picture may be seen on his mother's dressing table . . .

Ronald Fletcher

141

At one point, the match-makers Bryant and May asked permission to reproduce some of these gems on their boxes. Unfortunately, the copyright in all the scripts belonged to the BBC, who in those days didn't approve of any sort of commercial connection with the hallowed Corporation, so Frank and Denis lost their chance to pioneer the concept of commercial spin-offs.

◆　　◆　　◆

Somehow, *Breakfast with Braden* was becoming a cult, probably due to the combined talents of Muir, Norden and Nicol, all of whom had enjoyed the benefit of a classical education and were encouraged by Pat Dixon to use it. The rule seemed to be that if a joke required the audience to have heard of T. S. Eliot and, in Pat's view, it was funny . . . we used it.

I began to collect autographs . . . inadvertently. Among the people who wrote to me c/o the BBC were Rebecca West, Augustus John, C. A. Lejeune, Sir Compton Mackenzie, Robert Boothby, Sir Henry Moore and Christopher Fry.

In the spring of 1950 Christopher Fry was Britain's outstanding playwright. He'd written *The Lady's not for Burning*, and when that closed at the Lyric Theatre it was replaced by an Anouilh play, *translated* by Mr Fry. Sir Laurence Olivier was continuing his actor/manager season at the St James's Theatre with another play by Fry called *Venus Observed* while at the Lyric Hammersmith there were two one-act Fry plays, one starring Richard Burton.

During one of the recordings when I was allegedly recounting my life story, I'd reached a point where I was supposed to be navigating a solo trip around the world. My speech went: "Day followed day, mile followed mile. When I reached the Equator I leaned over the side and cut a little bit off to take home as a souvenir. Then into the Gulf Stream, the Bay of Whisky and the Sewage Canal. On and on I bore."

At that point Benny Lee contributed his first ad-lib to the series. He said, "You certainly do."

I wasn't ready for it and it showed. The orchestra realised it had been an ad-lib and didn't laugh. Benny himself was a little taken aback, and in my attempt to get us both out of it I said the first thing that came into my head which was, "This lad lusts to lose a limb or be lamed, 'ere he went."

Understandably, that didn't get a laugh either, so I added, "Sorry, Benny, I just threw that in on the off-chance that Christopher Fry is listening. Something for everybody."

Benny Lee

Well . . . Christopher Fry *was* listening, and took the trouble to write me a letter enquiring if I had coined the line, or if not, did I know its source? It was only then I realised that in my desperation I'd summoned up a line I'd said many times in Canada while playing the second shepherd in the York and Chester Mystery Plays. Happily I reported the source to Mr Fry who then invited Barbara and me to dinner. We were indeed profiting from the kindness of strangers.

The unexpected success of this unlikely radio show at such an unlikely hour was reflected in the relationships of everyone concerned with the show. We were all becoming celebrities of a sort and nothing draws people together quite so much as mutual success.

Eric Nicol, having told me that Ronald Fletcher was a gambling man, gave me an opportunity to have a little fun at Ronnie's expense. As I've said, Mr Fletcher paid little attention to our efforts, and seemed to look down his nose at me particularly. I took to looking up words in the dictionary, words with unusual pronunciations, and working them into conversations with Fletcher. The first one, I think, was "peremptory". When Fletcher announced we were in danger of running into overtime which would make him late for his next assignment, I said, "There's no need to be *pere*mptory about it, Mr Fletcher."

"*Pere*mptory, Braden?"

"Sorry. Did I say something wrong?"

143

"The word is 'per*em*ptory'."

"Really? I've always pronounced it *'per*emptory'."

"Well, you're quite wrong."

"I'm sorry. Would you like to make a small bet?"

"Any amount you care to name."

"How about five quid?"

"Done."

Having looked it up in the *OED* Mr Fletcher dutifully paid his debt, and the following week, I happened to mention that there was no point in my having a car because I hadn't a *gar*idj to keep it in.

"*Gar*idj, Braden?"

At that time the only pronunciation given for the word in the *OED* was "gar*idj*".

The following week I got him again on "sacri*leg*ious" as opposed to "sacri*lig*ious", and by the time he'd lost £20, Mr Fletcher was on to the joke.

Eric Nicol decided to use this little contretemps as a means of introducing Ronald Fletcher into the script. So on the morning of April 22nd, listeners heard the following:

FLETCHER: May I go home now? There are more important things on my agenda.

BRADEN: Don't you listen to what goes on between your two paltry announcements, Mr Fletcher?

FLETCHER: Oh no, I have other interests. I am studying for the Stuart Hibberd Bursary and Challenge Cup.

BRADEN: What's that?

FLETCHER: It's open to all announcers. The winners get an upgrading in salary, and are allowed to pronounce "controversy" any way they like.

BRADEN: Sounds fun. What do you have to study?

FLETCHER: Words. I've learned several new words today. For example "onomatopoeia".

BRADEN: Onomat o what a?

FLETCHER: A most interesting word, very worthy of the Home Service. From the Greek *omna* meaning "name", and *poeia* – to make. Thus giving us the complete definition "the formation of words in imitation of sound". Am I boring you?

BRADEN: Yes. Let me bore you. I also, in my small way, study words. For example, the word "rissole". That also comes from the Greek.

FLETCHER: (*sceptical*) Really?

144

BRADEN: Yes, he has a little restaurant round the corner. The word "rissole" itself is a corruption of "reincarnated soul" meaning something that returns from the dead in another form.

FLETCHER: Fancy. I'd quite forgotten that.

BRADEN: Oh, it was bound to come back to you. Generally in the middle of the afternoon. Or again, browsing through my dictionary I find the epithet, "umbraculiferous" meaning "bearing something like an open umbrella" . . .

FLETCHER: . . . Like an open umbrella? I'm afraid I don't follow that one.

BRADEN: I thought it would be over your head. But do you like it?

FLETCHER: I adore it. A very useful word.

BRADEN: Especially in wet weather. It saves quite a long sentence. Instead of saying, "I saw Pearl Carr in the street bearing something like an open umbrella," you can say, "I saw an umbraculiferous Pearl Carr in the street."

FLETCHER: Coming from a Latin derivative, I suppose?

BRADEN: I never pry into her private life. Then another nice word for Cup Final Saturday is "Vesiculata".

FLETCHER: Oh, I couldn't agree more. What does it mean?

BRADEN: It means the campanularian medusae.

FLETCHER: Oh yes. Well, I must go back to my studies now, I'm afraid.

BRADEN: I thought that would hold him.

BENNY: Oh, Mr Braden?

BRADEN: Benny?

BENNY: I couldn't help overhearing because I was listening. What are the "campanularian medusae"?

BRADEN: Benny, there's only one word to describe you and that I'm afraid is "nondescript".

BENNY: Nondescript. What does that mean?

BRADEN: It's been cut out of the *script*. Let us now abjure further procrastination and proceed with chanson.

BENNY: From the French?

BRADEN: From the music. Or as near to it as you think you can get.

Benny Lee had started his professional life as an acrobat in Scotland. It lasted for one evening, largely because of the shape of Benny's nose. In the finale of the act the twelve acrobats divided

145

themselves into pairs, each one grasping the ankles of his partner. They then executed a series of somersaults around the stage and as the manoeuvre proceeded Benny noticed that he was beginning to follow a circle of blood. His blood. Every time he was in the down part of the somersault his nose hit the stage, and that virtually ended his career as an acrobat.

He then joined the Glasgow Citizens Theatre where he served a useful apprenticeship and indeed became a very fine actor. It was as a singer, though, that he made his mark in British entertainment. And there are still songs that I would rather hear Benny Lee sing than anyone else.

Frank and Denis had cast him as the ultimate in naïvety. He fell under the spell of a gentleman called "Sid Greenblatt" who came up with a new scheme for Benny to make a fortune every week.

BENNY: Mr Braden, I have been in consultation with my partner, the man who bought up all the iron filings and became a big magnate.

BRADEN: Not the ineffable Sid Greenblatt?

BENNY: Who but, Mr Braden? I tell you, sometimes that man's business acumen and shrewd grasp of market activities amazes me. I wish I had a quarter of *his* brains.

BRADEN: Or anybody's.

BENNY: He's no ordinary businessman. He's a real typhoon.

BRADEN: Tycoon, Benny. A typhoon is just a whole lot of wind that . . . well perhaps you're right. What's the latest deal?

BENNY: He's gone up to the North Pole and bought a Goldberg.

BRADEN: You mean an iceberg.

BENNY: To you it may be an iceberg, but to us it's going to prove a goldberg. We'll make a million out of it. A *cool* million. Sid is going to moor it on the Thames just by Wapping Old Stairs during the hot part of the summer and sell little bits of ice to overheated white-collar workers.

BRADEN: Who wants to buy bits of ice?

BENNY: Who wants to – have you ever tasted a bit of ice, Mr Braden? It's delicious. I guarantee it'll melt in your mouth.

BRADEN: Sorry, I don't like the taste of it.

BENNY: You don't have to eat it, we also sell it in containers so you can take it home.

BRADEN: What for?
BENNY: Melt it down. Makes wonderful water.
BRADEN: What can I do with water?
BENNY: Make yourself some paving stones.
BRADEN: Paving stones?
BENNY: All you have to do is mix it with a little cement.
BRADEN: Sid's got this all doped out?
BENNY: I tell you that cold calculating brain misses nothing. He's planned it down to the last icicle. I've got my work and he has his.
BRADEN: What's your work?
BENNY: The preliminary stuff. I've got to go up to the Arctic and row the iceberg down to Wapping.
BRADEN: You'll be away some time.
BENNY: That's all right. Sid's taking care of my family. He's got my wife a job in a dancing troupe that's going to Buenos Aires, and he's wangled my little boy a lovely holiday riding pit ponies. I tell you, Mr Braden, you can't find a hole in Sid's logic.
BRADEN: Meantime Benny, why not make with the hole in your head.
BENNY: Pardon me?
BRADEN: We'll see. First, sing.

In fact, Benny Lee was never late for a rehearsal or a show, and was one of the most totally professional people I ever worked with. Our only problem with Benny was that he was very sensitive on behalf of other people in show business, and since part of

Members of band

Pearl Carr

our stock-in-trade was insulting fellow performers, Benny was always the one to suggest that we were being unfair. If I said that Charlie Kunz was the only pianist to play entirely with his thumbs, Benny was apt to remind me that "Charlie has been a sick man" and that if he heard a line like that it might retard his recovery. On one occasion I announced that "Music in Miniature" would be conducted next week by Wee Georgie Wood. Benny thought the line should be dropped because Georgie was very sensitive about his size. Fortunately, producer Pat Dixon paid no attention whatever to these protestations.

When Pearl Carr joined us she was the lead singer with the Keynotes, and when it came to music, one rehearsal was all Pearl needed. Her pitch was virtually perfect, and she was as skilled with point numbers as with ballads. In ballads particularly, she had a feel for a lyric that could be genuinely moving, even at 8.15 in the morning. Had she been born in the United States, I think she'd have become a major singing star, in a class with Jo Stafford, Anita Ellis, and June Christy.

In the Muir and Norden script Pearl was supposed to be in love with me. That, of course, was before she married Teddy Johnson.

BRADEN: And now a remarkable little example of British craftsmanship at its best . . . an ordinary pipe cleaner, bent

148

into a circle and plated with gold lacquer. If you take
this in your right hand, scrape off the lacquer and
straighten it out, you'll find it makes a perfect pipe
cleaner. Anyone shopping for tank traps will be interested in . . .

PEARL: Oh, I hope you don't mind me interrupting you, Mr
Braden . . .

BRADEN: Not at all. I didn't know how to finish that tank trap
gag . . . And what gives you that starry-eyed look
today, Pearl?

PEARL: You do, Mr Braden. You're so handsome and virile
and manly.

BRADEN: Oh, Pearl, come off it.

PEARL: So clever, so intelligent.

BRADEN: Oh, Pearl, come off it.

PEARL: Well then, not *really* clever, not *exactly* intelligent.

BRADEN: Pearl!

PEARL: Yes?

BRADEN: Get back *on* it.

PEARL: Oh, Mr Braden, you have such a ready wit.

BRADEN: Yes. Of course, it wasn't quite ready then.

PEARL: I suppose I deserved that snub. But *you* don't know
what it's like to love somebody out of your reach.

BRADEN: Oh yes, I do, Pearl. Every time I try to love anybody
she ducks out of my reach.

PEARL: But it's different with girls.

BRADEN: What do you think I've tried it with – ducks?

PEARL: You haunt me, Mr Braden. I've got pictures of you
everywhere. All over the walls, on the door, on the
ceiling –

BRADEN: On the ceiling!

PEARL: I like to look at you when I gargle. It brings it all back.

BRADEN: That's the most romantic thought I've ever heard. But
it's no use, Pearl. I'm not for you. You wouldn't love
me when I'm old and worn out.

PEARL: (*sobbing*) But I do, I do.

BRADEN: Now, now, dear, don't cry like that. Here, take my
handkerchief and wipe the tears from those lovely
lashes.

PEARL: (*sniffing*) Thank you . . . here's your handkerchief.

BRADEN: Thank *you*. Here are your lashes.

PEARL: Thank you. Oh, Mr Braden, can't you give me *some*
encouragement – some memento of you, something
lasting I can keep always. Something that won't go?

149

BRADEN: All right, Pearl, take this.
PEARL: What is it?
BRADEN: Benny Lee's wrist watch. That won't go.
PEARL: Oh dash . . .
BRADEN: Pearl Carr will now sing a song her mother taught her
. . . with specially cleaned up lyrics.

Nat Temple was a graduate of the Squadronairs, the official band of the RAF. He was Pat Dixon's choice to lead our band, with Malcolm Lockyer as pianist and arranger. The band itself varied from time to time in personnel, but never suffered in quality. The string section was led by Louis Stevens, Nat led the reeds with his clarinet, the brass section according to availability could include Kenny Baker, Eddie Calvert, Don Lusher, Don Hudson, George Chisholm, Jack Bentley and Tommy McQuirter, while on drums it was usually Eric Delaney or Jack Parnell. It took us a little while to realise that Nat was a personality in his own right with a dry sense of humour and an ability to read lines, so long as he didn't play anyone other than himself.
It started like this.

BRADEN: That was Nat Temple's Orchestra, conducted by the man who inspired the song "I Can't Tell a Waltz From a Tango". And now, friends, an exciting drama about —
NAT: Just a minute, Bern, can I interrupt?
BRADEN: Friends, it is Nat Temple! How about a big round of silence?

More members of band

NAT: Bern, I hope you're aware that by announcing to the listeners that I can't tell a waltz from a tango I could slap a sue on you. You see, Bern, from a conductor's point of view, there's not much to choose between a waltz and a tango. You see, a conductor is limited. Now take the baton. You got that bit of wood in your head? Right. You can make it go *up*, you can make it go *down*, you can make it go *sideways*. What else can you do with it?

BRADEN: (pause) Well . . .

NAT: No, Bern. See it from my point of view as the conductor. The man holding the stick — a waltz is just one up and two sideways. A tango is two down, one up, change hands. Least, that's how I did our recording of that famous tango, Jell.

BRADEN: I thought it was "Jealousy".

NAT: Yes, but I always leave out the "lousy" bit. You see, Bern, when it comes to music, I'm not a *complete* ignosserous.

BRADEN: Then how have you managed to maintain your belief that Puccini is a form of spaghetti?

NAT: Oh, you *are* maddening at times, Bern.

And it progressed as follows:

BRADEN: That was "Avalon" played by Nat Temple and his Orchestra — the sort of music you hear once in a lifetime . . . why did it have to be *our* lifetime?

Nat Temple

Now, friends, another chapter in our series, "Do It Yourself". This week we deal with laying eggs. Now you need a lot of grit to –

NAT: Pardon me, Bern. Can I interrupt?

BRADEN: Well, it's Nat Temple. And there's nobody I'd rather talk to. Or to put it another way, I'd rather talk to nobody.

NAT: (*gratified*) How nice of you, Bern. What I've always liked about you is the knack you have of making a person feel *wanted*.

BRADEN: I thought you *were*.

NAT: No no, that's all blown over. The girl's father agreed to settle out of court. Funny what a difference the last few months have made, isn't it, Bern? Here's me blossomed out into a lovable light comedian – while you – well, frankly, Bern, you've blossomed *in*.

BRADEN: Thank you, Nat. Now will you pardon Bern while Bern does a slow burn?

NAT: Not at all, Bern. And yet, when you come to think of it, Bern, success hasn't altered me, has it?

BRADEN: Oh no, you were big-headed before you started.

NAT: *That's* it. And now it's me on the up and you on the down. It's like with a herd of deer. There's the old bull, meaning you, Bern. Then one day he gets challenged by the young stag. Meaning *me*, Bern. And they fight over the doe. Meaning the money, Bern.

BRADEN: You've got this all doped out, haven't you, Nat? Well, I know one dope who's going to be out next series.

NAT: I'm not even worried, Bern. You see these days I've got so many irons in the fire. For example, there's my songs. I can place *them* any day.

BRADEN: Well, place them with the irons, Nat.

NAT: Not this latest batch of songs, 'cos I've got a smashing idea this time.

BRADEN: I don't know how you think of them. Or why.

NAT: Oh, I just get inspiration, Bern. I might be in Oxford Street when suddenly an idea hits me. I don't pause. I pick me hat up, put me clarinet away and start scribbling.

BRADEN: Well what are your latest scribblings?

NAT: Listen, Bern, this is what I do. I take *two* popular songs – two – shove the titles together and that makes a brand *new* song.

BRADEN: Does it work?

NAT: Like a charm bracelet. Listen, I've taken a popular song of Maurice Chevalier, and a popular song of Bud Flanagan and joined them together.

BRADEN: Result?

NAT: "You brought a new kind of love to me, underneath the arches." After that I produced, "It's my mother's birthday today, the old grey mare she ain't what she used to be."

BRADEN: Should be an evergreen. Like poison ivy.

NAT: Well, how about this one? "In a monastery garden there is nothing like a dame."

BRADEN: So true.

NAT: Well if you don't like that, I've got another idea. Look, you know songs like, "California Here I Come", "On the Road to Mandalay", "The Last Time I Saw Paris" – well, I want to do songs like that. But I want to compose songs about the land of *my* birth.

BRADEN: Mongolia?

NAT: Great Britain. Popular songs about the beauty spots of our own dear land. My first one is called, "Deep in the Heart of Brixton".

BRADEN: Great stuff.

NAT: Isn't it? My next is called "Does Your Mother Come from Aldgate?" And my latest is a wonderful duet: "You're not Sick, You're Just in Stockport".

BRADEN: May I wish you the very best of luck, particularly if you ever visit Stockport.

NAT: But you have to admit it, Bern, I've got a flair, haven't I?

BRADEN: You have, Nat. Please light it and apply it to your celluloid collar.

Nat, band and me

At some point we began to write Nat's wife, Freda, into the script. Not in person, but as someone who kept sending me notes demanding more air-time for "her Nat", much to his embarrassment.

On one occasion the entire cast was invited to do a late night charity show at a Lewisham music-hall. It needed rehearsing, and the only place we could all get together at the same time happened to be Nat's flat. Freda kindly fed us sandwiches during the break, and as we left and were going down in the lift Benny said to Nat, "You know, Nat, I definitely get the impression that where your marriage is concerned, your wife is definitely on top."

Nat thought for a moment and then said, "Well, Benny, Freda is better educated than I am, she's more intelligent than I am, she's more practical than I am . . . come to think of it, she's superior to me in every way."

We were very much an integrated group, enjoying our work, and we would be together for several years. In fact, to the best of my knowledge, when one considers the other comedy shows of the period, *Life with the Lyons*, *Ray's a Laugh*, *Take it From Here*, *Much Binding in the Marsh*, *The Goon Show*, and *Educating Archie*, at the time of writing, ours is the only show where all the main participants are still alive, and, with the exception of Benny Lee, still working . . . and with the right offer, I don't think it would be hard to persuade Benny out of retirement.

◆　　◆　　◆

Streetcar was continuing to play to packed houses, but its reputation continued to be pornographic. That's why I was slightly concerned when I received a letter from the Board of Trustees of my father's Church, telling me they'd advertised for someone to take my father's place and had had a number of applications which had been honed down to three. The one that appealed to them most had come from a clergyman in Dunoon in Scotland. They'd interviewed the two Canadian applicants, but still felt that on paper the man from Dunoon seemed to be the best bet. The trouble was that they didn't feel justified in having a member of the board travel all the way to Scotland (roughly seven thousand miles), or paying for the gentleman to visit them in Vancouver. If he didn't measure up in person to his written application it would be a matter of considerable embarrassment to everyone concerned. As my father's son, I was probably best qualified to assess the qualities of the person who would follow my father at Ryerson United Church. Was I prepared to travel to

Dunoon to meet him, or persuade him to visit me in London? They would be guided by my report.

If *they* were embarrassed, you can imagine how I felt. The likelihood that reports of this scandalous play and my connection with it had not reached Dunoon was slight.

There was no possibility of my going to Dunoon given my work schedule in London, so I decided that I'd take a chance on the Reverend Stevenson not knowing my name, and wrote him a letter asking if he could possibly come to London. I got a prompt and affirmative reply, with no indication that he'd either heard me on radio, or knew about *Streetcar*.

By now, Barbara and I had moved out of Chatsworth Court where our lease had expired and were living in a flat in Harley Street, due to the kindness of a BBC documentary writer, Margery Banks and her husband the Hon. Edward Ward. They understood that we needed temporary accommodation while we looked for a more permanent residence, and had made the flat available at a nominal rent because they had other accommodation. (Mind you, they could afford it.) Still, it was an act of kindness from people we barely knew.

Barbara and I planned the Reverend Stevenson's visit carefully. We would arrange to give him an early supper at the flat, between the Wednesday matinée and the evening performance of *Streetcar*. If the meeting went on longer than we intended, I would plead a previous engagement, not mentioning the theatre, and Barbara would continue to entertain him at the flat until it was time for him to leave, hopefully to catch a train in blissful ignorance of the reason for my early departure.

All was agreed, and because the flat was on the top floor of a building without a lift, we at least knew we'd be testing his physical stamina, since he'd have to walk up ninety-six steps to reach us.

On the specified Wednesday afternoon, after the curtain fell, I dashed out to the stage door to be met by a gentleman in a clerical collar who informed me that he was the Reverend Stevenson, and that he'd taken an early train so he could attend the matinée.

In the taxi en route to the flat we didn't discuss *Streetcar*. He expressed himself a fan of Vivien Leigh and that's where we left it. Having seen a copy of his application, Barbara and I didn't feel competent to do anything other than assess his personality, and had decided simply to talk about Vancouver, the Church, the parish, and the amenities of the area. Before and during supper we waxed enthusiastic and waited for him to ask questions. He didn't. Surely a man with a wife and two children considering a

155

seven-thousand-mile move to an unknown country would have a number of doubts as to whether or not he should consider such a move? It wasn't even an interview, either way. Eventually we were beginning to sound like a Chamber of Commerce handout from the City of Vancouver. Finally, it was time for me to leave, and I asked Mr Stevenson point-blank if there was anything he wanted to know.

He said, "We've just the one problem. My wife wants to know if there's central heating in the manse."

I assured him there was, and there were no further questions. That night I wrote my report with due humility to the Board of Trustees, and within months the Reverend Stevenson and his family were comfortably ensconced in the centrally heated manse where they stayed for the next fifteen years.

◆   ◆   ◆

On Friday evening, April 21st, 1950, the show we'd piloted in 1949, *Leave your name and number*, began as a series on the Light Programme, with Miriam Karlin, Stephen Jack, Norman Shelley and Lyn Evans. The orchestra was conducted by Stanley Black and the show, happily, written by Eric Nicol. Barbara and I did not expect it to be a success because the plot was still based on the fact that we were two Canadian performers trying to get work in London. That had been all well and good when we'd done the pilot, but there were now listed in the *Radio Times* two weekly series, *Breakfast with Braden* and *Leave your name and number* with at the bottom of the listing the announcement that I was appearing in *A Streetcar Named Desire* at the Aldwych Theatre, London.

Wolverhampton Express: "*Leave your name and number* is one of the freshest shows heard on radio in years. There's no doubt that the Bradens have something to show us in radio technique. I'd like to see both these artists on TV."

Manchester Guardian: "Among current variety broadcasts, *Leave your name and number* with Bernard Braden and Barbara Kelly is among the most amusing. These two have the laconic humour that seems to come from across the Atlantic rather than anywhere else."

Star: "Another new programme with popular appeal is *Leave your name and number*, a comedy vehicle for Bernard Braden and Barbara Kelly, the Canadians who established themselves with BBC audiences by their work in *Starlight Hour* and *Breakfast with Braden*."

Musical Express: "Isn't it surprising how Bernard Braden and Barbara Kelly keep up the tremendously high standard of their work on radio. Their new series *Leave your name and number* is a delight. The secret lies in script concentration. Most shows work to a formula, and there always comes a time when the writers are stuck for gags to fit the preconceived situations. The Bradens, it would appear, in co-operation with their writer, Eric Nicol, concentrate on story value first. The plot is created and then the gags are written into the plot formula. This seems to give them a great deal more scope than most of our radio stars. But don't try it all at once – maybe the little matter of talent enters into the picture as well."

Sunday Graphic: "Three months ago, Miriam Karlin had never seen the inside of a BBC studio, although her friends often told her 'you ought to be on the radio'. Brian Sears gave her a break in *Variety Bandbox*, and she was chosen as a resident comedienne with Peter Sellars to succeed Frankie Howard. Now she's co-starring with Bernard Braden and Barbara Kelly in the amusing new series *Leave your name and number*, produced by Ian Messiter. And it was only sixteen weeks ago that Brian Sears was told 'A Miss Karlin would like to speak to you.'"

Daily Express: "*Leave your name and number* made a successful début the other night with Bernard Braden and Barbara Kelly as two Canadians in contemporary England."

Evening Gazette: "*Leave your name and number* with Bernard Braden and Barbara Kelly and material supplied by another Canadian, Eric Nicol, is one of the delights of the radio week. If you haven't heard this programme take the next opportunity to listen – it is a classic example of what radio variety should sound like."

Daily Express: "I recently heard of a young Canadian radio actor who claimed that he was busy on the script of a new series called *Half an Hour without Braden.*"

Daily Herald: "Here's a show I forecast, will become as popular as *Take it from here*. Bernard Braden and Barbara Kelly's *Leave your name and number*. It's the BBC's biggest hit for years, fresh, funny and adult, with the Bradens getting into the kind of scrapes we've all been in. This show is full of laughs. The scriptwriter, Canadian Eric Nicol, has brought a crispness to radio which has not been experienced since Denis Norden and Frank Muir burst into broadcasting after the war. Eric has been here only three months. Highly recommended. Listen tonight."

Evening News: "The Braden/Kelly show *Leave your name and number* seems to me to have a nice proportion of laughs per minute. It sounds as if it's going to be as fearless as *Take it from here* when dealing with various aspects of life today."

Perhaps the show's success lay in the fact that the British public was used to the fact that rationing and austerity were still with them with no apparent end in sight. To Eric Nicol, and indeed to Barbara and me, rationing and indifferent food were not things we took for granted, and the fact that they were new to us featured heavily in the scripts.

In every script Miriam Karlin appeared as a cleaning lady who occasionally dropped in for a cup of tea to the "Kelly Actors' Agency". After each morning's job-hunting, we returned to the agency, which boasted one actor, to lick our wounds and call it lunch.

SOUND EFFECT: Door opens.
BRADEN: After you, Barbara.
MIRIAM: Coo-eee.
BARBARA: Well, look who's here, Mrs Grivel.
MIRIAM: Afternoon, ducks. Watch that floor, I've just –
BRADEN: Whoops!
SOUND EFFECT: Body thump follows quickly on the "Whoops".
MIRIAM: – waxed it.
BARBARA: Hurt yourself, Bernie?
BRADEN: Oh no. My spine broke the fall.
MIRIAM: Sorry, dear. My, the floor has got a nice polish now.
BARBARA: What brought this on, Mrs Grivel? You've never waxed our floor before.
MIRIAM: I was just waiting for my tea to steep, so I thought I'd do the bit by the door where the people see it.
BRADEN: Too late, you mean.
BARBARA: Do you think you could spare us a cup?
MIRIAM: Oh certainly, dear. You had masses in the caddy. Doesn't look like *our* tea. Got bigger leaves, but I suppose that's because it's Canadian. Everything grows bigger out there, don't it?
BRADEN: Yes, it's a wonderful sight in Canada, watching the elephants moving down the rows of tea trees, plucking the leaves with their trunks and blowing them into half-pound packages, untouched by hand.
MIRIAM: I'm sure. Here's your tea, dear.
BARBARA/BRADEN: Thank you.
MIRIAM: Some friends of mine emigrated to Canada last year. That was before petrol come off.
BARBARA: How do they like it?
MIRIAM: They're coming home next week.

158

BARBARA: They were disappointed with Canada?
MIRIAM: No. Mrs Pickley, that's Mr Pickley's wife, she's expecting an addition.
BRADEN: And she wants to have it for Britain?
MIRIAM: No, she wants to have it for nothing.
BRADEN: Of course. The ever-lovin' scheme.
MIRIAM: And Mrs Pickley says all them trees make her nervous. She says where she's at, it's like Regent's Park all over with the zoo let loose.
BARBARA: The wilderness doesn't agree with her, eh?
MIRIAM: No, it don't. My daughter Hedy's the one that likes the wilderness. She's pretty wild herself, you know.
BARBARA: Is Hedy thinking of emigrating to Canada?
MIRIAM: No fear. Not while she's with her old man. Lud detests America.
BRADEN: When was he over?
MIRIAM: Oh, Lud's never been there. He just detests it. He says he'll have nothing to do with any place that says everybody's created equal. He says if everybody's created equal, why ain't he got nothing?
BRADEN: He prefers to believe that the gods play favourites.
MIRIAM: Lud was born with nothing, and it's been all he could do to hold his own.
BARBARA: He still hasn't found a job?
MIRIAM: He's not looking, dear. He just sits in the kitchen, whittling toothpicks.
BRADEN: Toothpicks?
MIRIAM: Yes. He says he'll make a fortune when they take the ration off meat.
BARBARA: Well, speaking of cavities, Mrs Grivel, when you've finished your tea, the wash basin –
MIRIAM: Well, must be popping, ducks, or I'll miss my television. Cheeribye.
BARBARA/BRADEN: Cheeribye.
SOUND EFFECT: Door closes.
BRADEN: Mrs Grivel, our char, has television.
BARBARA: Uh huh.
BRADEN: I haven't even got normal vision.
BARBARA: What are we going to use for money as from now?
BRADEN: How much have we left in your purse?
BARBARA: I don't know. All I know is that last week the rustling stopped and yesterday the jingling stopped. There's something thudding around on its own, but I'm afraid it's my lipstick.

159

BRADEN: (*scoffing*) How many meals can you get out of a lipstick?
BARBARA: Plenty, if you know how to use it.

Miriam usually played several parts in each show, and in one script she portrayed a waitress in a BBC canteen where we'd gone to try and get a job.

BRADEN: Over here, Barbara. We get our trays at this end.
BARBARA: Oh goody. Mine has more gravy on it than yours has.
MIRIAM: Can I help?
BRADEN: Yes please, we'd like some lunch. Have you anything like meat?
MIRIAM: Yes. The raspberry tart's like meat . . . you know, red-like.
BARBARA: Oh, wait a minute. What's that over there? It looks like meat.
MIRIAM: That's roast mutton.
BRADEN: Roast mutton.
MIRIAM: Yes. It's a step between roast lamb and rubbish.
BARBARA: We'll have some.
MIRIAM: Both of you?
BRADEN: Yes, why?
MIRIAM: You're not related to each other, are you?
BARBARA: No, why?
MIRIAM: We don't like to serve it to members of the same family, in case . . . you know. Would you like some greens with it?
BRADEN: Yes, I think some sort of floral tribute would be nice.
MIRIAM: There you are. You can pass on now.
BARBARA: That's what I'm afraid of.
BRADEN: Just a minute. This plate is cold.
MIRIAM: That's all right, dear. So's the meat and greens. And for a sweet there's the raspberry tart and our special soggy trifle.
BRADEN: Which would you recommend?
MIRIAM: Well, it's difficult to say. The raspberry tart's been very popular with the flies all day.
BARBARA: We'll take the trifle.
MIRIAM: Anything to drink?
BRADEN: No thanks. We brought our own arsenic.

It was during the run of *Leave your name and number* that I received a script from a film producer offering me the leading role in a film about an American safe-cracker. I made the mistake of mentioning this one night when Barbara and I were dining with Gilbert Harding. Gilbert almost choked on his food and then went into paroxysms of laughter.

I said, "What's so funny?"

Gilbert took some time to recover, then explained rather bluntly that he'd never envisaged me as a potential film star. "You have a long, lugubrious face, and a jutting jaw, Bernie, and I doubt if a film screen could accommodate it all." He collapsed with laughter yet again. "I can see Barbara having a career in films, but *you*? I fear not, dear boy!"

Gilbert was one of my best friends, so I knew he meant it. When I took the script into my meeting with the film producer I said I couldn't see myself in the part. And the producer asked me why. I explained that since the role required the hero to be attractive to the ladies I didn't feel it was really me. He was a good-looking man and I suggested he might well play the part himself. He shrugged in a bewildered sort of way and said that "Perhaps something else would turn up."

I made the second mistake of recounting this story to Eric Nicol, and within a week it turned up, somewhat amended, in a script of *Leave your name and number*. I was supposed to be auditioning for television. The producer was played by Norman Shelley who did a fiendishly accurate impression of Gilbert Harding:

SHELLEY: Well now, Braden, so you'd like to go into television.

BRADEN: Yes, sir.

SHELLEY: And Miss Kelly is your agent?

BRADEN: That's right.

SHELLEY: Very attractive she is too.

BARBARA: Well, thank you, Mr Balsam.

SHELLEY: To be perfectly frank I'd have been less surprised if Braden here were the agent and you the performer. (*laughing*) Hm . . . hm . . . hm.

BARBARA: (*laughing*) hm . . . hm . . . hm.

BRADEN: Hah . . . hah . . . hah . . . hah.

SHELLEY: Not that Braden lacks charm of a kind which I personally find repulsive in the extreme, but you, Miss Kelly, seem to have all the requisites of the television personality . . . providing of course that you have two or three free evenings a week when we might go dining and dancing together.

Thorley Walters, Cicely Courtneidge and Norman Shelley

BRADEN: I'm the one that's going to take the audition, Mr Balsam.

SHELLEY: Yes, of course. I'll return to you in a moment, Miss Kelly.

BARBARA: That'll be nice.

SHELLEY: The question, Braden, is this: have we room for you on television?

BARBARA: Oh, I think if he pulled in his jaw, and taped down his ears . . .

SHELLEY: (*laughs immoderately*) Oh, that was very good, Miss Kelly, very good indeed. Didn't you think so, Braden?

BRADEN: (*a hollow laugh*) Excruciating.

SHELLEY: What can you do, Braden?

BRADEN: Well, I can act, imitate a dog and sing.

162

SHELLEY:	Let's hear you.
BRADEN:	Which one?
SHELLEY:	All of them.
BRADEN:	"To be or not to be that is the question" . . . (*barks*) . . . (*then sings*) "I love life so I want to live."
SHELLEY:	That will be sufficient, I think.
BRADEN:	It goes on, you know, there's more.
SHELLEY:	That's quite enough.
BRADEN:	Well, what did you think of it?
SHELLEY:	Well, judging your talent by that audition I can see you as the victim of a murder mystery. In short, a corpse.

The third of our regular performers in *Leave your name and number* was Lyn Evans. Released from his phonetic Southern accent in *Streetcar* he was a versatile actor and, like Miriam, capable of playing several parts in every script. In one episode, while I was being interviewed by a producer for a part Barbara stayed in the waiting room, and the man on the chair beside her said:

LYN:	'ullo.
BARBARA:	Hello. You waiting for someone too?
LYN:	Not me.
BARBARA:	I thought perhaps you were an actor.
LYN:	No. I'm a ar'ist.
BARBARA:	A ar'ist?
LYN:	'Sright.
BARBARA:	Must be a very interesting life.
LYN:	Only started last Sa'urday.
BARBARA:	Really?
LYN:	'Fore that I was a wri'er.
BARBARA:	A wri'er?
LYN:	An awfer. Worked under the name of Terence Ra'igan.
BARBARA:	And now you're an artist?
LYN:	'Sright.
BARBARA:	And what name do you *paint* under?
LYN:	Ginesbru.
BARBARA:	Gainsborough?
LYN:	I said Ginesbru.
BARBARA:	Ginesbru. I'm sorry.
LYN:	No offence taken. You prob'ly saw me last paintin'.
BARBARA:	I don't know, what was it called?

163

LYN:	You seen the Blue Boy, love?
BARBARA:	You painted *The Blue Boy*?
LYN:	*"The Blue Boy Luv"*!
BARBARA:	No, I don't think I saw that one.
LYN:	Pi'y.
BARBARA:	I'm sure it is. What are you doing here in a television studio?
LYN:	Thought they might let me try set designin'.
BARBARA:	D'you think they will?
LYN:	I doubt it. Closed shop here, you know.
BARBARA:	And you've no introduction?
LYN:	No talent. But they'll change their tune when they see what I've got in this 'ere briefcase.
BARBARA:	What is it?
LYN:	Nylons.
BARBARA:	Those should sell like . . . like . . .
LYN:	Nylons?
BARBARA:	That must be what I had in mind.
LYN:	You want a pair?
BARBARA:	Right now I have stockings.
LYN:	Yus, I no'iced. No offence intended.
BARBARA:	None taken, I'm sure.
LYN:	'Srigh'. You 'ave to be sportin' about these things.
BRADEN (*coming on*):	Barbara, I've got a job.
BARBARA:	Pardon me, Mr Ginesbru.
LYN:	Gran'ed.

We also revived Barbara's Uncle Gabby for this series, having first used him in *Starlight Hour*. Here, instead of being featured he became something of an interruption. We would be in the middle of a conference with an important producer or director and Gabby would bounce in and say:

GABBY:	HELLOOOOOO there!
DIRECTOR:	Who's this?
GABBY:	What d'ya say?
DIRECTOR:	Who are you?
GABBY:	Eh?
DIRECTOR:	Oh, never mind.
GABBY:	I bet you want to know who I am. Gabby's the name. G A double ABBEY, GABBY.
DIRECTOR:	Well what are you doing in here?
GABBY:	Oh . . . that's a tough one. Let's see now . . . 19 nought 3 the circus come to Moosegroin Saskatche-

wan, and I went into the tent that had the belly dancers. Come out in 19 nought 7. 19 nought 12 I moved to Alaska. It was cold up there. Woke up one morning and shot a bear in my underwear. How he got in there I'll never know. What was the question again?

DIRECTOR: I said how did you get in here?

GABBY: No . . . I don't think I played table tennis in, oh, twenty-three years.

As time went by Gabby became a bit of an embarrassment. Some people liked him, and others didn't. A few years ago I met Roy Hattersley who told me that as a boy (an endearing way to begin), he'd enjoyed my early radio shows, except for Uncle Gabby, whom he couldn't stand. On such occasions there was really nothing I could say, because I'd played the part myself.

Not long ago Benny Lee was in a club in Birmingham when a

Uncle Gabby

165

man came up to him and said, "I used to like you on that *Breakfast with Braden* show, but that old Uncle Gabby really drove me up the wall."

Benny said, "I'm terribly sorry to hear that, because the old man passed away just a few weeks ago."

All the aggression drained from the man's face and he said, "Oh, I'm terribly sorry to hear that."

◆　　◆　　◆

About two years before we arrived in England, Bonar had been engaged to play the lead in a film which required him to play scenes in their respective countries with Gina Lollobrigida, Anne Vernon, Eva Bartok and Lana Morris. The working title was *A Tale of Four Cities*. When the footage was all collated and shown in a London screening room nobody had the faintest idea what it was about, so it was written off as a mistake and filed in the vaults.

In the spring of 1950 someone got it out of the vaults and decided to look at it again with several colleagues. Bonar was invited to join them. When the lights came up there was a stunned silence and everybody looked at Bonar who simply shrugged. Then somebody said (of Bonar's character), "The guy looks like he's got amnesia," and somebody else said, "That's it! He's an American, a former GI and he's got amnesia. He knows something important happened either in Rome, Vienna, Paris, or London. He goes to the woman editor of a big magazine and persuades her to take him back to all those cities in the hopes it will cure his amnesia. Oh . . . since the editor lives in New York, we'll re-title it *Tale of Five Cities*."

And believe it or not that's what they did. There was no question of going back to the cities concerned, so the ladies were imported to London to shoot extra scenes. At Bonar's suggestion, Barbara was engaged to play the New York editor, and since all the actresses concerned were still virtually unknown, she was given top billing after Bonar.

In 1978 Barbara was the subject of the television programme *This is Your Life*, and during the preparation of the programme the researchers would occasionally phone me to check on some matter of fact. One day one of them called and said gleefully, "We've got Eva Bartok!"

"What for?"

"She was in that film with Barbara . . . you know . . . *Tale of Five Cities*."

166

Barbara and Eva Bartok

"Yes, but all their scenes were shot separately, and I don't think they ever met."

"Eva does. She's already got one foot on the plane from Los Angeles."

I think Barbara's biggest surprise that evening was when Eva Bartok was introduced and rushed on to kiss and hug her old friend Barbara Kelly.

♦   ♦   ♦

One Saturday afternoon Bonar and I were in my dressing room before the matinée of *Streetcar* when there was a knock on the door. It was one of the ladies in the cast, Mona Lilian, and she was in tears. She told us she'd just heard that her father was dying in Leeds, but that the Company Manager had refused to let her off the matinée or the evening performance, although she'd pointed out, quite rightly, that I'd been given two weeks off in the same situation. The Company Manager had told her he didn't have the authority to let her go, and that since it was a Saturday afternoon there was no one he could go to.

It was a ridiculous situation because Mona appeared as a nurse only in the last three minutes of the play and had a perfectly adequate understudy. Bonar went into immediate action. He banged on the dressing room doors of all male members of the staff and we all trooped down to the stage where he had us all sit down with our backs to the audience and against the curtain.

This was of course reported to the Company Manager who

167

stormed on to the stage and demanded to know what we were up to. Bonar said that unless Mona was allowed to go and see her father immediately we would stay in this position even when the curtain went up. While the man in authority raged at us Vivien arrived on stage and naturally enquired as to why we had taken this "recumbent position". The moment she was told she instructed the Company Manager to alert Mona's understudy and to release Mona immediately.

He was a good man to have around in a crisis, Colleano.

As the run of the play continued without any creative supervision some scenes inevitably became lax . . . and the fight scene was no exception.

Again, it was a Saturday matinée. I mentioned that there was one point in the scene which, properly executed, usually made the audience gasp. Sir Laurence had arranged that at a moment when I was facing upstage and Bonar downstage, I would throw a blow just short of his stomach which would jerk him backwards, then I would cross him with a right hook, just missing his chin. What made it look real was that just as my fist passed under his chin Bonar would jerk his head sideways, as if hit and at the same time clap his hands together, masked by my body, and collapse, apparently knocked out. Then I would drag him into the shower, turn it on, and leave.

On this afternoon, for whatever reason, when I threw the first punch, Bonar jerked forward instead of back. I was already throwing the second punch and it caught him full on the jaw. He looked at me for a moment and mumbled, "That wasn't right, was it?" then sank to the floor and passed out. The show must go on. I dragged his inert body to the shower and turned it on. Somehow Bonar managed to finish the scene, but in a decidedly groggy way and with a pronounced limp.

He recovered quickly enough from the blow, but by the time the play ended his ankle was swollen to twice its size. Obviously he'd fallen very badly. A doctor was called and diagnosed a broken ankle. While his understudy prepared to go on, Bonar phoned a physiotherapist who was employed by the Streatham Ice Hockey Team. Half an hour before the evening show he injected the ankle with God knows how much Novocaine, and Bonar did the entire play, although he was obviously in great pain during the last act.

I suppose it had as much to do with his circus upbringing as with the concept that the show must go on. Circuses tend not to have understudies.

Since there was no Monday night performance of *Streetcar*

Bonar took me one evening to the Palladium to see some of his circus friends, the Flying Ashtons. They were a quite extraordinary group of acrobats, with one of them dressed in a conventional suit, pretending to be drunk in the upper box stage left. At the climax to the act he literally fell out of the box, did a double somersault, landed on his feet on the high end of a see-saw, which automatically flipped one of his brothers on the other end of the see-saw who in turn landed on his feet at the top of a pyramid of Flying Ashtons.

Bonar suggested we go and have dinner then come back and see the second show. It was okay by me. When we got back to the theatre he said, "Now this time I want you to keep your eyes on the little guy, Micky."

"You mean the little blond one? I thought he was fantastic!"

"Just keep your eyes on him, that's all."

I thought I'd done that during the first show, and had been incredibly impressed by the speed at which the Flying Ashtons worked, particularly Micky, who seemed to be everywhere at once. When the act came on again, I did as I was told and Micky was a revelation. He never did anything. He never did any tumbling, or took part in any of the acrobatics, he just ran madly round all the time and when something pretty spectacular happened he would rush downstage, throw open his arms and say, "Hah", which automatically got a round of applause. Bonar said, "The Flying Ashtons believe that if Micky ever lost his voice they wouldn't have an act."

A few nights later Micky dropped into our theatre by way of the stage door, asked for Bonar, and was shown to my dressing room where as usual we were working out with the weights.

Now, I say "weights". In fact it was one bar-bell carrying about sixty pounds. For months we had been laboriously lifting this weight slowly to our chests then up over our heads then back down behind the neck, then up again, then setting it down. The way we did it it looked tremendously difficult.

After a few minutes' chat Bonar went to his own dressing room to get changed and I was left alone with Micky, who was slight and about five feet four inches tall. He looked at the bar-bell, then reached down with his right hand, centred it on the bar, then casually lifted it up over his head and back down again. Then he did it again with his left hand.

Well, I stood there with my jaw hanging open. He said, "All a matter of balance. Good night." Then he went out and closed the door. I stood and looked at this bar for about five minutes, then reached down and carefully found the centre of the bar, balanced

169

my feet as he had, and lifted it over my head with the greatest of ease. Then I did it with my left hand. He was right, it *was* simply a question of balance.

◆　　◆　　◆

Dressing room visitors at the Aldwych were fairly regular. As spring moved towards summer many of the people who'd been put off seeing *Streetcar* were hearing by word of mouth that it was *worth* seeing, and if they enjoyed it, and knew someone in the cast, they usually dropped around to complain about the critics.

Some very eminent people knocked on Vivien's door, and it was the custom at that time that the more eminent you were, the more likely you were to visit all the dressing rooms.

One night the stage doorman knocked on my door and ushered in a lady and a gentleman who was about six feet eight inches tall. He introduced them as Lilian Hellman and Robert Sherwood. Each had been distinguished playwrights and were the kind of people I'd hoped, but never expected, to meet. They were both very kind about my performance, but they went on to say how much they'd enjoyed the play and the production. Much more, they said, than the New York production.

As usual in those days when I disagreed with someone, I forgot they were important, and blurted out, "How could you possibly say that! I saw the New York production and it was far superior to this one. Brando alone was better than this entire show."

"Ah," said Mr Sherwood, "like so many you've missed the point of the play. The play is about Blanche, but in New York it was about Stanley, which threw Tennessee's writing totally out of balance. Tonight we have seen the play."

I swallowed three times, remembered who they were, didn't quite tug my forelock, and politely saw them out. Once again I sat alone in my dressing room thinking. Thinking I might possibly have been wrong and that Sir Laurence had been right.

◆　　◆　　◆

When Bonar had been given a contract with the Rank Organisation at the age of nineteen, he'd decided that his parents had worked long and hard enough and that it was time for them to retire. They had their own flat in London and he was now in a position to support them, as he thought, for the rest of their lives.

They had indeed worked long and hard. Like Bonar they'd been born and bred in show business and had started in the circus as

170

small children. Indeed, his mother Ruby had been one of several "Bettys" in the famous music-hall act, Wilson Keppel and Betty.

By 1950 Bonar was still doing well, but he was no longer under long-term contract to J. Arthur Rank or anybody else. He now conceived the idea that his parents were becoming too dependent on him and needed some form of independent activity to keep them interested. As usual, his idea was unorthodox.

"I'm going to set them up with a small country club. Nothing fancy, and not too far from London."

Just like that. He invited Barbara and me to accompany him and his lawyer one Sunday afternoon on a search for a suitable property. We were going to see two riverside houses in Shepperton, Middlesex.

"Must be on the waterfront, like Skindles, but not so far out as Maidenhead."

We had lunch at a riverside pub in Shepperton Square then walked a hundred yards to Creek House on the Chertsey Road. After a cursory walk through he dismissed the place as totally unsuitable.

"For one thing the rooms are too small. Second of all, it's not on the river proper, it's on a backwater so it wouldn't attract boat traffic on the Thames. Hopeless."

Then we drove down Ferry Lane to Lady Place, the former home of Sir Arthur Sullivan, which *was* on the Thames, with extensive lawns running down to the edge. It was situated just below Shepperton Lock, the rooms were larger, and Bonar guessed that with some additions and a good deal of renovation it might fill the bill.

On our way back Barbara asked if we could stop again briefly at Creek House. Ever the gentleman where Barbara was concerned Bonar agreed, but assured her it was a waste of time. We three men waited in the car while Barbara rang the doorbell and was admitted. Half an hour later she still hadn't come out and Bonar started pushing the horn. After another ten minutes he suggested that as a responsible husband it was my duty to ring the doorbell and instruct my wife to return to the car immediately. I reminded him that he should know by now that I didn't have that kind of control over my wife. He said he had a date in London and the lady concerned wouldn't wait for ever. I said that in that case *he* should go and ring the doorbell. He grunted and pushed the horn again.

Barbara joined us in her own good time. She got in the back seat with me and apologised for being so long. Apparently the owners had offered her a cup of tea, and it had arrived accompanied by scones, Devonshire cream, jams and cakes. It would have been unforgivably rude for her to rush out and equally crass to suggest we be invited in. Bonar muttered something about the unfairness of feminine logic and started the car.

As we rounded Halliford Bend Barbara leaned over to me and whispered, "I want it!"

I looked at her in amazement and raised my eyebrows, meaning, "Creek House?"

She gave me a beatific smile and nodded happily. My stomach turned to water because whatever Barbara really wanted I always tried to give her. However, I was confident that this desire lay beyond the realms of possibility.

Back in our rented flat in Harley Street, I tried to take the initiative by pointing out the disadvantages. The price would undoubtedly be beyond us, we were both working in London at different times and places which would mean needing two cars, and Bonar had said the rooms in Creek House were too small. Barbara reminded me that the three children along with Mr and Mrs Fulton were arriving in Liverpool on July 1st and I'd done *nothing* about finding a house; that houses in London were more expensive than in Shepperton; and that Bonar was looking for a country club not a house.

"You didn't really look at the place, did you?"

"No, not really."

"Well, there's a two-car garage which takes care of *that* problem –"

"Wait a minute, we don't have the two cars."

"And a self-contained flat above it with a large room looking out on the water for your study; the master bedroom suite is separate from the rest of the house including a dressing room for you; plenty of other bedrooms, *and* bathrooms; property on *both* sides of the river –"

"Creek."

"It's as wide as a river. There's plenty of room for a paddock on the other side –"

"We don't have a horse."

"The children should learn to ride."

"Maybe if Chris gets a paper round he can save up for a horse."

"There's a small orchard, a vegetable garden with *asparagus*, hedges and topiary –"

"Who's going to wield the shears?"

"A playroom with its own *stage*, leading to a sun-roof; a cabin cruiser and a dinghy – *with* an outboard motor."

"A cabin cruiser! What makes you think we can afford –"

"A separate games room big enough for a ping-pong table, a

dining room panelled in limed oak, and what's more, Charles Dickens wrote *Oliver Twist* in that house."

"I should think there are very few houses in Shepperton where Dickens didn't write something."

"There's proof. On one of the kitchen windows is a sketch of a girl's head done by Phiz."

"Who's Phiz?"

"Phiz was the nickname of the man who illustrated most of Dickens' books. Hablot Knight Browne." (This last with some scorn.) "He sketched a girl's head on the kitchen window and it's still there."

"How do you sketch a girl's head on a kitchen window?"

"He cut it into the pane with a diamond ring."

"Anything else?"

"Yes, Bernie." (Softly with a smile.) "I want it."

During the following week I chose my moment to suggest to Bonar that we were interested in buying Creek House, because after all he'd introduced us to the place.

"Why the hell should I care?"

"Well, I know you thought the rooms were small, but I thought you might change your mind and still want it as a night-club for your mother and father."

"Oh, that, I've changed my mind. I don't think it would be a good idea at all. When were you thinking of going back there?"

"Well, if you don't mind, we were thinking of next Sunday."

"Why don't I drive you down? We can have lunch together at the Anchor, and then drop in on the owners. But don't tell them you're coming. If you're going to buy a house, always drop in. Never make an appointment."

And so it was. Once inside, Bonar showed more interest in the place than I did. While Barbara was carefully showing me all the advantages, Bonar went off on his own, and we heard occasional exclamations of delight. I followed him into the main bathroom to find him posing in front of a large mirror over the bathtub, which reflected a kind of bronze colouring. As I entered Bonar said, "Robert Taylor, eat your heart out."

Bonar never bought Creek House, but he certainly made use of its guest room.

Negotiating to buy a house in England was something new to me. We'd done it several times in Canada which, by comparison, was simplicity itself. In the period after the war, the Canadian government funded mortgages up to ninety per cent. Surveyors were virtually unnecessary because Canadian houses had no history to speak of and the deed was all you needed. You paid a

173

solicitor to verify it and estate agents took a small percentage from the vendor. It could all be achieved in a matter of weeks or even days.

Creek House was a little more complicated. Part of the kitchen went back to the twelfth century and the various additions covered several other centuries. We were buying from an elderly couple for whom the house had become too large, and they wished to sell it fully furnished. The total price was £10,500, but that didn't include the cabin cruiser. I resolved to take a firm stand against paying another £2,000 for a boat, but Barbara pointed out that I was still recording five stories a week for the Canadian Broadcasting Corporation, and the revenue from that had been used to support the children in Vancouver. Now we would have no financial obligations in Vancouver, so we could bring that money over to London and use it to pay instalments on the cabin cruiser. I finally agreed.

The CBC series was, courtesy of the BBC, recorded once a week at 200 Oxford Street in the bowels of yet another BBC property. It consisted of my reading short stories by Canadian authors and was transmitted five afternoons a week by the CBC. My Canadian producer selected the best of the stories from those submitted and sent them over for me to edit so that each would run eleven minutes and fifty-five seconds.

I used to go through them the night before the recording and cut them to what I thought would be about eleven minutes and fifty-five seconds. I would then mark at the top of each page what the timing *should* be when I reached it and adjust the pacing of my delivery according to how many seconds I was either fast or slow so that the end result was eleven minutes and fifty-five seconds.

The BBC allowed me three hours every Friday morning for a week's recordings, but I don't think I ever used more than an hour and a half. This attracted some attention from the BBC technical staff who weren't used to recording without rehearsal. I think my record for recording five stories was one hour and eighteen minutes. The recording of these stories tied up a BBC recording line for the period I was using it which meant that any BBC executive switching channels in his office might accidentally tune it in . . . and this is exactly what happened one day. Tom Chalmers, who was among other things responsible for the nightly BBC *Epilogue* on the Home Service, happened to switch on to it when, the week before Easter, I was recording the Easter story (not by a Canadian author) from a composite of the books of the New Testament, compiled by a talented Canadian producer and writer, Andrew Allan. It was a sort of forerunner of the modern English Bible, but it retained much more of the flavour of the St James version.

Chalmers was so impressed that he asked me to do it again live as the *Epilogue* on Easter Monday. To my amazement it resulted in a flood of telephone calls and letters complaining that a Canadian comedian had been allowed to read the *Epilogue* on such a hallowed evening. Chalmers stood his ground, but those letters printed in the *Radio Times* the following week were vitriolic in the extreme.

Having been bathed in nothing but praise up to this point, I was seriously taken aback until I happened to bump into John Snagge, the doyen of BBC announcers, in the canteen. We had a cup of coffee together and John explained to me that to be asked to read the *Epilogue* any night of the year was an honour and privilege reserved for very few, mostly clergymen. He then told me a story that had gone the rounds of the BBC at a time when the puritanical Sir John Reith was Director General. The story involved Sir John walking along a BBC corridor one evening when he suddenly found himself face to face with Jesus.

"What are you doing here?" he exclaimed.

"Well," said Jesus, "I happened to be in the neighbourhood and thought I might do an *Epilogue* for you."

Sir John looked uncomfortable and lowered his eyes to his boots. "I'm afraid not," he muttered. "There was always that little doubt about your mother."

John's story relieved me greatly.

As it happened, the CBC had a programme meeting as soon as they learned the children were joining us in London, and the subject of my story series came up. One executive said he could see no reason why the Corporation should continue to subsidise the Braden family in England and recommended the series be dropped. I had several friends at executive level in the CBC but unfortunately none of them was present at the meeting, so it was agreed that the series would end that July . . . the very month we were due to move into Creek House and start paying for the cabin cruiser. Uneasily, I wondered if Sir John was striking back.

By a happy coincidence – for me at any rate – the property was flooded in early June and as the water rose, so did the cabin cruiser, which was crushed by the roof under which it sheltered.

Still, we now almost owned a house and an £8,000 mortgage, so there'd be somewhere for the children to live when they arrived.

♦ ♦ ♦

When a play runs longer than six months, there are not only lapses of concentration, but the occasional private joke which sometimes gets out of hand. In *Streetcar* the presence of Vivien precluded private jokes, so sometimes in the dressing rooms we'd do, "what if" jokes.

"What if some night on stage Mitch accidentally dropped Blanche on the floor?"

"What if the woman who lived above the flat fell down the staircase in the middle of a love scene?"

One night Bonar said to me, "What if during that long silent walk at the end of the play when Blanche is being led away to the asylum somebody flushed the on-stage toilet?" We had ourselves a little laugh then got on with the play.

The final scene arrived. Blanche was led to the door by her sister and, seeing two strangers, sensed something wrong and ran into the other room. The nurse ran after her, forced her to the floor and twisted her arm behind her back. The doctor ordered the nurse to release her, then bent down and helped her to her feet. He then offered his arm, as a gentleman to a lady. She looked at him for a moment, then slipped her arm through his and said, "Whoever you are I have always depended on the kindness of strangers."

Now came the long slow walk across the stage to the door. Just as Blanche and the doctor passed the poker table, Bonar and I exchanged a glance and burst out laughing. That was enough to ruin the end of the play. What made it worse was that the audience began to laugh *with* us. The curtain fell to roars of laughter and Vivien walked straight to her dressing room. There were no curtain calls.

Everyone else retired to *their* dressing rooms to change. Bonar and I waited for the inevitable summons. There could be no excuse for our behaviour, and we didn't plan to offer any. We had totally ruined the play and an entire audience had left the theatre believing that Vivien was supposed to be a figure of fun.

Now the danger with every actor in such a situation is that during the next performance he starts to tense up as that scene approaches again, and runs the risk of becoming genuinely hysterical. It has to be nipped in the bud and very quickly.

At last the stage doorman arrived to tell us that Miss Leigh requested our presence. We arrived at her dressing room and knocked on the door. A familiar voice said, "Come in", and, if two fully grown men can be said to troop like sheepish schoolboys that must be what we looked like. A two-man crocodile. All that was missing was the cap in hand. She looked at us for a long

moment and simply said, "That won't ever happen again, will it."
There was no question mark at the end of the sentence.

We mumbled our "Noes" and were rewarded with a smile.
"Good night," she said.

Outside, Bonar looked at me and said, "That was bloody
brilliant." And he was absolutely right. There was no danger of it
ever happening again.

♦ ♦ ♦

On the occasion of my final meeting with the vendor of Creek
House, *I* was served tea and scones and jams and Devonshire
cream after what I took to be the resolution of final details.
Already I was starting to look smug as I gazed round at "my
domain". I could see the beautiful inglenook fireplace in "my"
study, and imagine the two golden retrievers I would buy sitting
on either side. I would call them "Keith" and "Prowse" and when
visitors asked why I would say, "Because they have the best seats
in the house".

My reverie was interrupted by Mr Musgrave saying, "I've
assembled all the staff so you can meet them before you take
over." He called them in, one by one, the cook, the gardener, the
housekeeper, the downstairs maid, the upstairs maid and the girl
who came in to do the sewing twice a week. All but the gardener
curtsied.

I mumbled something to each of them, and waited in a daze
until the last of them had left.

"Mr Musgrave," I said, "I didn't understand that –"

"You're not to worry about space," he told me, "I realise you

Last scene of A Streetcar Named Desire

have three young children to accommodate, and probably a nanny as well. The theatre playroom upstairs will make an excellent day nursery and you'll still have space for a night nursery."

"But . . . but . . . but –"

"You see, the cook and the housekeeper are the only ones who live in. All the others live in either Shepperton or Walton-on-Thames."

"Mr Musgrave, there's nothing in our agreement about servants."

He looked stunned. "Servants?" he said. "Mr Braden, these are my friends! I couldn't possibly let the house go without them."

The inglenook fireplace had blurred and Keith and Prowse were nowhere to be seen.

"I do understand," I said, "but it was no part of our deal. We're already stretching our resources too far; you may have to find another buyer."

"Oh dear. Oh dear, oh dear!"

Reluctantly I broke the news to Barbara. "Well," she said, "we'll just have to find out how much they're paid, won't we? I suppose you didn't think to ask him that?"

"No, I didn't."

"Perhaps we can find a compromise. He didn't tell you about the servants until now. You didn't tell him about Mr and Mrs Fulton. We think of *them* as friends. We'll have to reach a compromise." She nodded as if the matter was settled.

. . . And it almost was. The staff wages varied between £3 and £7 per week. The housekeeper didn't want to stay anyway, and the downstairs maid left within the year to get married. The upstairs maid became the downstairs maid, and by the time we left nine years later she'd become the housekeeper. Mr Rosewall, the gardener, stayed on to work for the *next* owner of Creek House, actor John Gregson.

Only one problem remained. How did two Canadians like ourselves learn to cope with a household staff of that size? We were to find out that it was an art, and we'd have to learn it the hard way.

♦   ♦   ♦

One night Barbara and I went to the Caprice for dinner after the show and were seated at a table near Kenneth More and Elspeth March. Their names meant nothing to Barbara, but I'd seen them in 1947 starring in a Noël Coward play called *Peace in Our Time* and admired them tremendously. They were talking earnestly to one another and holding hands. As we finished our meal they spoke to Mario, the owner of the Caprice, who then came to our table and asked if we would join Mr More and Miss March for coffee and liqueurs. Well, of course we would. We moved to their table where Mario introduced us and retired discreetly to deal with the few other customers left at this late hour.

Elspeth and Kenny had seen *Streetcar* that very evening and were extravagant in their praise. Like so many others, they'd been put off it by the critics and friends of theirs who "hadn't actually seen it" for themselves. We discussed *Streetcar* at length, and eventually I was able to return the compliment by saying how much I'd enjoyed them both in *Peace in Our Time*, a play in which Coward had postulated an England that had lost the war and was under the rule of Hitler. Kenneth More and Elspeth March had played the leaders of the resistance, and all the action took place in the saloon bar of a pub with Dora Bryan as a barmaid. Coward was in one of his "out of favour" periods, the theme of the play was resented and it was not a success.

"Another one the critics killed," said Kenny. "The people who came to see it loved it, but there weren't enough of them."

I was prepared to return to the subject of *Streetcar*, but Barbara, with her usual tact, persuaded Kenny and Elspeth to talk about themselves. Kenny had spent years with a repertory company, in a theatre where he was so popular that eventually the theatre would be named after him. Elspeth, a fine actress, had been married to Stewart Granger by whom she had a daughter Lindsay.

Eventually we became so immersed in theatre conversation that time and place became irrelevant until we realised everyone else had gone home and only Mario (who could never be accused of hovering) was patiently waiting to shut up shop. With apologies we paid our bills and went our separate ways.

Many years later when we knew Kenny well and he was no longer with Elspeth, we were invited to a birthday party in his honour at Les Ambassadeurs. During that evening Kenny, well into his cups, took me aside and reminded me of that conversation at the Caprice. He said at the time he'd been out of work for a year and was planning to give up acting and emigrate to Australia, but our evening together had convinced him to stay on and give it another try.

Kenny, I knew from experience, was wont to put two and one together and come up with four when he'd had a few too many. Never mind the facts, it was the story that mattered. While preparing this volume, I phoned Elspeth's daughter and asked if she could check with her mother to see if the story was true. She said, "Why don't you check it yourself?" and gave me Elspeth's phone number.

Elspeth said she was about to be interviewed by a television company who were preparing a profile of the late Sir Robert Helpmann and wanted her to provide some reminiscences. "I'm trying to think of a clean story," she told me.

With some trepidation, I recounted Kenny's drunken recollection and asked if *she* recalled that evening at the Caprice forty years earlier.

"My dear," she said, "I remember it only too well. Kenny had his one-way ticket to Australia and was supposed to leave the next day. We were having a farewell evening. First we went to the theatre to see *A Streetcar Named Desire* then on to dinner. While we were sitting there you and Barbara came in, and Kenny said we should pay our respects. After our long conversation you left and Kenny said, 'That settles it. I'm not leaving.' I wish I could tell you he tore up the ticket, but he didn't. He needed the refund."

It was not long before Kenny was signed to play the lead in the West End opposite Peggy Ashcroft in Terence Rattigan's *The Deep Blue Sea*, a role which he repeated in the film opposite Vivien Leigh. Then came his great personal success in *Genevieve* after which he never looked back.

I hope all the restaurant proprietors I know now will understand and forgive when I say that in my view Mario Gallati was the best. He was a true lover of the theatre and provided not only the best food available, but an ambience fit for the brightest of stars. Today's stars shine as brightly on the stage but when the show's over like to be seen as ordinary people. I've seen Glenda Jackson striding down the Haymarket dressed like a militant school-teacher and Anthony Hopkins walking in Hyde Park looking like Everyman. Dame Judi Dench, especially when directing, seems always to be photographed in slacks. Receiving a BAFTA award for her performance in *Jewel in the Crown*, Dame Peggy Ashcroft said this was one of her proudest moments . . . not for the award, but for the privilege of having appeared on the same platform as Bob Geldof.

It wasn't like that in 1950. After so many years of austerity the public wanted their stars to behave and look like stars both on and off the stage and screen. Already there were ten top couturiers in London vying for the favours of the great and the mighty. As I write, only two are still alive: Hardy Amies and Ronald Paterson.

Mario provided a perfect setting for both the stars and the dressmakers. Sir Michael Balcon, no stranger to glamour, once told me that his most glamorous moment took place in the Caprice. It did not involve the Oliviers or the Lunts. It was the sudden appearance in the entrance of Marlene Dietrich on the arm of Alfred Hitchcock. Apparently everyone in the room stood and applauded.

By the same token, Mario looked after actors regardless of their current status. Someone I won't name who'd fallen on hard times received a phone call from Mario asking why he hadn't been to the restaurant recently. The actor said, "I'm sorry, Mario, but I can't afford it. No work. All the producers seem to have forgotten me."

Mario said, "We can't have that. Come in once a week, I'll give you a prominent table, and there'll be no charge. You can pay me back when you're on your feet again."

It took nearly six months, but it paid off. John Huston saw exactly the face he was looking for. Mario not only got his money back, but a friend for life.

Barbara and I learned about food and wine from Mario. As Canadians we were used to simple food, even without rationing, and hardly ever drank wine. Mario it was who introduced us to gull's eggs with cayenne pepper, smoked sturgeon with tiny onions; caviare, smoked salmon with scrambled eggs or hard-boiled egg yolks and lemon juice, and pâté de foie gras. When it came to oysters, though, I felt I was an expert, having been brought up on the Pacific coast of Canada. I didn't want them neat with lemon juice, I wanted them in a cocktail sauce for which I gave a precise recipe. "Two parts mayonnaise, two parts cream,

Mario Gallati

two parts tomato ketchup and a dash of Lea and Perrins." Mario winced, but served it as ordered. With time and confidence I took to experimenting with my orders, culminating with a request for smoked salmon and water melon. It too was served . . . by the chef, who sat down opposite me and said, "This I have to see." It was my second most embarrassing moment at the Caprice. The worst was when Mario recommended a dish I'd never heard of, saying he could only get it two weeks of the year. It was the tenderest and most succulent meat I'd ever eaten. What was it? And why was it only available two weeks in the year? "It's unborn kid," said Mario . . . I never ordered it again.

In the late spring of 1950 Mario threw a party for clients and staff. It took place at a sports ground in Elstree, and was run like a miniature Olympics. Everyone had to enter something, and when I saw Sir Godfrey Tearle going red in the face as he staunchly acted as anchor man in the tug-of-war, I quickly volunteered for the four hundred yards relay. At least that would be over quickly.

Our team consisted of Jimmy Hanley, Dirk Bogarde, Bryan Forbes (as captain) and myself. Bryan decided that I (as an un-known quantity) would run the last leg. Presumably he hoped that the other three would give me such an overwhelming lead that however slowly I ran I wouldn't be overtaken.

Now in those days the baton was passed differently. The runner held it tightly by one end and as he approached the next runner he offered it horizontally. As his successor grasped the other end the first runner would give a mighty push of the baton to add impetus to his team mate's start.

No . . . I did *not* fall over. When Bryan reached me we had a sixty-yard lead. He handed me the baton and gave a mighty push, after which I continued to run as fast as I could. Barbara said it looked for three strides as if I were going to break the world record. "Then," she said, "it looked as if you stood stock still." I was overtaken by my three competitors, all of whom were my seniors by several years.

One of my team mates (you'll have to guess which) greeted me at the finish line and said, "I know you're supposed to be funny, but did you have to *run* like a comedian?"

Back in the grandstand people were kinder. They just looked away.

♦   ♦   ♦

Lunchtime at the Caprice presented an interesting ritual. At 12.45 every banquette was occupied by a well-known journalist, each of whom had made a one o'clock appointment to entertain a celebrity who would be interviewed during lunch. The game was to notice which journalist was kept waiting the longest, and the ultimate fun was when the celebrity never showed up at all. I managed to improve on the ultimate.

John Junor invited me to the Caprice one Wednesday lunchtime to be interviewed for the *Sunday Express*. I arrived precisely at 1.00 p.m. feeling greatly honoured, only to find that my interviewer hadn't shown up. During the next fifteen minutes various celebrities arrived and were greeted by their interviewers, but Mr Junor was conspicuous by his absence. By 1.30, waiters were asking if I'd like to have my first course but I steadfastly refused. The next half hour was acutely embarrassing, and I finally asked if I could make use of the telephone. When I was put through to Mr Junor's office his secretary informed me that he had indeed arranged to lunch with me at the Caprice a week from this very day. Mario, ever on the alert, invited me back to the table to have a free lunch. I didn't have the guts to face all those other banquettes and took my leave.

♦   ♦   ♦

One morning early in July I took a train to Liverpool to meet the *Empress of Scotland* when it docked from Canada with our three children, Mr and Mrs Fulton and what had been my father's car. Again the press was in attendance and accompanied me on board to get pictures of the family, minus Barbara who was filming *A Tale of Five Cities*. Again, the obligatory shot of the happy family together was totally ruined because Kim, at eighteen months, didn't recognise me, and cried every time I made a move to pick her up. She was finally persuaded to sit briefly on my knee and the only picture on record shows Chris and Kelly looking happy enough, me looking wary of what might happen next, and Kim looking as if she's about to break out of the cage.

My plan had been for all of us to drive back to Creek House in Shepperton, leaving me time to get to the evening performance of *Streetcar*. The problem was that Customs and Excise refused point-blank to release the car until a substantial amount of duty was paid. I didn't have the money, and a phone call to my bank revealed that they couldn't authorise payment until a number of forms had been filled in. In the end we boarded the Liverpool boat-train called *Howard of Effingham* and hired a car at Euston Station to take us "home".

Fortunately, Barbara had been released from the film set early so was on hand to take over. The children ran happily round the house and were then let loose into the garden which they explored, then up and over the bridge above the creek to the *corale* on the other side. We sat and waited until they returned . . . waited for them to express their joy and delight in what were certainly the most glamorous surroundings they'd ever encountered.

Kim ran straight into the arms of Mrs Fulton, Kelly said, "What's for tea?" Chris said nothing. Finally I asked him what he thought of the garden.

"Not bad," he said, "for a back yard."

It was understandable. In Vancouver, most homes have a large front garden, and what's behind the house is usually known as "the back yard". Creek House fronted on to the Chertsey Road with no garden. This wasn't the time to explain.

◆　　　◆　　　◆

Breakfast with Braden, having originally been booked for eight weeks in January, was coming to the end of its run in mid-July. It would return under the new title *Bedtime with Braden* on September 19th as an evening show, but the BBC planners had arranged a repeat at the old time, so listeners would also be able to

Chris, me, Kelly and Kim

hear *Bedtime with Braden* at 8.15 in the morning. Meantime, *Leave your name and number* would continue and Barbara and I were asked to do yet another series called *Mr and Mrs North* about an American couple who solved mysteries, with hopefully a degree of humour. *The Concert* was to be repeated on June 23rd.

This plethora of Bradens caused Collie Knox to write in the *Daily Mail*: "By the way, the BBC have no intention of discontinuing the Third Programme. They plan to extend it. The report that a Fourth Programme is being organised so that Mr Bernard Braden can have a little more scope is, curiously enough, without foundation."

With *Breakfast* about to go off the air, Frank and Denis were still up to their trick of incorporating real-life incidents into the script. As someone who'd started in radio as an engineer in 1935 I sometimes quarrelled with the BBC's concept that it had invented radio and everything in it. There was yet another apocryphal story that the BBC had arranged a postponement of a Royal Tour where North American networks planned to use tape recorders, because they hadn't invented theirs yet.

One day in the studio I found myself complaining that a certain sound effect wasn't accurate, and outlined a method by which I

Creek House

thought it could be achieved. The sound effects man on duty folded his arms and said, "It can't be done." I then walked over to his working area and did it. For a performer to cross into the hallowed precincts of a BBC engineer constituted a mortal sin and the atmosphere in the studio for the rest of that recording was not conducive to a great deal of laughter.

Trust Muir and Norden to smooth the waters. When the script for the following week arrived it contained the following sketch.

BRADEN: That was "Pink Champagne", sung by Pearl Carr, accompanied by Nat Temple and his Orchestra, the finest bunch of musicians ever to pluck chickens at the back of Bethnal Green Road. And now . . .

Record: disc of a funfair.

BRADEN: Hold it! The script says, *"Fan*fare!" not *"Fun*fair!" Really, the sound effects people we get on this programme nowadays. They're all kids!

BENNY: (*Cockney*) Just a minute, please, Mr Braden. I am the head sound effects man on this programme and I resent being told I'm incompetent.

BRADEN: Do you deny it?

BENNY: No, I don't, but that don't stop me resenting it. (*Raising his voice*) I'm not here to be walked over by the likes of you, nor your crummy hangers-on.

NAT: (*Off MIC*) Would you two mind lowering your voices. Some of the band are trying to get to sleep.

BRADEN: I'm sorry. (*In a low intense voice*) I'm not asking the impossible. All I ask is for you to give the sound effects as they're marked in the script.

BENNY: (*same pitch*) That's *all*, he says. If I could *read* d'you think I'd be doing this! I'd be an announcer. It's no picnic standing here with two coconut shells shoved under me pullover.

BRADEN: I'm sorry, Miss, I didn't real –

BENNY: I've got a very temperamental wind machine over there to look after. One false move, it goes into reverse and I get sucked into its interior. Don't get workman's compensation neither.

BRADEN: All right, I'm sorry. I'm very sorry.

BENNY: My mother didn't bring me into the world to be sucked into a wind machine. Nor to be sneered at by broken-down Canadian actors who can't make a living in their own country. And another thing, Braden . . .

186

BRADEN: Yes?
BENNY: Can I have a couple of free tickets for your play?
BRADEN: Providing I get a fanfare.
Record: fanfare.

♦   ♦   ♦

The cast of *Streetcar* read in the paper that Vivien Leigh was leaving the show to go to Hollywood and prepare to make the film. At first we assumed that the show would close, but then we read that she would be replaced by Betty Ann Davies.

Betty Ann was an actress of some stature both in films and in theatre, and came into the part slightly on the defensive because it had been published that Ann Todd had turned it down, on the grounds that *she* did not follow another actress into a West End play. Since Sir Laurence was not available for rehearsals, it was decided that they would be taken by the Company and Stage Managers. Betty Ann insisted that she should have a proper director, and this put Irene Selznick back in the saddle.

Streetcar had just been revived at the City Centre in New York with Uta Hagen and Anthony Quinn, under the direction of Daniel Mann. Irene pointed out, not unreasonably, to Binkie Beaumont that Renée Asherson was also leaving the cast to be replaced with an unknown Canadian girl, Frances Hyland, who'd just won the Silver Medal at RADA. She insisted that Daniel Mann be brought over from New York to redirect the new performances. Since she had not liked Olivier's production, this obviously meant "re-direct" the *play*.

And so we embarked, during a long hot summer, on rehearsing a totally new production all day, and playing it every evening with Vivien and Renée as directed by Olivier.

Mr – "Call me Danny" – Mann was something of a revelation. It was his first trip to England, and throughout rehearsals he persisted in his belief that everyone in the cast was English and had never been to North America, including Bonar and myself. He told us who Tennessee Williams was, and also Marlon Brando, on the assumption we'd never heard of either. This didn't go down too well with Bonar, since throughout the run of the play I kept telling him how far short he fell of Brando in the part of Stanley.

Danny's relationship with Bonar came to a head fairly early on. In scene five, Blanche and Stanley, who are not getting on, have a conversation in which Blanche asks what sign he was born under. Stanley says, "Sign?" and Blanche says, "Astrological sign. I bet you were born under Aries. Aries people are forceful and dynamic.

187

They dote on noise! They love to bang things around! You must have had lots of banging around in the army, and now that you're out, you make up for it by treating inanimate objects with such fury!"

Stella says, "Stanley was born just five minutes after Christmas," and Blanche, laughing, says, "Capricorn – the goat!"

STANLEY: What sign were *you* born under?
BLANCHE: Oh, my birthday's next month, the 15th September;
            that's under Virgo.
STANLEY: What's Virgo?
BLANCHE: Virgo is the Virgin.
STANLEY: (*contemptuously*) Hah!

Since our audiences on the whole tended to side with Stanley, this usually got one of the biggest laughs in the play.

One morning we had our first rehearsal of this scene with Danny, and he stopped it at that point and said from the stalls, "Bonuh. I want ya to try dat a different way."

Bonar asked how there could *be* a different way.

"I'll tell yuh. I've had Tony Quinn doin' it dis way and it woiks bettuh. Instead of Saying 'Hah!', you *think* the word 'Hah!' You don't say it, you just think it. I guarantee yuh it'll have twice the impact."

Betty Ann looked perplexed, Bonar looked heavenwards for guidance.

"C'mon, try it for me once. You'll see."

They went through the scene again, and Bonar didn't say "Hah!"

With a shout of triumph Danny leapt up on the stage, threw his arms around Bonar and said, "You got it in one. Bonar, you're gonna kill the people!"

Bonar slowly disengaged himself from Danny's embrace and said gently, "Danny . . . I kill the people *now* . . ."

But it was poor little Franny Hyland who took the brunt of the strain. It wasn't all that long since she'd come from the plains of Saskatchewan, and she was very proud to have won the Silver Medal at RADA and to have been put under contract by H.M. Tennent at £10 per week, then catapulted into a feature role in London's most talked-about play. She was not familiar with Danny's methods, or indeed his vernacular.

Danny was obsessed with the idea that Stella's feelings for Stanley, her husband, however much they argued, were always conditioned by the fact that she was carrying his baby. At one

188

point, in trying to get this point across, Danny said to Franny, "Honey, not only do youse love dis guy . . . you got his turkey cookin'!"

Franny burst into tears and fled to her dressing room.

In addition to trying to change dialogue, Danny was restructuring the movement of all the actors, which made it rather difficult in the evening with Vivien. We had to remember the old moves, having spent all day learning the new ones.

One day, in an attempt to "get to know us better" Danny took Bonar and me to lunch at the Waldorf Hotel, near the Aldwych. Once seated he began to fill us in yet again as to what things were like in New York, and how different they were from England. At one point he said, "I went to PS 174 . . . PS . . . that means public school. All the public schools in New York are numbered and I went to PS 174 and —"

Bonar said, quite truthfully, "I went to PS 174."

Danny said, "*You* went to PS 174? Well, like I was tellin yuh. In New York PS stands for public school and they divide the schools into numbers and . . ."

And he went on with his explanation, having totally missed the significance of Bonar's remark.

About halfway through the meal he pointed to two men who'd just entered the restaurant and were sitting down. "You know who dose guys are?"

Before we could say we did, he said, "Dere names are Richard Rodgers and Oscar Hammerstein. You probably won't have heard of dem over here, but in New York dey are real comers. Dere over here to do a musical, I tell ya, it'll knock the English on their ears. When dat musical opens, everybody in England will know dere names. But the great thing about them is that successful as they've been, they're real people. I'll introduce you on the way out."

He was as good as his word. As we passed their table Danny stopped and said, "Hi, Oscar, Hi, Dick."

Hammerstein looked up and said in a very non-committal voice, "Hello, Danny." Rodgers didn't look up, just continued eating.

"I want you to meet a couple of boys I'm working with over here in *Streetcar*. Bonar Colleano and Bernie Braden. We're re-doin' the show."

Hammerstein said, "Hi", and went back to his food. Rodgers continued eating. There was no alternative but to leave.

As we reached the outer door, Danny stopped, turned round and faced us. "See what I mean?" he said. "Real people!"

I told Bonar later I thought I'd seen a glint of humour in Danny's eyes as he said it. Bonar didn't agree.

It was during this period of travail that I came up for air after a morning rehearsal to find a message at the stage door asking if I'd care to join Miss Leigh for lunch at the Savoy Grill. The Savoy was not that far away from the Aldwych and Danny had allowed us an hour and a half for lunch.

I was shown into the Grill and seated at a corner table for two where Vivien was apparently engrossed in *The Times* crossword puzzle. I wasn't impressed by that, because I knew she could do it in twenty minutes. We ordered our food, Vivien chose the wine, and I waited. Finally she asked how the rehearsals were going.

I wanted to spare her the details, so I said something like, "As well as can be expected."

"I only asked, because although I'm leaving the play in a few weeks, it's not too late to learn, and if Mr Mann is doing interesting things that you think might be worked into the evening performances I'd be only too pleased to try them."

"Vivien," I said, "we're having enough problems as it is. Trying to adapt Danny's suggestions to your performance would drive us all right up the wall."

"I just thought there might be something that could be useful in the film. I know he's tried to do a production different from Kazan's original, and since Kazan is directing the film, it would be nice to come up with one or two new ideas."

I said I doubted if Danny had anything to offer that hadn't already been tried and discarded by Kazan.

Suddenly she said, "You and I have something in common."

I gave her a wary "Oh?"

"We both had TB."

It was true, but I wasn't sure where it was leading.

"I have a theory that tuberculosis gives people like us an advantage over other actors. We've suffered in a particular way that they don't understand, and we can incorporate that suffering into our performances."

Fortunately our first course arrived at that time, along with the wine, which Vivien asked me to taste. Well, given that good wines were new to me I had no hesitation in accepting a 1947 Gevrey-Chambertin. I was a bit staggered she'd chosen it because it cost nearly a pound.

During the meal Vivien launched into a long discourse about her return to Hollywood and how delighted she was to go back as "Lady Olivier". She said that while she was making *Gone with the Wind* she and Larry, who were not then married, were allowed to live together in a Beverly Hills house, surrounded by a very high brick wall, but they had to go to and return from parties separately. It had been a matter of deep humiliation for both of them. Now she could go into the Hollywood studios in the full knowledge that she was the wife of the most respected actor in the world, and that her own star status would be unquestioned.

Since I was still very much in awe of both of them, it struck me as odd that she'd want to unburden this sort of sentiment to someone as unimportant as myself. I was fascinated though, until I looked at my watch and realised it was time to get back to rehearsal. I made my apologies, stood up and kissed her on the cheek, hoping that some of the other diners in the room might think there was something between us.

When I got about ten feet from the table she said, "Just a moment." I stopped and turned back.

In a voice unkindly loud, she said, "I suppose you're wondering why I invited you here for lunch today."

I gave her an embarrassed nod.

"I was supposed to lunch with Noël Coward, but he stood me up."

A last little head butt from Vivien.

During the last week of Vivien's tenure as Blanche, I was in my dressing room, waiting to go on for the last scene of the play. The previous scene had ended at a point when Blanche and Stanley were alone in the apartment, Stella having been taken off to hospital to have her baby. Stanley had made an overture to Blanche who'd broken a bottle and threatened to twist the broken end in his face. He'd disarmed her and thrown her across the table before carrying her to the bed as the curtain fell.

Bonar suddenly appeared in my dressing room, white-faced (which wasn't easy for him), and said, "Have you got a drink for Christ's sake?" I handed him a bottle of whisky and, as I went to get a glass, watched him take a hefty swig from the bottle.

"What's the matter?"

"You don't know what happened out there."

"What happened out there?"

"You know when I throw her over the table in those two bright follow spots?"

"Yeah."

"One breast came right out."

"Jesus! What did you do?"

"Well, I had both arms around her, what *could* I do? I put my mouth over it."

Again there were no complaints at the box office. It was no more than the audience had been led to expect.

♦   ♦   ♦

The only things that made up for the anguished hours spent in Danny's company were the long summer weekends at Creek House. First we had to get to know the neighbours.

On our immediate left were the Harrisons, people of no mean repute. Mr Harrison was the King's printer. He called on us and invited us to tea. After a few days our two gardens became communal for their children and ours. On our right were the Kinross's, who lived in the White House. They too had children and a proper punt, which Chris much preferred to our dinghy.

But the real test of our acceptance in the community would come when we received an invitation to the home of Mr and Mrs Haddon Howard, who lived in the Manor House on the Thames. Rumour had it we were already in Mr Howard's bad books because the pleasure steamers which went up and down the Thames had a guide with a megaphone and it had been discovered that we'd moved to Shepperton. Since the steamers weren't able to negotiate the creek on which we lived the guides took to describing the "big" house as "lived in by Barbara Kelly and Bernard Braden". Mr Howard was right to be annoyed. He'd been born in that house and expected to die there. It was said to have the largest expanse of green lawn on the whole of the Thames.

"Nevertheless," said Mr Harrison, "you will receive an invitation and when you arrive will be offered a single glass of dry sherry. Mr and Mrs Howard will be polite and introduce you to their son, and her mother, who refers to her late husband as 'my Governor'. Before she can get launched on life with her Governor, it will be made clear that it's about time for you to leave. You will probably never see them again. You may invite them to your house, but they'll find a way of declining the invitation. You will then be considered a member of the community."

Eventually the invitation arrived for late on Sunday afternoon and when it emerged that Barbara and I were interested in lawn tennis we were offered a second glass of sherry. Mr Howard then took us on a tour of the grounds, which included a lawn tennis court, and the local cricket pitch and pavilion. Mr Howard, it emerged, had once qualified for Wimbledon and took his tennis very seriously. Also prominently displayed on a tripod was an enormous telescope, captured from the Germans during the war and used by Mr Howard to spot planes. Whatever he was doing, when he heard a plane he rushed to the telescope. Since we were only about four miles from what was then known as London Airport, these interruptions were fairly frequent.

Then we were shown through the house itself, and Barbara complimented them on the reproduction lights over the dining table which looked for all the world like the old gas-mantle lamps.

"They're not reproductions," said Mr Howard. "I don't hold with electricity and won't have it in the house." He then took me to the cellar and showed me his television set, which ran off batteries.

When we left an hour or so later it was with an invitation to dinner the following Sunday.

"Come early," said Mr Howard, "we'll have a game of tennis."

We got there about 4.30 and while Barbara had tea with the ladies, Haddon (as I was now asked to call him) joined me on the tennis court. I was in whites, he wore nothing but a pair of extremely brief swimming trunks and a pair of tennis shoes. When he served he held three balls in his left hand, two in the palm, and one halfway up his wrist, and anchored by the pressure of his palm on the other two balls. I asked him why. "In case I serve a net cord," he said. "Saves bending down to pick up another ball."

It seemed reasonable, but I never did figure out how, with his left hand supporting three balls, he ever managed to throw one of them in the air.

I had many games with Haddon over the years, but they were always slightly frustrating, because, even if we were in the middle of a rally, the moment he heard the sound of a plane, he dropped his racquet and ran to the telescope. On almost all these occasions, after a few moments he'd say, "Missed it", walk back to the court and say, "Where were we?"

After that first game we "joined the ladies" when more tea was wheeled out by a lady of not less than eighty-six years, name of Basset. Balanced on the trolley was an eight-tier stand of sandwiches, scones, muffins, crumpets, biscuits, cream cakes and chocolate. Haddon scoffed most of them, and then said he must change for dinner. While Barbara chatted with Mrs Howard (Iris), I walked the two hundred yards home and also changed for dinner.

During the meal, which was served under the genuine gas-mantle lamps, Barbara enquired as to what Haddon did. He said he was the chairman of a building and renovation company – mostly renovation, which included long-term contracts with organisations such as Sadlers Wells and the Drury Lane Theatre.

193

How had he got into the business?

Through his father, who'd owned it. He'd been put in charge of a crew on a particular job when he left school at eighteen.

Any training?

None.

Then how had he known what to tell the crew what to do?

"Ah . . . well, I found myself on this site with a number of workmen. The foreman seemed to understand the job in hand. It was just where and how to begin. I gathered the crew around me and asked their opinions, then acted on the one that seemed most reasonable to me . . . and that's roughly the way I've done it ever since."

During the meal Iris's mother chattered amiably to no one in particular, and no one paid her the slightest bit of attention. At one point in a conversational lull I heard her say, "My Governor and I used to go for picnics on Sunday afternoons to Pharaoh's Island."

She noticed that I was listening, and that nobody else was. With a shrug in my direction she said, "It's probably not even there any more."

The only time I ever knew her to laugh out loud was when she

Chris, me, Jackson, Barbara, Jason, Kim and Kelly

heard on the radio that Gordon Richards had been knighted. As she recovered from what sounded like a fit of hysterics she said, "Imagine knighting a jockey. Such absurdity. My Governor will be spinning in his grave."

After dinner, we were shown into yet another room which can only be described as a ballroom. It was lit by gas-mantle chandeliers, each of which was set alight by the eighty-six-year-old retainer, who'd also served the entire meal. Once we'd looked round Haddon ordered her to extinguish all the candelabra lights and showed us back to the living room. We never saw the ballroom again, and to the best of my knowledge it was never used.

Each morning of the week, Haddon took the Shepperton train to the City, wearing striped trousers, a cutaway coat and a wing collar. Also gloves. The gloves, he stressed, were absolutely essential for one in his position. Barbara asked what he'd do if he found he'd left his gloves on the train.

"I should turn up my coat collar, make my way to Moss Bros and buy another pair."

The Howards became fast friends and by the end of the summer were known to our children as Uncle Haddon and Auntie Iris.

Barbara and me

Kelly, our older daughter, who was six at the time, remembers being granted the privilege of being allowed a short-cut entrance to the Manor House through a hole in a brick wall, rather than having to walk all the way round to the long driveway. This privilege was also granted to tradesmen, because it was called the Tradesmen's Entrance. She loved to call on Auntie Iris, but was terrified of Uncle Haddon, so before each visit, two-year-old Kim was required to reconnoitre the property. If there were no signs of Uncle Haddon, she and Kelly would pay their call. Kelly remembers that whatever time of day they arrived, Auntie Iris always made them welcome, and they were offered tea or lemonade.

Pushed for a touch of hindsight, Kelly recalls that Auntie Iris's actual words were, "My God, not you again! How nice!"

♦   ♦   ♦

In addition to the neighbours there were visitors from London. Summer weekends attracted virtually everyone we knew who had a car.

"We just happened to be in the neighbourhood and thought we'd drop in and say hello." Most of the time the place looked like a garden party, and for a while we considered changing its name to Open House.

Creek House

Later in the year when November fogs covered the Thames we tried to arrange a few dinner parties with some of our summer visitors, but somehow they always had another engagement.

Still, it made for a stimulating summer . . . Dickie and Sheila Attenborough, Johnny and Mary Mills, Bonar and somebody-different-every-time (they usually stayed the weekend), Ronnie Waldman and Lana Morris, Laurence Gilliam, Head of BBC Radio Features, and Cecil McGivern, soon to be Head of BBC Television, Leslie and Phyllis Mitchell, and Roy Rich and Brenda Bruce.

Brenda Bruce and Roy Rich

One Sunday evening, the Riches and the Bradens went to one of the local pubs, the King's Head, run by a wonderful plump woman called Dot Soper. The King's Head boasted the only wine cellars in the area that were situated upstairs. The place was, after all, built on the water. The four of us were sitting outside because it was a warm evening, and as we talked, I noticed that Brenda had lost the thread of our conversation and was examining the faces and figures of the people sitting around us. Suddenly she put her hands behind her head and said, "God, we're an ugly race!"

It was, in fact, simply an indication of what austerity had done to people. The men were drably dressed, and most of the women wore kerchiefs on their heads, rather than bother with a hairdresser. Given time, all that would change, and by the sixties the British had become "the beautiful people", setting styles and fashions for the rest of the Western world.

◆　　◆　　◆

Vivien Leigh played her last performance of *Streetcar* on a Saturday night, and we all wished her luck with the film version in Hollywood. I said earlier that Vivien was not a "natural" actress, and didn't really explain what I meant. A natural actress (or actor) is born with a gift that can't be taught. It starts in very early childhood when it is usually called "a tendency to show off". It has nothing to do with professionalism, it's simply an instinct.

If an actor turns professional, and is taking part in a play which goes on for some months, there is a natural tendency to "deviate" in movement, and from the script, out of sheer boredom. For example, playwrights sometimes require actors in the course of a speech to interrupt the thought of a character, and start a new thought. The true actor will find different ways of doing this. It may consist of something as simple as breaking the thread of the speech on a different syllable of the same word, before starting the new thought. Vivien would always end the first thought on exactly the same syllable, and time the beginning of the new thought in exactly the same way. Only the actor playing with her would realise from her eyes that she was not actually changing the thought. She was simply doing to the best of her ability what had been agreed between herself and the director.

True actors recognise each other immediately. When I overheard Olivier say of me, "I don't care if no one's ever heard of him, the man's an actor", he wasn't so much paying a compliment as saying "He's one of us." An actor who also directs can recognise someone who's "one of us" within seconds of the beginning of an

audition. I once put this theory forward to Stirling Moss, and asked if the same thing applied to racing drivers. How soon did he know if someone with the ambition to be a racing driver had the natural talent necessary? Stirling said, "Before he ever gets on the circuit."

No one was more aware of this deficiency than Vivien herself. And never did anyone work so hard to offset it. Technically she was as near perfection as was possible to get, and not just for herself, for others as well. I've seen her walk off stage at the end of a scene and call up to an electrician: "Light seventeen on bar three needs to be replaced."

Sir Laurence once told me that when they opened a tour in Australia rehearsals became impossible because the lighting cues were all wrong. Nothing was where it was supposed to be. He and his assistants worked for hours, poring over the lighting plot and trying to make sense of what was happening. When Vivien arrived to take part in the rehearsal nothing was ready. She looked at the lighting plot and said, "Larry, in this theatre the prompt corner is on the other side."

"If she hadn't noticed it," he told me, "I'd have had to phone our lighting director in London. It might even have delayed the opening."

Something else Vivien had to fight as an actress was her quite incredible beauty. In *Streetcar* she wore an unflattering blonde wig, and covered her face with garish make-up; but I, who sat beside her on a bench for twenty minutes every night while she poured out Blanche's story, could see through the make-up, and there were evenings when, knowing the script as well as she did, the only way I could pretend to be hearing it for the first time was to concentrate on the line from the bottom of her chin down to her throat, when I could have wished I was Michelangelo.

No challenge was too great for Vivien, and she took on some of the greatest Shakespearean roles in an effort to prove she was worthy of them, but it was only in films that she truly came into her own. I'm told she never appeared in a picture that didn't make money. A box office manager in Leicester Square told me when I'd queued up for *The Roman Spring of Mrs Stone*, which hadn't been well reviewed: "That's all we need. Her name above the title."

When I saw her in the film of *Streetcar*, I was watching an actress I'd never met on stage. She even managed to diminish Brando's performance, and it was significant that she won the Academy Award and he didn't. Without in any way detracting from her performance, I suspect that her knowledge of film techniques and possibly womanly wiles with the director had something to do with that. The Brando I'd seen on stage was someone who riveted attention, and for me the other performers hardly existed. On screen there were numerous cutaways to Blanche, and the rhythm of Stanley's performance was constantly interrupted. The pity is that he never again appeared on stage.

The next time I saw Vivien was shortly after the film of *Streetcar* opened in London. She'd been well aware of my fascination with Brando during the months we worked together, and after I'd complimented her on her own performance, I chose what I thought was the right moment to ask her what she thought of Brando.

"Such a sweet naïve boy," she said. "He came on the set one day bursting with news that he'd got clap. I never saw anyone so proud."

In the years that followed I saw her quite often, sometimes happily sometimes not. People in theatre don't usually tell colleagues in advance that they're going to see a play in case they don't like it. That didn't work with Vivien. She had an uncanny knack of finding out if someone she knew was out front, and invariably you'd be handed a note in the interval inviting you backstage where you could either genuinely praise her performance or pretend.

She and Olivier appeared at the St James's Theatre starring in, on consecutive nights, Shaw's *Caesar and Cleopatra* and Shakespeare's *Antony and Cleopatra*. Sir Laurence sent me tickets for both performances, and asked me to come round to his dressing room after the *Caesar*. "Ho ho," I thought, "perhaps he has another part for me." As it happened both Barbara and I were entranced with the Shaw play and the performances, and it was all too easy to tell him how much I'd enjoyed the show. "There's something I wanted to ask you," he said.

"Yes?" (It was all I could do not to say "Yes, yes?")

"Vivien and I are taking these two productions to New York when we finish here, and I've had to find another production for this theatre while we're away."

"Yes, yes?"

"I've chosen a Canadian play called *The Happy Time* by a man called Robert Fontaine. Do you know it?"

I did. It had started in French Canada as a radio soap opera, and been translated into a full-length play by the author. It was about the domestic misadventures of a family of French Canadians during the twenties and when it was filmed in 1952 the leading role was played by Charles Boyer.

Olivier continued, "I played a French Canadian myself during the war, in a film called *The 49th Parallel*."

I knew that too, and bloody well he'd done it.

"I learned the part phonetically with the help of a wonderful little book by a man called Drummond, written entirely in French Canadian dialect."

"*Leetle Bateese*," I said.

"That's the one. Now my fellow producers are trying to get me to bring over a cast from Paris to do this play, but I understand that Montreal and Quebec have a number of excellent actors who could do it more authentically than Parisians. Do you agree? That's what I wanted to ask you."

I took a moment to reply, partly because I realised there was no part for me, and partly because I'd become fascinated by his body make-up. In his attempt to make Caesar look an older man he'd drawn with make-up blue lines vertically down his arms, anatomically placed to represent the appropriate veins. What bothered me was that it must have taken the best part of an hour, and with the stage lighting I hadn't seen them from the fourth row of the stalls.

"I agree totally," I told him, and then proceeded to extol the virtues of French Canadian actors at too great a length. Sensing this, I congratulated him again on his performance and made my exit.

En route to the stage door I passed the entrance to Vivien's dressing room, which was open, and she caught sight of me in the mirror.

"Bernie," she said, "did you enjoy it?"

With hand on heart I was able to tell her how much I had enjoyed it, and particularly her own performance.

"You're coming tomorrow night?"

"Of course," I said.

"Will Barbara be with you?"

"Yes."

"Well, be sure you both come and see me afterwards. The Shaw thing is just a romp. The other's a play."

The following night Barbara and I watched "The Play" and hated it. Afterwards I said, "I'm sorry, dear, but we just have to go round to Vivien's dressing room."

"I'm sorry, dear," said Barbara, "I'll wait for you in the pub."

Now during the interval we'd exchanged pleasantries with Mr and Mrs Robert Sherwood who were sitting next to us. As I approached Vivien's dressing room, which was again open, I knocked on the door and took one step inside. Vivien said to the mirror, "Well?"

I said something I hoped would sound non-committal, but it certainly didn't please her. For the next ten minutes she gave me the equivalent of a present-day *Guardian* lecture on the reasons why the Shakespeare was superior to the Shaw, while I shifted from one foot to the other and noted out of the corner of my eye Mrs Sherwood sitting on a chaise-longue at one end of the dressing room.

When Vivien felt I had done my penance, and seeing me glance at Mrs Sherwood, she said, "I'd like to introduce you to Mrs Sherwood, but I've forgotten your last name."

Our last meeting, though, was a happy one. Barbara and I were in New York and went to see a musical version of the play *Tovarich* starring Vivien and Jean-Pierre Aumont. I still find this hard to believe, but during the interval I was handed a note from Vivien inviting us backstage after the matinée. We duly showed up and were met by Jack Merivale with whom Vivien was then living. We both knew Jack, having worked with him in television, and Vivien was in fine fettle. We talked of many things, and on the spur of the moment she invited us to join them for dinner that evening at a hotel after the evening performance.

Again the four of us talked well into the night and my last memory of Vivien was of a "happy time".

Incidentally, the leading role in *The Happy Time* as produced at the St James's Theatre was taken by Ronald Squire, a jovial British character actor of some talent, as long as his parts didn't stray too far from playing the captain of a suburban golf club.

During the weekend following Vivien's departure from *Streetcar* all the ashtrays were replaced on the theatre seats, and the Monday night performance restored. Betty Ann Davies, made up to look as much as possible like Vivien, gave an excellent performance, and Bonar continued to say "Hah!" He continued to "kill the people" – but not nearly so many of them.

Sad to say, the judgement of those who'd suggested that audiences came only to see Vivien Leigh get raped proved to be fairly accurate. The advance bookings plummeted and box office takings were minimal. Within a few weeks the play closed and was sent on tour, minus Bonar and myself. We both had other commitments and our contracts only covered the London run.

This also concluded my professional relationship with Sir

Vivien and Larry

Laurence Olivier, though we'd meet again through the years.

I've already paid myself the compliment of suggesting we were both born actors, and it is a truism to say that every actor worth his salt must believe himself to be the best actor in the world.

There's the story about a bit-part player who was called as a witness in a trial. Under cross-examination, asked if he considered himself a "good actor", he replied that he was the best actor in the world. Later, a colleague said, "How could you bring yourself to make such an extravagant claim?"

"What else could I do?" he said, "I was under oath."

Olivier was one of a very small group of actors with "charisma". Those who possess it can coast to success, but if they're to be "great" they must work as hard as lesser actors to learn their craft, and carry this charisma into whatever medium they find themselves.

It continues to amaze me when people refer to film, radio,

theatre and television as "art forms". They are not. They are media through which art can be purveyed, and the only challenges they offer are in techniques. An artist of Olivier's calibre had no trouble in mastering these techniques.

I went through a period in Canada when radio was my only professional outlet, and those of us engaged in it believed it to be an art form. During the war various film and stage stars from America came to Toronto on behalf of the war effort to take part in radio shows supported by Canadian actors. These included Walter Huston, James Cagney, Helen Hayes, Walter Pidgeon and Pat O'Brien. They fell into two categories: those who were nervous of the medium, and those who thought of it as simple because "you only had to read it". It made no difference to us because by the time they appeared on the stage of the Massey Hall before an audience of several thousand they were quivering with nervousness. They just didn't realise there was a technique involved.

There was one exception. Ingrid Bergman arrived to star in a radio version of Paul Gallico's *The Snow Goose*, supported by one actor, myself. The director was a man called Rupert Caplan, and at the end of the readthrough in the morning he began to outline rehearsal plans for the rest of the day. Miss Bergman interrupted and said, "Mr Caplan, I consider myself an actress, but I'm totally unused to radio. I need a crash course on technique. Would you be kind enough to give me that course during the rest of today? Then I will do one rehearsal, and hope to be ready for the show."

I was dismissed, and spent the rest of the day smiling to myself at the idea that a film star could become a radio artist in one day. That night when we came to do the show Miss Bergman played the microphone like a flamingo and it was suddenly clear to me that a talented actress could mould any medium to her artistry.

When the Old Vic Company appeared in New York after the war, it was arranged that radio versions of their stage productions should be done live on a series of Sunday evenings. I listened to every one, and was astounded that these distinguished British stage actors had not bothered to emulate Miss Bergman and learn what was basically technique. They declaimed. Again, with one exception. In Ibsen's *Peer Gynt*, Laurence Olivier in the relatively small role of the button moulder breathed life into our living rooms. Unlike his colleagues he'd bothered to learn a relatively simple technique.

He and I shared the birthright of being sons of the clergy. This meant that we'd been brought up in a formal situation. As far back as I can remember, Sunday was a day when I attended Sunday school, and two church services. Although I belonged to a non-conformist Church, I took Communion regularly from an early age, and was aware that I was symbolically eating the body and drinking the blood of Christ. As time went by I attended Bible Class, and Prayer Meetings. I sang in the choir. By the time I was nineteen I'd had my fill of formality, and decided to leave it behind. To this day I am restless at christenings, weddings and funerals. I fight formality whenever possible . . . I was thrilled when I first read Mark Twain's line about the Bible. He said: "It is full of interest. It has noble poetry in it; and some clever fables; and some blood-drenched history; and some good morals; and a wealth of obscenity; and upwards of a thousand lies . . ." But if the formality attending religion did not exist, I'd have nothing to fight.

My guess is that Laurence Olivier continued through most of his life to embrace formality, and that he revelled in exploiting it both as actor and director.

During my rebellion against formality, director Andrew Allan arrived in Toronto to produce his first play for radio in that city. The leading part was played by Lorne Greene, later to become Ben Cartwright in *Bonanza*. During rehearsals, Mr Allan kept addressing Lorne as Mr Greene. Lorne finally said, "I'm sorry, but I'm not used to being called Mr Greene. Couldn't you make it Lorne?" and Andrew Allan replied, "During rehearsals I'd prefer to call you Mr Greene. As soon as rehearsals are over, Andy would be happy to buy Lorne a drink."

I witnessed something similar in 1947 at Pinewood Studios where two productions were in progress on adjoining sound stages. One was Laurence Olivier's *Hamlet*, and the other was *Private Angelo* directed by Peter Ustinov. Outside the Olivier sound stage were signs saying, "No visitors", and outside the Ustinov sound stage were signs saying, "All visitors welcome".

I was in the studio commissary at lunchtime when Peter came in with a coterie and took over his regular table, and their meal proceeded with loud laughter and much hilarity. Rumour had it that during the morning Sir Laurence's directing zeal had caused him to allow a tracking camera to run over his foot. Suddenly Olivier, dressed as Hamlet, but supported by a cane, appeared at the canteen entrance and just stood there. All eyes turned in his direction and laughter died in the throats of the Ustinov contingent. It left an inference that they'd been laughing at Olivier in his absence. The table reserved for Olivier was nowhere near that of Ustinov. Slowly, and like a man anxious not to show how much pain he was in, Olivier and his cane made a substantial detour which took him to Ustinov's table. He then stopped and looked at everyone present in total silence. Then, "Good morning, Peter," he said quietly, and continued at the same slow pace to his own table. Anyone *could* have broken the spell with a single giggle. There wasn't a murmur until he was seated. I thought that was class. It was also consummate acting of the kind that rule-breakers don't have.

Charisma, talent, technique and a love of formality. There was one other quality required and Olivier had it in abundance. Audacity . . . the ability to make an audience believe "this can't really be happening".

The headlong bound from the top of the ramparts in *Richard III* that left him hanging upside down from Ralph Richardson's shoulders . . . the opening night of *Titus Andronicus* in Stratford-upon-Avon when, by using a magician's trick, he persuaded Richard Burton that he'd actually cut off his hand . . . the stunning effect of appearing to have gouged out his eyes in *Oedipus Rex* . . . and his amazing use of adrenalin when he realised in rehearsal that he could not climb a flight of stairs carrying his leading lady under one arm and a sword in the other. He simply postponed that event until opening night, when he did it with apparent ease – and continued to do it for the run of the play. All these were acts of audacity performed within the rules of formality.

If there was an area in which he performed uneasily it was when he was required to be life size, rather than larger than life. In 1951 the Boulting Brothers made a film in honour of the Festival of Britain, starring Robert Donat as William Friese-Greene in *The Magic Box*. Friese-Greene was Britain's contender for the invention of the moving-picture camera. Because of the prestige of the film the Boultings were able to call on the most prestigious British actors and actresses to play cameo roles.

There was a crucial scene in which the inventor finally managed to produce the illusion of moving pictures by projecting images on to a white sheet at one end of his laboratory. It happened some time in the middle of the night, and he found it so exciting that he had to show it to someone . . . share it with someone . . . He rushed into the street, and took hold of the only person he could find, a local bobby on his beat. He hurried him up the stairs and into the laboratory, then told him to stand still and watch the white sheet on the end wall. When the camera cut to this simple policeman watching what seemed a miracle, bemused and amazed, it cut to the face, not of a local policeman, but clearly the face of the world's greatest actor, Sir Laurence Olivier.

Robert Donat, a great actor himself, was aware this would happen. He found reasons for delaying the shooting of that scene for three days.

In calling Olivier the world's greatest actor, I'm expressing a personal opinion. I once had a barber who didn't agree. "Have you seen Olivier in *Richard III*?" he said (meaning the film). I hadn't. "I don't know what he thinks he's up to," he said. "For a start he keeps talking to the camera like he was Groucho Marx. And when he gets to the last scene where he says 'My horse, my horse, my kingdom for a horse', everybody falls on him and plunges daggers into his body. Then they all stand back. Why? You may well ask. It's so he can have his spasms."

I didn't go to see the film.

We live now in times when actors are so used to breaking rules and imposing informality that there are virtually no rules left to break, and no formalities to fight. In Kenneth Branagh's *Diary* of the making of his film *Henry V* he records that as a neophyte director he was more in awe of Paul Scofield than any of the other legends working on the film. During the course of the rehearsal Branagh gave some notes to Brian Blessed who was playing the role of Exeter and Blessed yelled, "You never give Paul Scofield any fucking notes. You're just a bloody arse licker. You've destroyed my performance."

I think under similar circumstances Olivier would have *ended* his performance.

Kenneth Branagh may indeed be ushering in a new school of acting and directing that will make Shakespeare more understandable and more interesting to more people. On the other hand Olivier "saw off" many new styles of acting during his long career, including "the Method" . . . of which, I must confess, my other hero, Marlon Brando, was the most successful exponent.

Olivier once told me a story about the Group Theatre, which I mentioned earlier. It was unashamedly a left-wing group, believing that all actors were equal, and that, when in the mood, they should not hesitate to improvise. They should "live" their roles, rather than act them. As part and parcel of this philosophy, it was their policy never to take curtain calls. The young Franchot Tone started his career with the Group Theatre and played a part in which he was stabbed to death between the first and second acts. Since there was no curtain call he used to get changed in his dressing room, and go home in the interval. Every night about two minutes before the curtain was due to go up after that interval, the actor who was supposed to have killed him crept into his dressing room with the rubber dagger in his hand and, as Franchot Tone sat at his dressing-room mirror, pretended to plunge it into his back. He timed this so that as the curtain rose he could come on stage with the bloodstained dagger and say, "I killed him, I killed him."

One night Tone hid in the wardrobe. As the curtain rose the actor went on stage and extemporised, "I couldn't find him, I couldn't find him."

If Olivier was larger than life on stage, he had no trouble being "one of us". In the early sixties, he and I sat next to each other at the head table of a Variety Club Lunch at which we were both to be presented with awards, his for acting, mine as "Light Entertainment Personality of the Year".

I assumed I was expected to be funny, and made a rather ill-judged acceptance speech which began, as I recall, with the words: "I always thought the Variety Club was an organisation that met regularly to tell scatological jokes and rationalise by giving milk to children." This jest was met with utter silence, and I hastily extemporised with a series of unplanned jokes, some of which hit the target, and others missed by a mile. Fortunately, my closing line got a good laugh and even some applause. As I sat down, Olivier leaned over and said, "You reminded me of a scrum half who gets hold of the ball by accident and starts a broken field run, runs the length of the field apparently about to be brought down at any moment, but somehow managing to get through for a try. A very messy try."

Later, at a press reception in an adjoining room, photographers were milling about looking for the shots they wanted, and Olivier took over. He knelt on the floor and got the shortest of us to stand immediately behind him, and the rest of us to stand immediately behind each other in order of height. "Think of it as an ABC film press release," he said. "For maximum coverage they have to get us all in one column."

Lord Olivier, over the years, encouraged me to call him Larry, but I could never bring myself to call him anything other than Sir Laurence.

And that from a rebel.

◆　　◆　　◆

The demise of *Streetcar* hadn't been anticipated and I'd spent most of the summer assuming it would run until at least the end of the year. With *Bedtime with Braden* due to start in mid-September, and a third Gracie Fields's series in October I hadn't really been looking for work.

209

The family

Whenever possible during the entire summer I'd been spending time at Creek House and with my children . . . getting to know them. During that time Olive Harding had gone on holiday, and the Head of the Myron Selznick Agency in London, Cecil Tennant, had agreed to look after our affairs in her absence.

One day while I was basking in the sun there was a phone call from Mr Tennant. I came in from the sun, blinking and drowsy. Mr Tennant said, oozing lassitude, "Bernie." Matching his mood, I confirmed that I was on the other end of the line.

Jason, me, Jackson, Barbara, Kim and Kelly

The family

"I'm getting awfully tired of war films, aren't you?"

"Yes, Cecil. Awfully tired of war films."

"I thought you'd agree with me. There's been an enquiry for you to take part in yet another war film. I forget the name of it. But it doesn't matter, because you agree with me, don't you? Awfully tired of war films."

I couldn't wait to get back into the sunshine. "Yes, Cecil. Awfully tired of war films."

"I'll tell them you're not available then, all right?"

Me and Kim

"Whatever you say, Cecil."

This exchange caused me to lose a leading role in a film I won't name because the actor who played the part they had in mind for me was so good in it.

Cecil's next call was fused with energy and excitement.

"Bernie, can you get out to the clubhouse at Wentworth Golf Course as soon as possible? It's very important!"

I said I could and jumped into my Hillman Minx without a map. I drove through Chertsey and Staines at breakneck speed, turned left at Runnymede, broke speed limits through Egham, then ran into the most horrendous traffic jam. It was coming from the other direction and since the road had only two lanes, one each way, the drivers coming towards me were so frustrated by the hold-up they kept trying to overtake on the wrong side of the road. An hour later I finally made my way to the Wentworth clubhouse, and eventually found Cecil seated at a table in the bar with friends.

"What is it, Cecil?" I asked him. "What is it?"

"Ah, Bernie," he said, "there you are. Sorry to have brought you on a wild goose chase. When I called you, it looked very much as if one of your Canadian chappies was going to win this important tournament. I thought you should be here to greet him. Unfortunately he faded badly on the last nine. Have a drink."

I never lost my affection for Cecil Tennant, but I felt much more at ease when Olive returned.

Now the prospect of more work was welcome. Barbara was still travelling to Riverside Studios every day filming *A Tale of Five Cities*, but that was due to finish fairly soon. Something else happened in early September that made the prospect of further work imperative rather than just welcome. Now that the entire family was living in England my accountant informed me that we had achieved "resident status". This meant that the BBC could only pay us into a resident account and he advised that we should transfer whatever money we had in Canada into that account. We managed to achieve this two days before the Labour government devalued the pound from $4.25 to $2.80. We no longer had any dollars, and some years later when Harold Wilson devalued British currency and announced that, "It would make no difference to the pound in your pocket," I permitted myself a wry smile.

The two eldest children were attending fee-paying schools,

Chris at a primary school in Walton-on-Thames, and Kelly at a convent school just across the river. It was the first school that Chris had attended where he was required to wear a uniform but when I asked him what he thought the main difference between his schools in Canada and in England, he said succinctly, "In Canada there were girls."

The situation with Kelly was a little different. As a son of a non-conformist clergyman I was slightly sceptical, but was assured by my Catholic friend, Gilbert Harding, that if I had a chat with the Mother Superior and explained the situation she would see that efforts were not made to convert our daughter to Roman Catholicism. This proved to be absolutely true, and both she and later her sister attended St Mawe's for several years.

The next time that Gilbert came to Creek House, and I told him that Kelly was settling in nicely he said, "People as dedicated as nuns can get along with almost anyone without inflicting their own religion on them."

Barbara and Bonar in A Tale of Five Cities

He then told me a story about a convent school where one of the pupils was about to become a novitiate. She came of an important Catholic family and the ceremony was to be conducted by a Cardinal. The Mother Superior decided that some renovations of the chapel were required on such an important occasion, and put the job out to tender. Out of four estimates, she found that the most comprehensive and cheapest came from a small building company consisting of a father and two sons, all Jewish. Although this gave her pause for thought, her sense of economy overcame her reservations and she gave them the contract.

As the work progressed, she found them efficient and at pains to avoid disrupting other activities in the convent. At one point the father of the family approached her and asked her to explain the nature of this event which was so important that she required renovations. Patiently she told him that in effect the girl was to become the bride of Christ, and that the attendance of the distinguished prelate made it doubly important. She'd grown rather attached to her builders once she became used to the fact that they tended to address her as "Mother Shapiro".

The father then asked if it would be possible for him and his two sons to attend the ceremony. They had become used to the chapel, and would be delighted to see to what use their handiwork had been put. Again with patience the Mother Superior explained that it was a private ceremony and only the family of the bride and certain distinguished guests were invited.

The builder persisted, and suggested that since he and his sons were now so familiar with the architecture of the chapel, they could find a place to hide in the rafters where no one would notice them or even know they were there. Reluctantly, the Mother Superior agreed.

On the great day the Cardinal spoke at length in Latin, but being a bit of a ham, in the middle of his peroration he suddenly rolled his eyes upwards and interrupted his own discourse to say, "What are you doing up there?"

And a meek voice replied, "Friends of the Groom."

After we'd enjoyed our laugh at this joke, Gilbert suddenly turned serious, and said, "You know, I studied for the priesthood myself."

This was a new one on me, and I asked him where and when.

"It was many years ago near a godforsaken place called Antogonish in your own godforsaken country. Nova Scotia, to be precise. I entered a monastery there and one of the rules was total silence which, as you can imagine, was particularly hard on me. After about six months we were told that an important Jesuit was coming to visit, would have dinner with us, and that on this occasion the vow of silence would be lifted. During dinner I plied the Jesuit with questions, and when we rose he invited me to walk with him in the cloisters. I looked around at my colleagues and couldn't resist a superior smile at having been singled out by so distinguished a man. As we walked he asked me what had brought me to the monastery, and I replied that I had heard the 'call'. We then sat down on a stone bench, and he said, 'My son, I'm sure you appreciate, having taken the vow of silence, that this was considered by your colleagues a special occasion, where they were joined together to listen to what I had to say. You behaved as if we were all there to listen to what *you* had to say. Are you sure it wasn't something *else* you heard?' "

Gilbert gave up his ambition to be a monk.

Kelly had a choice of going to school "the long way round", that is by crossing the Walton-on-Thames bridge and then all the way back to Weybridge, or directly across the river. As we hadn't had to pay for the cabin cruiser, I acquired a second-hand slipperstern launch in which she was ferried to school and back again by the gardener. When she arrived home on the first day I asked her what she'd learned.

"The alphabet," she said.

Kelly

215

"That's very good. Can you recite it to me?"

"Certainly. A-B-C-L-X-T-R-Y-N and so on."

"Interesting. I think they must have changed the alphabet since I went to school."

"Yes," she said. "They mentioned that."

After about a week Mr Rosewall, the gardener, told us that although he was due to pick Kelly up in the launch at a specific time, he usually had to wait anything from ten to twenty minutes before she arrived. I, in turn, mentioned it to her.

It emerged that Kelly was the only girl in her class who could tie her own shoelaces, and that in a spirit of charity she also tied the shoelaces of the other girls, which meant that they got away before she did, and explained her lateness. There was more . . . all the other girls had ballet shoes. Kelly didn't have ballet shoes. Madame had said it was important that Kelly have ballet shoes. All the other girls had white ballet shoes. Madame insisted that Kelly should have gold ballet shoes.

A few words with Madame sorted that one out, and Kelly ended up with ballet shoes. White ballet shoes.

◆   ◆   ◆

Until *Streetcar* closed it had been more than a year since Barbara and I had been able to attend a theatre together. We returned first to the Aldwych to see *Streetcar*'s successor, a play called *Accolade* by Emlyn Williams, who also starred. It was about a distinguished man who'd been led to expect a knighthood and discovered that the seamier side of his life was to be revealed by a blackmailer . . . and very seamy it was. John Gielgud, who *would* become a knight in due course, was heard to murmur on the way out, "A jolly good play, but Emlyn made it rather too autobiographical for my liking." Then a revival of *Home and Beauty* by Somerset Maugham, which we attended largely because Brenda Bruce took a leading role. *Cocktail Party* was an undoubted success, partly because of the performance of Alec Guinness, but mainly because Barbara's former impresario, Henry Sherek, had persuaded T. S. Eliot to write a play for the theatre . . . his first.

I'd always wanted to see (and we did) *Harvey*, because it involved the theatrical trick of presenting a six-foot invisible rabbit and a star who could apparently see him. It originally starred Sid Field, but after his death James Stewart had taken over the leading role, and we enjoyed it thoroughly.

216

The fact that Gilbert accompanied us on most of our theatre excursions wasn't always a blessing. If he imbibed too freely before the curtain went up he was apt to fall asleep and start snoring. If, on the other hand he was sober and alert, any defect in play or performance would elicit verbal criticism that could be heard in the auditorium and on the stage. There were occasions when he would snort angrily and leave the theatre.

One evening, many years later when Gilbert had moved to Brighton, Barbara and I attended a first night at the Theatre Royal there. As the curtain rose we were aware of agitated movement behind us. A whole row was standing to accommodate a lady who'd apparently arrived late. Not so. The lady turned out to be Gilbert's housekeeper, who stopped when she got to us and said, "Gilbert asked me to tell you that if he leaves after the first act it will be because of his asthma, not the play." She then made her laborious way back to the aisle.

We saw no sign of Gilbert in the interval, but as the curtain rose on the *second* act, the incident was repeated, except that this time she said, "Gilbert asked me to tell you that he left because of the play, not his asthma."

We also went to see *Top of the Ladder* at the St James's Theatre with Johnny Mills, and several weeks later, also at the St James's Theatre, *Captain Cavallo* with Peter Finch, whom we'd come to know when he was appearing in *Daphne Laureola* at Wyndham's Theatre, which backed on to the New Theatre, when Barbara was doing *The Male Animal*. Peter had been discovered in Australia by the Oliviers who'd signed him to a long-term contract of which he was already trying to divest himself.

With Dickie Attenborough and his wife Sheila Sim we went to see *Mister Roberts* starring Tyrone Power and Jackie Cooper. We'd been invited back to the Attenboroughs' after the show and travelled in Dickie's 1934 Bentley. The Attenboroughs lived in Richmond, and as we turned right after Hammersmith Bridge we were given the siren by a following police car. To our amazement Dickie simply speeded up and the police car gave chase. As we reached Barnes Common the police car turned left while we stayed on the road by the Thames. Dickie continued to gather speed, but when we reached his house the police car was waiting for us. Two officers got out and said, "Ha ha. We beat you again." In some ways London was a freer place in those days.

On another occasion, after seeing Noël Coward's musical *The Ace of Clubs* and then going to dinner at the Ivy, Barbara and I got into an argument on the way home. As we proceeded along the old Cromwell Road (long before the overpass was built) the argument

217

grew more heated until Barbara, who was driving, stopped the car and ordered me out. I did as I was told and waited patiently, knowing that eventually she'd come back for me. When she did, I hid behind a tree, causing her to drive about a mile further back into town than she'd intended. On her return journey I flagged her down, got back into the car and we both had a good laugh. Within minutes the argument started again. By the time we reached Richmond roundabout the car was stopped once more, and I was ordered out again. This time I was pretty sure she wouldn't come back, so I went to the police box at the roundabout and asked the officer on the other end of the line if he could think of some way of getting me safely home. A police car arrived in less than three minutes. I gave them the address and we hurtled our way home using short cuts they knew about and I never learned. I invited them in for a drink and when Barbara arrived we were sitting calmly in the living room exchanging stories. There wasn't much she could say about that, but her eyes spoke volumes. The two policemen refused a second drink, and I saw them out to the car, thanking them profusely. The driver rolled down his window and said, "Oh, just one thing, sir. Sometimes on occasions such as these, well-known people like your good self write letters to the superintendent thanking *him* for our courtesy. We'd be most grateful if you didn't."

◆　　◆　　◆

Before *Bedtime with Braden* started there was a long meeting with Muir and Norden, Eric Nicol, Pat Dixon and myself. There had been some indication, according to the press, that *Take it From Here* was getting into a bit of a rut. Certainly Frank and Denis felt that its new season would require more of their time, and their faith in Eric was such that they felt it safe to hand over most of the *Bedtime* writing to him, with their own contribution limited each week to a single sketch. The producer and all three writers believed that some changes were needed in the format in switching it from *Breakfast* to *Bedtime*. Pat suggested that adding Barbara to the cast might help, and Eric agreed that it would give him more scope. The only problem was that up to this point Pearl Carr was supposed to have a crush on me, so it was decided that Pearl would have a new boyfriend and, to complicate matters further, Ronald Fletcher would have a crush on Barbara.

I was still obsessed with the fact that I'd never had a chance to play Stanley, so I suggested that Pearl's new boyfriend be an

At work

uncouth American called "Brandy Marlow", which would give me a chance to do my impression of Marlon Brando. It would have to stand on its own, because Brando was still totally unknown in Great Britain, and so it was agreed.

The other dimension added by Eric was that whereas I played myself as brash and bossy in the studio, the sketches I played with Barbara, allegedly at home, allowed her to score off me rather than the other way around.

In one episode Barbara was consoling a distraught Pearl.

BARBARA: Now then, Pearl, what's the trouble?
PEARL: It's Brandy, Miss Kelly, he's in jail again.
BARBARA: What was it this time?
PEARL: Well, the police aren't quite sure yet, but somebody said Shakespeare should swear out the warrant.
BARBARA: Shakespeare?

PEARL:	Yes, he's a man who wrote plays.
BARBARA:	Oh, that Shakespeare.
PEARL:	You've heard of him?
BARBARA:	Only by hearsay.
PEARL:	Then you've probably heard of the Walthamstow Button Manufacturers Little Thespian Society.
BARBARA:	I don't think Hearsay mentioned that one. Why?
PEARL:	Well, they asked my fiancé Brandy Marlow to play Mark Antony in their version of *Julius Caesar*. It would have been all right if Brandy hadn't agreed.
BARBARA:	You mean he came down out of his tree just to play Mark Antony?
PEARL:	Oh, Miss Kelly I wish he was still up there.
BARBARA:	What happened?
PEARL:	Well, I attended the first performance last night and (*fade out*)
BRANDY:	(*Bernie*) Friends, Romans and countrymen, lend me your ears. I come to bury Kaiser, not to praise him.
RONALD:	Caesar.
BRANDY:	You do the Hazlitt version if you want. I'm sticking to the Folio.
BENNY:	If thou consider rightly of the matter, Caesar hath had great wrong.
RONALD:	Shakespeare hath had great wrong.
BENNY:	Read the will, Antony.
BRANDY:	I haven't got to that part yet. I still gotta do all that malarky about Brutus bein' an honourable crook, and judgement bein' fled to brutish beasts, and all like that there.
NAT:	Stand from the hearse. Stand from the body.
BRANDY:	Relax, Jack, he ain't been dead *that* long.
RONALD:	Treason, treason.
BRANDY:	Look, Buster, you handle your part and I'll handle mine, see. I'll be Antony and you stick to bein' fourth citizen. Got it?
NAT:	Please, you're standing on my feet.
BRANDY:	You shut up, Kaiser. You're supposed to be dead.
RONALD:	Oh, do be careful of the bier.
BRANDY:	What beer? You guys been drinkin' beer and didn't offer me none? (*Shouting*) Pearly, you hear that? These guys been drinkin' beer instead of –
PEARL: (*off*)	Please, Brandy, don't lose your temper.
BRANDY:	I'm gettin' the red mist, Pearly. I mean I came to bury the creep, not to praise him.

RONALD: Ring down the curtain somebody!

BENNY: I'm getting out of here.

BRANDY: Listen, Kaiser, you're dead. You stay where you are, or I'll bop you on the noggin.

RONALD: No, no . . . please . . . the bier.

BRANDY: If you guys can't take it serious like I do, I'll bop the lot of you.

Effects: Mighty crashes.

BRANDY: (*over screams of cast*) Go fetch fire, pluck down benches . . . mischief, though art afoot, take thou what course thou wilt, and . . . (*fade out*).

BARBARA: So Antony's oration really *did* move the people, eh, Pearl?

PEARL: Yes, but then the police came and moved Brandy.

BARBARA: Never mind, he'll find his way back to that tree.

PEARL: Sure, but what am I supposed to do?

BARBARA: Sing, Pearl.

Now to Ronnie Fletcher and my relationship with Barbara.

RONALD: Oh, Braden.

BERNIE: Yes, Mr Fletcher.

RONALD: I noticed in the newspaper recently that one of the television critics expressed his admiration for the lovely Barbara Kelly for her mixture of good health, good looks and good sense, and wished that she could be seen more often without her husband. (*Pause*) That's you, of course.

BERNIE: Yes, that's me.

RONALD: I don't suppose there's any chance of you and Miss Kelly separating? Professionally as well, I mean.

BERNIE: None. And you can pull in that old school tongue. (*Fading*) Barbara and I have always worked as a team, and we ignore what the critics say about us.

BARBARA: Say, Bernie.

BERNIE: Yes, Barbara?

BARBARA: You remember one day last week you brought in the morning paper with a chunk torn out of one page, and you said the dog must have been chewing it?

BERNIE: Yes. I'm sure it was Jason.

BARBARA: Well I found where Jason hid the piece after he'd finished chewing. Up on the picture rail in the front hall.

BERNIE: Yeah, he sure is one tall dog.

BARBARA: The piece of paper was a television critic bit about me.

BERNIE: Oh really?

BARBARA: Uh huh. He expresses admiration for my good health, good looks and good sense, and wishes that I could be seen more often without my husband. That's you, of course.

BERNIE: Yes, that's me.

BARBARA: Funny Jason should have torn out *that* piece, isn't it?

BERNIE: Very funny. (*Laughs weakly*)

BARBARA: You don't think he could be jealous of my success, do you?

BERNIE: Who, Jason?

BARBARA: You know any other mutts in the house that could reach the picture rail?

BERNIE: No.

BARBARA: You're sure you didn't see that piece about my mixture of good health, good looks and so on?

BERNIE: Well, what if I did?

BARBARA: Nothing. Except that someone besides me has been using my pot of skin food.

BERNIE: You're right, Barbara. I want to be glamorous like you. Maybe you *would* be better off on your own, Barbara.

BARBARA: Bernie, I was only teasing –

BERNIE: No, you go on alone in television. I'll find another part some place. Sooner or later they're bound to make *The Man in the Iron Mask* again. You've got good health, I'm ... (*coughs*) I'm not likely ... (*coughs*) where are you going, dear?

BARBARA: Out to order the flowers. If you feel yourself falling, try to fall *away* from the good china.

SOUND EFFECT: Door slam.

BERNIE: (*fade in*) ... So you see, Mr Fletcher, there is no professional rivalry between Barbara and myself.

RONALD: Oh, that's a pity. I too had been hoping to see Miss Kelly alone. (*Dirty laugh of a sort*)

BERNIE: That, friends, is a dirty laugh as taught by the Cheapside Academy of Dramatic Arts and Laundry Works. Sing, Benny.

But back in the studio it was the usual chaos.

222

Enjoying our work

PEARL: Some day, Mr Braden, Brandy and I will find our dream cottage, far from "the madding crowd".

BERNIE: That's the maddening crowd, Pearl.

PEARL: Oh, I'm sorry. We'll be far from the maddening crowd, just Brandy and I.

RONALD: (*coming on*) You were quite right, Miss Carr. It's *Far from the Madding Crowd*.

BERNIE: Well, if it isn't Fowler's older brother, Fowlest.

RONALD: I'm sorry, Braden, but the girl's right. I assure you I'm just as surprised as you are.

PEARL: If Mr Braden says I'm wrong, I'm wrong.

BERNIE: It's *Far from the Maddening Crowd*.

BENNY: What is?

BERNIE: Oh fine!

RONALD: We are discussing the title of Hardy's work.

BENNY: Oh I remember that. It was *Two Dopes in the Desert*.

BERNIE: That's *Laurel* and Hardy.

BENNY: That's right. I remember one terribly funny scene where Hardy kisses a camel and then Laurel scratches his head –

BERNIE: Benny! Back to your Plasticine. There's still some you haven't eaten.

223

With Pearl Carr

NAT: What's the discussion?

BERNIE: All right now. Who's watching the cash register?

RONALD: Mr Temple, as leader of this stout orchestra, I'm sure you will support me when I say that it's *Far from the Madding Crowd* and not *Far from the Maddening Crowd*.

NAT: Correct. It's just in Bayswater. Mr Bentley my trombonist can give you the address. Bentley!

PEARL/BENNY: Mr Braden . . . Laurel and Hardy –

BERNIE: That's enough. Somebody sing a song before this chaos grows into a ministry.

My radio reputation was getting me offers to speak in public. The first came purely by accident. Ted Heath's band used to give regular Sunday night concerts at the London Palladium where his compère and singer was Paul Carpenter. Late one Sunday afternoon Paul phoned Ted to say that he was suffering from almost total laryngitis and wouldn't be able to appear that night. In a panic search for a substitute they finally arrived at me. Paul was a popular compère and usually went on to a large round of applause.

Glasgow Evening News: "Bernard Braden was at his very funniest when 'Breakfast' returned as 'Bedtime' on Tuesday. The addition to the cast of Barbara Kelly was a tonic. Benny Lee and Pearl Carr gave splendid support."

Evening Gazette: "Braden returned to the Home Service on September 19th with his new show *Bedtime with Braden*. There is no doubt that the man who could make us laugh at the thought of getting out of bed will keep us out of it a bit longer at night."

Edinburgh Evening Despatch: "I'm strongly tempted to vote for Bernard Braden as the outstanding radio personality of the year on the strength of his new series: *Bedtime with Braden*. Night or day Braden is the man for the laughs. He is a 'do not miss' for me from now on. I don't know of any other variety star who can appear on the Third Programme 'straight' either."

"Radio's most talented and versatile performer, Bernard Braden, commenced his *Bedtime with Braden* last week. Now that's a much better time for an artist of Braden's importance."

Northampton Chronicle and Echo: "Bernard Braden has made the transition from Breakfast to Bedtime smoothly enough and now reaches twice the number of listeners that used to enjoy him over the toast."

Sitting nervously in my dressing room I knew that as a substitute I might well be a disappointment and decided that the important thing was to have a good first line, but by the time I was introduced over the microphone I still hadn't thought of one. I walked on to enormous applause which threw me a little, and during the pause allowed by the audience reaction, something flashed into my mind and I said, "Well, what do you know? A Canadian at the Palladian." It wasn't very funny, particularly since Paul Carpenter was also a Canadian, but it brought the house down. From then on I could do no wrong. It just hadn't occurred to me that I'd reached a point through radio where whatever I said sounded funny.

A little later I was invited to be one of the speakers at the Dockyards Settlement Ball at the Savoy Hotel in the presence of Princess Margaret. I was seated at the head table next to Lord Mancroft, who at that time was reckoned to be the best after-dinner speaker in London. It didn't bother me because I'd never heard of Lord Mancroft. I thoroughly enjoyed the dinner, and the wine that went with it. Then Lord Mancroft got up to speak and I sank lower and lower in my chair, as his erudition and wit took hold of the audience. I knew he was definitely out of my class. He sat down to an ovation that lasted several minutes, and as I was introduced to follow him I could feel waves of sympathy coming in my direction from the audience. "Who could follow that?"

Again I sensed it was time for audacity, and I began by saying, "I would like first to congratulate Lord Mancroft on the wittiest and funniest after-dinner speech I've ever listened to in my life, and I would like to congratulate him on speaking so lucidly and intelligently to such tremendous effect. It's amazing to me that anyone could be so fluent as Lord Mancroft, particularly when he's as drunk as I know him to be." The laugh that followed was more of relief than anything else, but again, if you get off to a good start, the rest comes fairly easily.

Then I was invited to compère a concert at the Old Lyceum Ballroom, introducing some of the biggest stars in Britain. One of these was Leslie Henson, whose reputation as a musical star and comedian was certainly not lost on me. In the days when Fred and Adèle Astaire were doing musicals in London, Leslie Henson was billed above them. I introduced the great Leslie Henson and walked into the wings. What went wrong, I don't know. Perhaps it was because it was mainly a crowd of young people, some of whom might never have heard of Leslie Henson. He was due to stay on for ten minutes, and came off after six or seven . . . in tears. As I shook his hand he said, "They don't like me any more. They don't like me."

There was a lesson for me there, but I was so full of my present success that I missed it completely.

About twenty years ago my wife started a business supplying after-dinner speakers all over the country. Organisations of all kinds phone up and request after-dinner speakers. Unlike Leslie Henson I've never come off stage in tears, perhaps because during the past ten years no one has ever requested me as an after-dinner speaker.

On October 4th, 1950 Gracie Fields and I began the third series of twenty-six shows for Radio Luxembourg, and Gracie was her usual ebullient self. There was no audience for Gracie's show, but two young ladies appeared regularly and were given seats in the control room. They seemed to know Gracie well, and one day she introduced them. One was Hilda Gilbert, the wife of film director Lewis Gilbert, and we came to know her and her husband well. Indeed it was Lewis who'd enquired about my availability for a war film from Cecil Tennant earlier that summer which had been turned down out of hand because Cecil was "awfully tired of war films".

Some years later Lewis and Hilda invited Barbara and me to a private screening of a film, along with Ronald Paterson, the couturier, and his wife Steve. It wasn't one of Lewis's films. It was an early picture by Carl Reiner called *Enter Laughing*, which I don't think was ever released in Great Britain, but Lewis loved seeing it again and again and often invited friends to share it with him.

After the showing the six of us went to the Ivy Restaurant for dinner. It was quite late, and shortly after we sat down I saw George Brown, then Foreign Secretary of Great Britain, come in alone and sit at a table for two. He ordered coffee and what appeared to be a triple brandy.

After a few minutes he looked up, apparently at me, and beckoned with his finger. I looked behind me, because I'd never met George Brown, but there *was* no one behind me. When I turned around Mr Brown nodded and beckoned again. I walked to his table and he said, "Brother, I've had a tiring and difficult day. There are pressing matters of state weighing on my conscience and soul. My wife and I have had a quiet meal and a walk. Now she's gone home and I've come here because I need a cup of coffee and the opportunity to think things out by myself. May I join your party?"

Two minutes later he was seated at the head of our table embroiling us all in political discussion as if we were members of the Cabinet or the opposition. Mostly he asked questions, and shot down the answers, but two things were clear. One, that he cared desperately about his country and his party and two, he was genuinely interested in our opinions, even though we were total strangers.

At one point he suddenly said to me, "Bernie, phone my wife at the Foreign Office and ask her to join us. She'll enjoy this."

Obediently I went to the Reception desk and got through to the Foreign Office, explaining that I had a message for Mrs Brown from the Foreign Secretary. I was put through and a sleepy voice said, "Yes?"

"My name is Bernard Braden. I'm at the Ivy with some friends and your husband, and Mr Brown thought you might like to join us."

There was a long pause . . . Then, "Mr Braden, I'm in bed, and don't really feel like getting dressed and going out again. Thank you for your invitation, and I'd be most grateful if you could see that my husband gets safely home."

Walking back to the table I realised that the restaurant was empty except for our party and some restless waiters.

"All right," said Mr Brown, "now I'm going to ask you one at a time starting on my left. If you were Foreign Secretary of this country, what would *your* priority be?" . . . and all of us tried our best under his piercing gaze to put ourselves in his place and give a sensible answer. "China . . . Russia . . . the European Community . . . developing countries . . . the United States."

Finally his gaze came to Barbara who said, "If I were a member of this government, I'd stop talking and start doing something. It seems to me that all we've got since you came to power is words and more words, but very little action."

It was the sort of challenge he'd been looking for, and from then on the rest of us were ignored as George directed his arguments to Barbara. This gave the rest of us the opportunity to get the bill, pay it and make ready to leave.

As the grateful waiters saw us out I asked one of them to summon the Foreign Secretary's car. He said, "What car?" And it emerged that Mr Brown had no transport and no escort of any kind. It was after 1.00 a.m. and there wasn't a taxi in sight.

"That's all right," said Mr Brown. "One of you can give me a lift back to the Foreign Office."

Which was fine, except that we'd only one car between us. It was a five-seater and we were seven. We all piled in with Hilda Gilbert seated on George's lap. It struck me that his American counterpart Dean Rusk wasn't likely to find himself in such a situation in the early hours of the morning.

As I saw Mr Brown up the steps of the Foreign Office I muttered something about wishing him luck in his difficult task.

He turned and looked at me. "Not a chance," he said quietly. "I want to get things done too fast. My colleagues move more slowly, and in my heart I know they're right. You can't rush government decisions and implement them quickly. But I'm too impatient." He waved a hand at the Foreign Office. "I won't be here much longer. You'll see."

Then he turned and went inside.

He was right, of course, and in his later years, it became fashionable to think of George Brown as a sort of joke. But after his visit to the United Nations in New York as Foreign Secretary, his impact was such that Alistair Cooke said, "He's the first

Foreign Secretary of Britain who's known to everyone in the United States since Anthony Eden."

The morning after our night at the Ivy Hilda Gilbert received a phone call from a reporter identifying himself as being with the *Daily Express*. He said, "I understand that you dined with the Foreign Secretary at the Ivy Restaurant last night."

Hilda said this wasn't true, but admitted they'd had coffee together. "We were with a party," she added quickly.

"But you left rather late, didn't you? I understand there was no one left in the restaurant."

Hilda said again that she was with a party and it included her husband.

"But isn't it true that you sat on Mr Brown's knee during the journey home?"

Hilda, definitely trying to walk a fine line, pointed out that they hadn't driven home, but that Mr Brown had been dropped off at the Foreign Office.

After a few more questions the *"Express* reporter" finally broke down and admitted that he was Lewis Gilbert, her husband.

◆ ◆ ◆

Having made a point throughout this book of stressing the importance of writers and the fact they rarely get credit for their work, mention of the name Lewis Gilbert reminds me that the same is often true of directors.

Lewis Gilbert directed his first British film in 1947, and although he's worked all over the world has always stayed based in Britain. He directed *Reach for the Sky*, *Carve her Name with Pride*, *Ferry to Hong Kong* and *The Greengage Summer*, among others; and should be particularly remembered for *Alfie*. He set that film up himself, but backed by Paramount who, as Lewis said, "Thought it was a good bet because it was going to be made for $500,000, normally the sort of money spent on executives' cigar bills". He'd arranged his production schedule, but since Paramount had the final veto on the casting, it looked as if he wouldn't be able to start on time. Without reference to Paramount Gilbert cast the leading part and started production. After two weeks of solid work Paramount sent a memo informing him they'd found the perfect person to play Alfie: a new film had just opened in the States called *The Ipcress File* and they thought the leading man would make a perfect Alfie. Lewis was ordered to stop shooting and start again with Michael Caine. There was no need to stop shooting, because he'd already cast Michael Caine.

Lewis Gilbert directed more of the Bond films than anyone else, two with Sean Connery and three with Roger Moore. He directed Michael Caine and Julie Walters in *Educating Rita*, and more recently, Pauline Collins and Tom Conti in *Shirley Valentine*.

It occurred to me that I'd never seen a film profile on television or anywhere else on the subject of Lewis Gilbert, so I phoned him and asked him if I'd missed something. "No," he said. "After all I've only made thirty-five pictures."

In March 1990 he won the Michael Bakon award from BAFTA for distinguished service to the British film industry.

◆　　◆　　◆

Meanwhile, back in 1950, Gracie Fields and I completed our last series together and went our separate ways. I only met her once again, in the mid-fifties when I was appearing in a play called *The Man* at the Lyceum Theatre in Edinburgh and Gracie was giving a concert at the Usher Hall. Since we were both staying at the same hotel we decided to have dinner together one evening . . . a late dinner, and talked far into the night. At some point, she noticed that all the other diners had gone and we were alone with the waiters. Unlike George Brown she realised we were keeping them up and ended the evening in typical Gracie fashion. Knowing that the waiters were hanging on her every word she pushed her chair back, stood up and said loudly to me, "Well, as you haven't asked me to go to bed with you, I think I'll return to my room now." . . . which of course she did.

◆　　◆　　◆

Bedtime with Braden was popular, but the BBC never did pay much money, and I felt the need to do something else. Olive Harding took me to lunch with Val Parnell, then the Head of Moss Empires, and Val suggested that I might play Buttons in *Cinderella*, one of his Christmas pantomimes. Olive had assumed that after nearly two years in the country I understood what English pantomimes were about, but I didn't. I'd never seen one, and the idea of playing Buttons in a children's entertainment after appearing with Vivien Leigh in *A Streetcar Named Desire* and having gained a radio reputation as witty and sophisticated appalled me. I said so in no uncertain terms (I'd never heard of Val Parnell either), and Mr Parnell made a rather hasty exit before the lunch ended. *Then* Olive, head in hands, explained the nature of the British pantomime and the amount of money one could earn doing it. Too late.

Next she introduced me to the producer of a current review called *Sauce Piquante*. It was in the French style, and because of other commitments the French star who'd compèred the show had to leave. Olive arranged for me to see the show and meet the producer afterwards. He was a flamboyant continental of the type who wore a camel-hair coat draped over his shoulders. He explained that I could start the following Monday, but of course would have to write completely new material to suit my own personality. This sounded like too much work on three days' notice, and although I'd enjoyed the show, I felt it somewhat beneath me, and turned it down . . . although with one slight misgiving. There was a very attractive girl in the chorus with a petite figure and enormous eyes. Her name was Audrey Hepburn. Also Christmas was on the way, and if I went on like this there'd be no extra money coming in, and I could well be on the verge of losing my agent.

Meantime, a film called *The Men* opened at the London Pavilion, starring Marlon Brando . . . his first film. After seeing it, Barbara and I went to the Embassy Club to watch Tommy Trinder in cabaret. During the evening I saw Bonar Colleano sitting at a table across the room. He'd obviously had far too much to drink and while friends talked round him he sat slumped in his chair with his eyes closed. After all I'd put Bonar through about Brando and his superior performance I knew Bonar would have been one of the first to see *The Men*. Making my way through the tables around him I approached him from behind and squatted by his chair. Then I tapped him on the knee. He roused himself enough to get his eyes together and recognise me, then said, "Hi".

I said, "What did you think of Brando?"

He looked at me for a long time and a number of expressions crossed his face. Finally, he got himself into full focus and said belligerently, "I fought him for twenty minutes."

Having turned down several lucrative offers on the grounds that they were beneath me, I was even more taken aback when Olive phoned to say that bandleader Ted Heath wanted to present me as the top act on a variety bill for one week at the Ardwick Hippodrome in Manchester. Supporting acts would include Max Wall and Anton Karas, the zither player from *The Third Man*. Max Wall was my idea of a music-hall star. Why would I get top billing over Max? Olive explained that Max was a familiar figure in music-hall and that audiences loved to see him, but were so used to him they wouldn't pay for the privilege . . . at least not

231

enough of them. I, on the other hand, had a successful radio show, my voice was familiar; now people would pay to see what I looked like. Whether they liked what they saw was a matter for conjecture . . .

I didn't like that last bit and wondered if there were any other offers for the taking, until Olive explained further that if I filled the Hippodrome twice nightly for a week I could be paid as much as £3,000 depending on the percentage she was able to negotiate! It was a deal. The first problem was, as I'd explained so many months ago to Pat Newman, I didn't have an act. Frank Muir and Denis Norden agreed to put something together to display my myriad talents adequately. They wrote the act, but I thought up the opening. That was all my own work.

Now in those days it was the custom for comedians to open with a song. If they could sing they'd also *close* with a song, but if they couldn't, it was still obligatory to open with one. I decided to confront this problem head on. I would come out and sing sixteen bars of "I Get a Kick Out of You", break off and say, "Don't you find it ridiculous that comics always start with a song, even if they can't sing . . . I mean, after all, we're hired to tell jokes, not sing. You didn't come to hear me sing, you came to laugh at jokes, so let's forget the song and get down to business. Joke . . ."

I would then tell a joke so bad that no one would laugh, then finish the song. Brilliant? I thought so. I then asked Frank and Denis to provide me with a joke guaranteed not to get a laugh and they came up with: "Lady walks into an ironmonger's shop and says to the man, 'Do you have long nails?' Man says, 'Yes', lady says, 'Good. Scratch my back.'"

After due preparation, I set out to drive to Manchester on a rainy Sunday morning. Although this was long before the motorways were built, I didn't need a map because I was accompanied by two friends, both of whom knew the way . . . or rather each of whom knew the way. One was Bonar Colleano, the other was Gilbert Harding. Their differing concepts as to the correct route varied considerably, and because Gilbert had booked us for dinner at a well-known inn in Knutsford, Bonar finally agreed to give way and I followed Gilbert's directions. This resulted in a side journey to North Wales, where pubs didn't open on a Sunday, and Gilbert's embarrassment was compounded by the frustration of not being able to get a drink.

By 7.00 p.m. we were safely out of Wales but had no idea how to get to Knutsford. Deeming it Gilbert's responsibility Bonar and I made him get out at every pub and enquire the way. At each pub his visits grew longer and he emerged from the seventh or eighth soaked to the skin from driving rain, and announced, "It's become a kind of eccentricity to want to go to Knutsford. They say of a man, he's an adulterer, yes, a pervert, yes. He indulges in incest and sodomy, but *he doesn't want to go to Knutsford.*"

We finally gave up on Knutsford and the delicious repast promised by Gilbert, settling instead for the Grand Hotel in Manchester, which we finally reached about midnight and were grumpily served with limp lettuce sandwiches by the night porter.

The following morning I attended "band call" at the Ardwick Hippodrome. Bonar and Gilbert were still abed. The rule was first come, first served, regardless of billing. Each act laid down his music on the apron of the stage, the orchestra leader passed out the parts, and rehearsal began. As the last to arrive, I was privileged to watch the others and horrified to realise that they weren't really rehearsing at all, but just using a kind of shorthand to outline the act from the orchestra's point of view.

One comedian hadn't even bothered to turn up, he'd sent his dresser. This gentleman said, "Right. We start with the play on music." The band duly played four bars of "Dark Town Strutter's Ball", the dresser cut them off and said, "Right, now Mr So and So sings 'There'll be a Hot Time in the Old Town Tonight'; just play the last few bars, that's fine, then he goes into his routine about the nit nurse." There was an interruption here while the dresser went into paroxysms of laughter at the mere thought of his boss's "nit nurse" routine.

Then . . . "He ends with the old man who was supposed to be at death's door, but then took a turn for the nurse – that last line should be written into the music, right? – that cues you into 'The Skater's Waltz' dum, dumty dum, dum, dumty dum; and you play that right through while he does his skating routine on sand, then straight back into 'Dark Town Strutter's Ball'. He makes a false exit, back on to stage, fade out, 'Dark Town Strutter's Ball' and he does his main monologue – there's no music there – except for the bit where the drummer cues him into the tap dance and won't let him stop because – oh, Mr Wall is doing that routine? Okay, I'll have my man cut it, so your next cue is where he says, 'Let's just remind ourselves of that great performer, Vesta Tilley,' and he does the Vesta Tilley medley in falsetto. Big finish on 'Burlington Bertie' and exit. Back into 'Dark Town Strutter's Ball'; be prepared to keep playing it for about seven curtain calls, and then off!"

Every act did the band call in roughly the same way, simply making sure that the parts were properly marked and in the right order. I was totally unnerved, because I'd planned to rehearse my whole act. In addition to "I Get a Kick Out of You", I proposed to sing a chorus of "I'm Through with Love", then fade the band while I did a monologue of my love life when I was working in a circus. Sample joke: "I got a note from the bearded lady asking me to meet her for a chin wag" (!), finishing singing the last eight bars of "I'm Through with Love". Then there were my singing impressions which included a baritone and tenor duet of Bach's "Good Fellows be Merry", a tenor with a slow vibrato singing, "Where my Caravan has Rested" and a loud baritone shouting, "Singing a Vagabond Song", right up to the last loud note but stopping short of it and saying, "Oh hell, the place isn't big enough", and walking off stage. (*False exit*) But most importantly, there was my stolen version of "Fine and Dandy". I'd had Malcolm Lockyer lift the arrangement from a Mel Tormé record. It was basically simple, but there was a tricky obbligato for a muted trumpet and that was the key to its originality.

When we reached the point in my band call where the orchestra turned a page to be faced with "Fine and Dandy" the trumpeter said, "What's this, then?"

"It's a trumpet obbligato," I informed him.

He studied it briefly, turned the next page, studied that, then closed the music. "Not bloody likely," he said.

We cut it.

Back at the hotel I told Bonar that this experience had to some extent diminished my confidence. "My fault," he said, "I should have warned you." He was particularly amused by the comedian who had planned to pinch part of Max Wall's routine and told me about a famous occasion when the American comedian Joe Frisco had walked up to Enrico Caruso as *he* was about to start a band call for a charity performance, and said, "Hey, buddy, lay off of 'Alexander's Ragtime Band', will ya? I use it to finish my act."

Later, when I'd got used to band calls, I was told about the chorus girl who embarked on her first music-hall tour. She was third from the left in a line of eight and during the first show the trombone player winked at her. She smiled back, and after the show he took her out to dinner. In fact they had dinner together every night that week and some fun afterwards as well. Then she moved on to another town and another and another. Four weeks later she was lying in bed with yet another musician and said, "You know something funny? Every Monday night I get winked at by someone in the orchestra, and it's always the trombone player. I wonder why?"

234

The musician looked at her and smiled. "Third girl from the left," he said. "It's written on the music."

Still in the company of Bonar and Gilbert, I made my way to the theatre. There was my name up in lights, above and bigger than Max Wall's. As I sat in my dressing room making up, Gilbert and Bonar sat on either side of me making suggestions and offering advice. Much in the same way they'd given me directions to Manchester. Ted Heath was hovering in the background, and I heard someone ask him, "What's all that about?" Ted said, "It's called the blind leading the blind." I stood in the wings and watched a tall, imposing man speak into a microphone off stage. "And now, a gentleman who has been recognised throughout the world as the greatest impressionist of all time . . ." Music played, the man handed me the microphone and walked on stage to justify his claim. During his act I wished I were at home, then suddenly they were playing my music. I walked into a blinding spotlight and began to sing: "I Get a Kick Out of You" . . . at the appropriate moment I cut off the band, and went into my routine about "tell jokes, not sing, so let's get down to business. 'Joke: -Lady-walks-into-an-ironmonger's-shop-and-says, - Have-you-got-long-nails? - Man-says, - Yes, - Lady-says, - Good-scratch-my-back.'" This was followed by the biggest laugh I got all night!

For the bandleader, his not to reason why, he raised his baton, struck up, "I Get a Kick Out of You" where I'd left off and I meekly finished the song to a bemused audience wondering why I hadn't carried on telling jokes. From then on it was downhill all the way.

After I'd thrown up in the dressing room I sat there realising with horror that I had to do it all over again to another audience before I could go back to the hotel and commit suicide. Bonar walked in and looked at me. "Don't say it," I told him.

Bonar said, "After the act was over I went to the men's room and stood next to a man who said, 'What an act to top a bill.' I said, 'What was wrong with it?' He said, 'The guy doesn't do anything, he just stands there.' I said, 'Have you ever seen Jack Benny?' He said, 'Yes.' I said, 'What does *he* do?' He said, 'Nothing.' I said, 'Well?' And he said, 'Benny does it better.'"

For the second performance I left out the most successful joke, and simply sang "I Get a Kick Out of You" all the way through without interruption. There were no other changes and the result was slightly worse.

For reasons I'll never understand, Bonar had arranged a celebration . . . (Wake?) back in my hotel suite. Guests included Ted Ray, Al Read, and Max Wall. Ted and Al hadn't seen the show, so in a sense it *was* a celebration. Ted, Al and Gilbert vied with one another as to who could be most amusing, and the entire disaster got lost in their badinage. My only consolation was that the hotel manager, John Wheeler, told funnier stories than any of the professionals. Before I passed into unconsciousness, Max took me to one side and arranged for us to meet the following day.

"The main problem," said Max over lunch, "is that you're playing to the first row of the stalls. You're looking desperately for eye contact with the least important members of your audience. They're local tradesmen who've been given free seats for advertising the show in their window. The important people are at the back of the stalls, in the circle, the upper circle, and the gods. There's no way you can reach them with your eyes, but you must pretend to. You must open up, move around, take in everybody. Or appear to. There's another thing. The act is too sophisticated. We're north of Watford. [I'd never heard of Watford.] Some of these people resent you because you've been a success in London. It's not a question of getting down to their level, it's more a question of proving that you understand people everywhere. Your Canadian accent removes you from the class system, and you should capitalise on that. I tell you what I'll do. I'll leave some jokes in your dressing room every night and you can try them out." What a lovely man!

The first part of his advice was flawless. I did learn to "open out" and take in the entire house. The second part was also useful, and I suspect that Norden and Muir would be the first to admit now that my material was a bit sophisticated for the Ardwick Hippodrome. The only problem was that the jokes Max left in my dressing room were wilder than anything Frank and Denis had provided. About a year before, the great boxer Joe Louis had retired. But he'd already come out of retirement three times to my knowledge, and been soundly beaten. One night I came into the dressing room to find a note from Max saying, "Have you heard about Joe Louis, he's coming back for good!" Trying to re-write the act was not helped by the fact that in the adjoining dressing room Anton Karas insisted on rehearsing the theme from *The Third Man* for an hour every night.

Max's greatest contribution to my act was fortuitous. He was to appear in an ice extravaganza at Earl's Court that Christmas, so he was practising ice skating every day at a local rink. On the Thursday he sprained his ankle and could not appear in the evening.

"What you do," said the theatre manager, "is you come on in Max's spot in the first half and do your act. Then in the second

236

half you come on in your usual spot and do something else."

So this was show business! I managed to get through my act in Max's spot, and in the second half I walked on stage with an empty mind. What I did was talk to the audience. I told them about Max's misfortune, about my journey north with Bonar and Gilbert and about the first performance on Monday night. Gradually I could sense warmth coming up towards the stage, and at last I understood . . . thanks to Max Wall.

Apart from the money, the only good thing that came out of my sojourn into music-hall was a lifelong friendship between John Wheeler, the manager of the Grand Hotel, and Gilbert Harding.

Many years later Barbara and I were touring a play and the management had booked us into the Midland Hotel in Manchester. One night we returned from the performance to find Gilbert waiting for us in the residents' lounge. "Welcome to Manchester," he said. "Since we're so well met, you can buy me a drink."

I ordered drinks for the three of us, but the waiter said, "I'm sorry, but I won't be able to serve Mr Harding. It's after hours and he's not a resident."

"Don't be insolent," said Gilbert. "Use your eyes, my man. I'm wearing bedroom slippers."

The man replied, "I realise that, Mr Harding. I also know that you walked here in them from the Grand Hotel where you happen to be staying."

There was no answer to that.

Something else happened during my music-hall week in Manchester. Barbara and I were booked to do our first television show together as guests on *Kaleidoscope*. When the producer learned that I was already booked and would be in Manchester, he decided it was no problem. "Since you can't be in the studio, we'll arrange a telephone link to your dressing room at the Ardwick Hippodrome, and we'll simply write a telephone conversation between you and Barbara, played visually entirely on her." The first hitch was that the management of the theatre flatly refused to allow us to have the phone conversation live because if it was advertised people would stay away from the theatre and watch the television show.

"No problem," said our producer. "We'll pre-record your side of the conversation and leave space for Barbara to say her lines live in between."

And so it was arranged. Barbara told me later that it seemed to work well enough in rehearsal, but she spent most of her time imagining all the things that could go wrong and looking for ways to deal with them.

The sketch opened with Barbara being led into the studio by a dinner-jacketed compère. They walked past a prominent sign saying, "No Smoking" and sat on a settee. Barbara took out a cigarette, then offered one to the compère, saying, "Do you smoke?" He nervously replied, "No," and glanced away to the sign. After a moment or two Barbara said, "Do you light?" and at this point the telephone rang and was passed to Barbara. As my voice was heard saying, "Hi there," the one thing Barbara hadn't allowed for happened. The telephone came to pieces in her hands. She and the compère began to laugh helplessly while my recorded voice droned on in the background with my side of the conversation.

Some people thought it was planned that way.

♦   ♦   ♦

During November, BBC Television planned its most ambitious programme yet. A full-scale musical from the studios of Alexandra Palace lasting two hours, it was adapted and written by Eric Maschwitz with music by Hans May and produced by Walton Anderson. It had a cast of nearly a hundred, headed by Barbara and Norman Lawrence, and was billed as "a musical romance entitled *Carissima*".

Recalling those two minute studios in Alexandra Palace it seems impossible now that they had eleven sets, and in addition to the cast the George Mitchell Choir and a full orchestra directed by Eric Robinson . . . and it would be live! No expense was spared. Barbara's gowns were specially made by Norman Hartnell.

It really was too much to ask. In the event, the dress rehearsal was only halfway through when it had to be stopped so they could arrange sets and costumes back to the beginning again. This was barely managed before the show went on the air.

At one point Barbara was in an office in tailored clothes. She then had to change for a scene in a night-club wearing a shimmering evening gown and dash down a seventy-five yard corridor to arrive at the night-club set. One minute was allowed for this, and when Barbara arrived at the end of the corridor, she realised there was no way to get to the night-club set without crossing a camera already in use. She got down on her hands and knees and literally crawled in Mr Hartnell's masterpiece past the cameras to the set. She came home almost in tears thinking her reputation was ruined.

Somehow they got away with it.

Manchester Evening News: "Television's first big musical, *Carissima*, was a major technical and artistic triumph. For an hour and three-quarters one basked in the sunshine of Venice, joined in the swinging choruses of the gondolieri, and sipped vino on shaded balconies. The illusion was complete. The marvel was that it was created in two small studios augmented by adroitly mixed film shots and minute sets which had the appearance of spaciousness. The cast gave of their best, particularly Barbara Kelly."

The Sketch: "This is all too rare a type of production. The adaptation by Eric Maschwitz from his stage version was so thorough that no trace of stage technique remained discernible. The action moved swiftly from place to place, pausing long enough to give full value to the musical numbers. Barbara Kelly, who has been typed as a comedienne, sprang quite a surprise on us by proving that she is a most accomplished straight actress. In the role of Lisa Marvin, she achieved a fine characterisation."

Television Weekly: "*Carissima* had too much of the stage version remaining in this small screen version. The author and producer had been so busy cutting down and simplifying the spectacular ensembles that they had overlooked the necessity for toning down their actors.

While they were singing, Norman Lawrence and Eugenie Castle were quite delightful; and if their acting had been rather more restrained it would have been doubly effective. The only artist to emerge with full marks was Barbara Kelly. She acted the part of the heroine as if she really believed in it, and succeeded in appearing completely credible from her opening scene right to the fade-out. Here is an artist obviously at home in the television medium."

Daily Mail: "The first big musical attempted by television, namely *Carissima*, was a triumph of invention over lack of space. Barbara Kelly played with such feeling and sincerity that she nearly threw the entire production out of gear."

At home, Barbara was still trying to cope with what we couldn't bring ourselves to call "the servant problem". Forty years ago the word "servant" was quite acceptable in some parts of British society, but we'd been brought up in North America where servants were supposed not to exist, except in the British aristocracy. We saw them regularly in films, mostly Hollywood films, where at least half a dozen actors during the thirties and early forties earned a sizeable living playing comedy butlers in Hollywood. There was Robert Greig, the fat one; Eric Blore, the hysterical one; Alan Mowbray, the smooth one; Edward Everett Horton, the stuttering one . . . and several others.

Mr Musgrave, who'd sold us the house, had insisted that these people were his friends rather than his servants, and that he felt a responsibility for them. He'd probably grown up as a child with such friends, but it took a lot of experience to walk the fine line between friends and servants. We didn't have that experience, and though we did the best we could, one thing we hadn't been prepared for was that the people who worked for us weren't necessarily friends of each other.

One Sunday Cecil McGivern came to lunch with his daughter, and Ronald Waldman, the new Head of TV Light Entertainment, with his wife Lana Morris. It was a social occasion, but given that Mr Waldman was considering us for a series on television, and Mr McGivern was the Head of Television, it *was* rather important. Towards the end of the meal, a row broke out in the kitchen, and I do mean row. It was one that certainly couldn't be ignored in the dining room. Barbara suggested we all take our coffee to another room, picked a bottle of brandy out of the sideboard and marched into the kitchen to settle the row. She joined us half an hour later, somewhat the worse for wear, but with the row apparently settled. Within a few minutes it emerged that Barbara must have consumed most of the bottle of brandy.

That evening she said, "I know what I want for Christmas."

"What's that?"

"You to take charge of the staff."

Well, I tried, but it seemed a losing battle, and took up too much of my time. One night in a pub, I tried to explain my predicament to a friend, going into some detail, until we were interrupted by an amiable drunk who said, "I couldn't help overhearing your conversation, and wish to express my sympathy with your problem. As I understand it, you have a fifteen-room house on the Thames, a housekeeper, a gardener, a nanny, a cook, an upstairs maid and a downstairs maid. As if that weren't enough, you are burdened with a Slipper-stern launch plus two automobiles in which you and your wife commute regularly to London, but often at different times, which means that on occasion you must, having attended some smart party in London, convoy each other home using the two cars in the early hours of the morning. Your friend, as I understand it, recommends acquiring a chauffeur to overcome this difficulty. I have no advice to offer. I simply wish to express my extreme sympathy with all your problems."

Everyone in the pub had stopped to listen to him. My friend and I slunk out like a couple of wet terriers.

♦   ♦   ♦

Cecil McGivern had taken over BBC Television shortly after the surprise resignation of the Controller, Mr Norman Collins. Mr Collins's view was that in the long term, television would inevitably become the primary BBC service and sound radio secondary. While accepting that radio had arrived first, he objected to television being kept as a "department" of the BBC in which radio was regarded as the senior service.

It was in this atmosphere that Cecil McGivern had taken over as a kind of peace-maker. He ran it rather like a cottage industry, watched every programme that was transmitted, and made a point of meeting everyone who appeared on television. But there was an iron fist within the velvet glove. He had, for example, a direct line from his office to a telephone on the desk of the newsreaders. One night I was watching McDonald Hobley read the evening news when something struck him as funny, and he got the giggles. He tried to begin again several times, but kept breaking up, until he was virtually hysterical. Suddenly the telephone rang on his desk. He picked it up and we could hear a distorted voice, although we couldn't hear what it was saying. Mr Hobley listened, said, "Yes, sir" three times at intervals, replaced the receiver and read the rest of the news with total composure.

When TV Headquarters were moved to Lime Grove, Mr McGivern occupied two adjoining offices. One for business, one for entertainment. If a new series went on the air, he arranged to have in the entertainment office a table set for a formal dinner for the leading members of the cast. It was catered not by the BBC canteen, but by an outside organisation offering the best in food and wine.

Mr McGivern would watch the show in his business office, and,

Cecil McGivern

241

if he liked it the dinner would be served in the adjoining room with congratulations all round. The cast would be informed by a telephone call to the control room. If he didn't like it, there would be no phone call, and Mr McGivern would dine alone in stately splendour.

Mr Collins, whose resignation had been made in good faith, and realising that the BBC was not going to change its attitude in the near future, went on to become the architect of Independent Television, and was mainly responsible for the Bill that got it through parliament. (Interesting to note that one of the main lobbyists against Independent Television was the Advertising Association, who maintained that the economy of the country could not support television advertising.)

All this was important to Barbara and me because we were prominently featured in Ronnie Waldman's plans for Light Entertainment on television in the new year. Light Entertainment was to be based at Lime Grove, with producers Bill Ward, Michael Mills, Walton Anderson, Richard Afton and Henry Caldwell. An article in *Television Weekly* said:

> Foremost among the new recruits will be Bernard Braden and Barbara Kelly, the Canadian pair who have scored so many successes in sound radio. The Western Brothers have also signed TV contracts for a series called *Cads' Club.* Terry-Thomas will shortly be back with a new series of *How Do You View?*; and Bobby Howes is now in script conferences about an entirely new series to follow his *Such is Life* series.

Meantime, a small tempest had blown up in radio, a wind that was to blow us some good. It started when a repeat of a radio play called *Party Manners* was cancelled – because of its alleged anti-government bias – by Mr Lindsay Wellington, the Head of the BBC Home Service. Pat Dixon always maintained that the programme schedule of the BBC Home Service was totally controlled by a railway porter in Stevenage New Town. Mr Wellington, Pat said, never listened to any programmes, but always consulted this railway porter, who was an inveterate listener, before boarding his London train. What made this cancellation into news was that the play had been written by Val Gielgud, the Head of Radio Drama at the BBC.

Twenty-four hours before the decision to ban *Party Manners*, we'd broadcast in *Bedtime with Braden* an innocuous sketch in which Benny Lee, on behalf of his friend Sid Greenblatt, was ranting about bureaucracy.

BENNY: You have to send in a form in triplicate, and we have only one piece of carbon paper.

BERNIE: You won't let that lick you?

BENNY: No fear. Sid said it's just a tangle of red tape of the lousy bureaucracy that is throttling the country. Sid has some friends on the inside –

BERNIE: Dartmoor?

BENNY: No. Whitehall. Cabinet people too. You've heard of Bevin and Bevan? Well, Sid knows a man called Bevoon.

BERNIE: That's a new one on me.

BENNY: Bevoon is the only Minister in the Cabinet without a portfolio. And he needs it to keep his sandwiches in.

And so on. Somehow this little sketch attracted the attention of Victor Feather, Assistant Secretary of the TUC. He was quoted in most of the Sunday papers as saying: "Mr Braden seems very fond of trying to take the mickey out of government and our movement. I know one fellow who's had insomnia for twenty years, but *Bedtime with Braden* cures him."

Well, we couldn't really let that one pass, and most of our listeners knew it, so we were assured of a good audience for the next programme. We opened the show with a monologue in which I said:

It's come to my attention that some politicians are now using jokes in their speeches. This I consider grossly unfair to those of us who feed and clothe our loved ones by this method. If it continues, we, the organisation of alleged comics, may ask for a cancellation of the next meeting of the House of Commons, scheduled to be a repeat of the session of 1784. We feel that being a politician is a full-time job, and making a fool of oneself is a full-time job too. Now here's Nat Temple to play "Feel Like a Feather in the Breeze".

This got us unprecedented publicity. Apart from being heavily reported, it was the subject of editorials, and one said:

The public will always side with comedians in thinking that politicians, like mothers-in-law, are fair game for wit. Once upon a time politicians liked to boast that "they could take it". They knew that the man who stands up to good-humoured heckling is always a favourite with the crowd. Why are the present holders of high office so thin-skinned? Resentment against the wisecracks of the comics is bad political psychology, as well as evidence of a poor sense of humour.

I was grateful to Mr Feather, who doubled our audience for the rest of the series.

◆   ◆   ◆

Pat Dixon introduced something new to *Bedtime with Braden*, which he spread out over the season: virtually unknown guest artists. They were written into the script and interviewed by me. They were very funny, but didn't seem to belong in our show. Two of them were quite mad, and departed from the written script to an extent that brought out all my alleged skill as an ad-libber. One did quite brilliant impressions, and one, after a bit of badinage, sang a song in a beautiful tenor voice. They were part of a plot by Pat Dixon and his colleague, George Inns, to get a new show started, and this was one way to let the hierarchy hear them . . . as individuals. Their names were Michael Bentine, Spike Milligan, Peter Sellers and Harry Secombe. Pat and George got their way. And within a year the Goons were on *their* way.

◆   ◆   ◆

Looking back on those days I get the feeling that the relationship between performers and the press was . . . how shall I put it . . . more cordial than it is now. There was a pub in Grosvenor Street just round the corner from Aeolian Hall where the Light Entertainment crowd mingled happily at lunchtime with reporters. You could find Ted Ray, Tommy Trinder, Richard Murdoch, Ben Lyon, Eric Barker, Jimmy Edwards, and Dick Bentley exchanging jokes with Jimmy Thomas, George Campey, Robert Cannell, Leslie Ayre, Richard Findlater, Peter Noble, Jonah Barrington and Roy Rich. Some of the latter group appeared on radio themselves, and I don't think we ever talked about anything being "off the record". The reporters knew instinctively if something would be best not printed.

I recall Arthur Askey coming in one day having just returned from a music-hall tour where he'd shared the bill with Eddie "Monsewer" Gray. With two shows a night, filling the days could be pretty boring, and through the years Arthur had begun to take an interest in attending court trials. So much so that he'd made friends with many of the circuit judges. On this last tour he'd learned that Assizes were in progress in Birmingham and one day persuaded Eddie to join him in the public gallery.

The judge, recognising Arthur, sent him a note inviting him to tea in his Chambers during the afternoon recess. Arthur took Eddie with him. Now Eddie, who wore an obviously fake moustache on stage was, like Groucho Marx, usually not recognised in public. After exchanging some words with Arthur the judge realised that he might be being rude to Mr Gray, as Eddie had been introduced.

"Have you ever been in a court room before, Mr Gray?" he asked. Eddie said he hadn't.

"Well, if there are any questions you'd like to ask, now is the time, don't hesitate."

"Well," said Eddie, "there is one thing that's been puzzling me."

"What's that?"

"Is that a wig you're wearing?"

Not quite sure if it was a serious question, the judge admitted that he was indeed wearing a wig.

Eddie nodded solemnly. "I thought so," he said. "I was sure I could see the join."

Peter Noble was one of those who crossed the line, sometimes writing about radio, and sometimes appearing, but Peter's main interest was films, and in *What's On?* he wrote an amusing, but never vindictive gossip column. In fact, I don't remember Peter ever writing unkindly about anyone. When he entertained you in his home he was a quite different man and sometimes surprised guests who thought of him as a man with no particular opinions. Peter had very strong opinions, and political convictions, so it could come as a surprise to find yourself contradicted, however eminent you considered yourself to be.

Peter and his wife Mary went out of their way to be kind to us from the moment we met, and I think they're the only couple we know who still live in the same house where we first met them. I often think of Peter when reading those film reviews of what can be seen this week in the *Radio* and *TV Times*. They seem to be either written by film buffs interested in showing their own knowledge, particularly of obscure directors and even film editors; or simply copying bits of old reviews from films they've never seen, which is not what *I* want to read when I'm trying to decide what films to watch on television.

As far back as 1950 Peter Noble was known as the walking encyclopaedia of film, and was appearing as film critic on *Woman's Hour*, where he recommended films he thought the listeners might enjoy.

There's never been any side to Peter and Mary, although I can remember a time when they found their car too small to accommodate the family. In a burst of frustration Peter acquired an elderly Rolls-Royce which lasted about three months . . . not because the car broke down but because it was one of those Rolls-Royces designed for maximum comfort in the back seat and minimum comfort for the chauffeur in the front seat. Peter and Mary found themselves totally cramped in the chauffeur's area, while the children appeared to have room to play table tennis in the back. It wasn't quite what Peter had in mind, so he reverted again to a small car.

George Campey of the *Evening Standard* was particularly helpful to Barbara and me in his reviews, and when he found that Barbara enjoyed riding, arranged for her to have access to the polo ponies kept at Richmond Park. George went on to become Head of Publicity for BBC Television.

Jimmy Thomas of the *Daily Express* was unquestionably the most mischievous of the television reporters. At press conferences he would bide his time until the rest of the reporters had asked the usual questions, then as everyone was making ready to leave he would shove in the one question that nobody wanted to hear.

During my days with ATV I attended a press conference where Lew Grade was announcing autumn schedules. One reporter was highly critical of "Beat the Clock" which was a regular feature of *Sunday Night at the London Palladium*. The reporter waxed

George Campey and Barbara

eloquent on his theory that a quiz game had no part in a variety show, which *Sunday Night at the London Palladium* purported to be. "Besides," he said, "people are getting tired of it."

Lew, who was no slouch when it came to press conferences, asked for a show of hands, and most of the press agreed that "Beat the Clock" had had its day.

"Right," said Lew, "I don't want any of you saying that Lew Grade doesn't pay attention to the press. This autumn 'Beat the Clock' will not appear in the Palladium show." Aware that this was a scoop, the representatives of the *Evening Standard* and *Evening News* rushed out of the press conference to the nearest telephones and filed their stories for the evening editions. At last they had something over the morning papers.

Jimmy watched them leave, waited until the door closed behind them and then launched into an impassioned plea for the retention of "Beat the Clock". It had been an integral part of *Sunday Night at the London Palladium* from the very first week that ITV had gone on the air, hosted originally by Tommy Trinder, and then by Bruce Forsyth. To drop it now would be to throw away a bit of history. Surely Lew didn't want to upset so many of the *Palladium* fans?

Lew changed his mind immediately, and said that "Beat the Clock" *would* be included in the autumn series. Jimmy smiled the smile of the Cheshire Cat.

Among the "really important" critics was Godfrey Winn. Godfrey had his own weekly programme on the BBC as well as being a critic of the medium on which he appeared. We were flattered when he asked to come and interview us at Creek House. It was a Saturday afternoon. Godfrey arrived with pad and pencil and a square cardboard box. He interviewed us in the garden and the children hung about, I think because they felt that whatever was in the cardboard box might be something for them.

When the interview was over, Godfrey summoned his photographer to take pictures of the three of us . . . i.e. Godfrey, Barbara and myself. There was also a make-up girl who, after she'd touched up his eyebrows and applied pan make-up, opened the box and lifted out Godfrey's toupé, which she also applied while he looked at himself in a hand mirror. The children were fascinated.

♦   ♦   ♦

Fan mail had become a factor for both of us, and autographed pictures. Whenever you read that some superstar takes the time

247

Portrait-time

to read all his or her fan mail and, in some cases, claims to answer
it personally . . . forget it. We were by no means superstars, but
there was enough mail to guarantee that if we'd answered it all
personally we wouldn't have had time to take part in any radio or
television shows, so we were lucky indeed to find a lady called
Edna Barrett, known as Dan, to deal with our post. I'd first met her
on the opening night of *Streetcar* which she attended as the guest

of a Canadian friend of mine who was Head of Features for the CBC. He'd represented the CBC in London during the war and Dan had been assigned to the CBC offices.

The CBC representatives, who had to work through the BBC, had proved somewhat of a thorn in the flesh of that organisation, and Dan's escort of that evening, J. Frank Willis, had been the prickliest of them all. He'd been allowed to sit in on many of the BBC policy meetings where politeness prevailed, except for Frank, and, in fairness, Laurence Gilliam, Head of BBC Features. Whenever Frank had a bee in his bonnet, Laurence urged him to get it off his chest. On one occasion Frank stood up and said apropos of nothing, "I've just been going through your staff figures in the BBC, and according to my reckoning administration personnel outnumbers programme personnel by eight to one. This means that for every poor son-of-a-bitch trying to put on a programme, there's eight bastards trying to stop him." (I think it's worse today.)

In any event Dan had enjoyed the informality of working for the Canadians, and I think it was that which made her accept the offer of being secretary to Barbara and me. She stayed with us for twenty years, except for a three-month period in 1950. Dan and I were having a drink one day in the King's Head when we got into conversation with the production manager of a film being made at Shepperton Studios. It was called *The Mudlark* and starred Irene Dunne as Queen Victoria. Apparently Miss Dunne needed a secretary to deal with *her* mail for the next three months, and they were having trouble finding someone.

Back at the house, as we started work again, Dan mentioned demurely that Irene Dunne was her favourite film star. I looked at her, shrugged and picked up the telephone. By the time we got

Edna Barrett (Dan)

249

Dan back from Shepperton Studios there was a small mountain of mail waiting for her to deal with.

◆　　　◆　　　◆

Kenneth Tynan was beginning to make his name on the London scene, and for some reason took an interest in Barbara and me. He'd invite us to dinner and we'd find ourselves in the company of Richard and the first Mrs Burton. One night we went on to Al Burnett's Stork Club where from time to time people would be asked to come up and perform. Richard, always a heavy drinker, to our amazement volunteered to sing. To our further amazement he sang a Welsh ballad in a beautiful tenor voice that totally stilled the audience and was followed by prolonged applause. It wasn't until *Camelot* that he sang professionally and revealed a talent few people knew he had.

As well as being star-struck, Ken was a political animal, and it was through him that we met most of the "Hollywood exiles". The anti-Communist fear that gripped the United States when Senator McCarthy came to the fore in 1952 became news in Britain, but in 1950 the Un-American Activities Committee was already active, and the major Hollywood studios had been ordered to get rid of anyone in the industry who might at any time in the past have been *thought* to have had Communist leanings. They included writers and directors and a few performers. Most of them fled the country. Some went to Mexico, some to Paris, and a good number came to London. They included Joseph Losey, Cy Enfield, Sam Wanamaker, Ben Barzman, Robert Parrish and Carl Foreman. Ken cultivated them and in turn introduced them to us.

Any hopes they had of getting work in this country were quickly dashed. Although Britain was producing films, those films depended heavily on American distribution and the mere mention of any of those names was automatically blackballed by Hollywood's major studios.

One who stayed in Hollywood was Dalton Trumbo the writer, who went to jail as one of the "Hollywood 10", and subsequently alleged that within three years he'd been nominated for five Academy Awards under an assumed name.

Sam Wanamaker got work here by producing American plays in the West End such as *Winter Journey*, and *The Rain Maker*, in which he also starred. Years later when he played Iago to Paul Robeson's *Othello* at Stratford-upon-Avon, he suffered from the fact that the production was built entirely round Robeson and Iago was reduced very much to a supporting role. I asked him why he'd taken it on, and he said, "It's the first part I was ever offered in Britain."

In the early fifties they were a very tightly knit group, these exiles united in a common cause, but the tragedy was that they couldn't win. To get work in this country or be allowed back into the States they all had to present themselves to the FBI in Washington, subject themselves to ruthless questioning and recant before they got a seal of approval.

One by one they did that, but it totally broke up the group. Those who hadn't recanted wouldn't speak to those who had. The last to make the journey to Washington was Cy Enfield. By then Senator McCarthy and the Un-American Activities Committee were history. Cy found himself faced with three young FBI crew cuts, and when he began to recount his history they had no idea what he was talking about.

In 1950, though, they were an education for someone like me. Fine minds, and full of skills they weren't allowed to exercise.

One I particularly liked was a man called Bob Roberts. He'd started as John Garfield's manager, but once in Hollywood became aware that writers were underpaid and that their value was underestimated. He set about signing up writers in the forties and acquired a building with separate offices for each of them. They comprised most of the Hollywood 10, and Roberts devised a plan which literally held the big studios to ransom. MGM or 20th Century Fox would find themselves two or three weeks into the production of a film which obviously wasn't working. Even in those days the daily cost of a feature film amounted to thousands of pounds. The script would be rushed to Roberts, who would hand it over to all ten of his writers. They would work all night and the new script would be delivered to the studio the following morning at a cost of anything up to $100,000.

What with ten per cent of the takings and handling the then successful career of John Garfield, Bob Roberts was . . . doing . . . all . . . right. One morning his receptionist called through to say, "A man is about to barge into your office. I couldn't stop him."

As if on cue a man barged into his office and said, "Roberts?"

Bob admitted his identity.

"It's all very well using a number of writers to work on one script, but the concept is doomed. What you need is one man to write a film script that will get Academy Awards and make your name. I am that man."

Well, as Roberts said, when you've got a nut on your hands you have two choices. Throw him out, or go along with it. The man said his name was Polonsky, he needed $25 a week, an office and a typewriter. Roberts had one small office available, roughly the size of a broom cupboard, and the typewriter was no problem. He hired Polonsky at $25 a week, and then forgot about him. Occasionally he'd open the door of the broom closet and Polonsky would say, "Can't you see I'm creating? Get out!"

From time to time in his meetings with Hollywood moguls Roberts, to amuse himself, would hint that he'd acquired the services of a superb writer, name of Polonsky, who was working on a blockbuster film, which in due course he would show to studio heads. This went on for about a year, until Polonsky had become something of a legend in the industry.

One day Roberts found himself extolling the virtues of Polonsky at a board meeting of 20th Century Fox, chaired by Darryl Zanuck who said, "We're getting fed up with these stories about Polonsky. You've told us nothing about the film, or what it's about. It's time to deliver, Roberts. It's time you produced Polonsky."

Knowing he was in a tight corner, Roberts panicked and phoned his office, ordering them to produce Polonsky immediately in the boardroom of 20th Century. Half an hour later he arrived and outlined the story of a boxer caught up in the claws of the Mafia, who promoted him through to the world championship which he won, and then ordered him to throw the next fight. Polonsky acted out all the parts and when he got to the boxing sequences leapt on to the boardroom table and acted those out too.

The boxer double-crossed the Mafia and won the fight. As the tough guys closed in on him he smiled at the Mafia chief, gestured to the cheering crowd, smiled and said, "What are you gonna do, kill me?" Polonsky then jumped down off the table and said, "That's it."

The executives stood and applauded. Some of them pounded the table and cheered.

Polonsky said in wonderment, "You like it?"

More applause, more cheers.

"Good," he said. "Get somebody to write it."

He then left the room.

The Fox executives were on Roberts like hawks. "Get him back here and now," they chorused.

Too late. By the time the message got through Polonsky had cleared the studio gates and disappeared.

Roberts, hoping against hope, returned to his office, walked to the broom closet and opened the door. There was Polonsky, sitting at the typewriter.

"Why did you leave? They loved it!"

"What do they know?" said Polonsky. "They don't understand a writer's problems. Come over here."

Roberts walked over and stood behind Polonsky, and watched him laboriously type out the word "t-h-e-i-r", then cross it out and type "t-h-e-r-e". "You see what I mean? What do they know about a writer's problems?"

It emerged that the boxing script had been fully written, and that put Roberts in a powerful position. He made a deal for distribution and exhibition but stipulating that it would be an independent production by his own company, which he called "Enterprise". By now he was totally in thrall to Polonsky and asked him who he thought should direct the film. Polonsky said, "There's only one man who can direct this film. His name is Hal Rosson."

Roberts took Rosson to lunch and asked him if he'd like to direct *Body and Soul*. Rosson said he wouldn't. He was a cinematographer, and a good one. His credits included *The Wizard of Oz* and went back all the way to 1924 when he'd been lighting cameraman for the silent version of *Gentlemen Prefer Blondes*. He was not interested in directing.

Roberts went back and reported this to Polonsky who said, "Did I say Hal Rosson? I meant Robert Rossen."

Another lunch, another meeting with Robert Rossen who explained that he wasn't a director, but a writer. His credits included *They Won't Forget*, *Dust be my Destiny*, *The Sea Wolf*, *Blues in the Night* and *A Walk in the Sun* . . . but he was a writer, not a director. In desperation Roberts said, "Would you like to *be* a director?" Rossen said he would.

The deal was made at the lunch table, and over coffee, Roberts said, "I think I should tell you, you have Polonsky to thank for this."

Rossen said, "Who's Polonsky?"

The film was made with, again at the suggestion of Polonsky, James Wong Howe as lighting cameraman. Howe worked out a method of shooting the boxing sequences as boxing sequences had never been shot before. He had an apron built on all four sides of the ring where he squatted on something very much like a skateboard and was moved around the apron so that for the first time a boxing match was shot through the ropes rather than from above.

The film was released in 1947, starring John Garfield and Lilli Palmer, and Academy Award Nominations went to Abraham Polonsky and John Garfield. Rossen went on to write, produce and direct *All the King's Men* for which he won the Academy

Award the following year. In 1949 Polonsky wrote and directed *Force of Evil* which critics described as being almost as hypnotic as *Citizen Kane*. Dilys Powell said, "It credits an audience with intelligence in its ears as well as its eyes." He then fell foul of the Un-American Activities Committee, and disappeared until 1969 when he had another spectacular success with *Tell Them Willie Boy is Here*, starring Robert Redford.

Books have been written, plays produced and films made about those unfortunate enough to have fallen foul of the Un-American Activities Committee. I would just record that it was a privilege to meet some of them in London in the early fifties and, through *Bedtime with Braden*, make some of them feel at home. I remember a gleeful phone call from Carl Foreman after we broadcast an alleged interview with an American tourist who said she was in Britain "to see your wonderful country, and help hound Charlie Chaplin".

◆   ◆   ◆

After the fiasco of our first appearance on *Kaleidoscope* when the telephone came to pieces in Barbara's hands, we continued the series of "First Date" within the *Kaleidoscope* magazine, which was Eric Nicol's concept of how different types of people behaved on a first date.

The magazine *Scan* reported that:

> during the comparatively short time they have been known to British TV audiences, Bernie and Barbara have distinguished themselves as an acknowledged acting couple. Both of them display wit and charm. Both of them can project their personalities from studio to fireside. Their "First Dates" in *Kaleidoscope* were a joy. Now they are to have their own series and I'll chance a long-range forecast and tip them as winners in the race for TV personalities in 1951.

Sandwiched between these was my first television appearance *without* Barbara. It was a game show appropriately called *The Game Show*. In one form or another it's been on television ever since and is currently known as *Give us a Clue*. On the night I took part, our team consisted of Nigel Patrick (captain), Constance Cummings, Yolande Donlan and myself. Nigel Patrick undertook to explain the game to us ten minutes before we went on the air, and suggested the possibility of short-cuts. "For example," he said, "the most popular film in England at the moment is *The Fallen Idol*. If it should happen to come up, I suggest that whoever gets it simply folds his arms in front of him and falls over."

When it was my turn I walked to the desk of the chairman, Robert McDermott, and he handed me a piece of paper on which were written the words, "The Fallen Idol". I got credit for very fast thinking, credit which really belonged to Nigel Patrick.

Barbara and I were delighted to be invited to the Annual "Water Rats" Ball, the Water Rats being an association of variety performers. On this occasion the master ad-libber, Ted Ray, was to be installed as King Rat, a signal honour. Ted could handle pretty well anything, but his duties on this night included saying grace, about which he was somewhat embarrassed. The toastmaster was one of those sergeant-major types who called us all to attention with the gavel, then said in a loud voice, "Pray silence for your new King Rat who will now say grace." It was a somewhat uneasy silence in which Ted was barely heard to mumble a few words which didn't reach the back of the hall. The toastmaster, still playing the sergeant-major, shouted, "Speak up, sir, your guests cannot hear you!"

Ted turned on him in a flash. "You mind your own business," he said. "I'm not talking to them." I'd never heard quite such a fast riposte.

◆　　◆　　◆

Among the strangers who were particularly kind to us in England were radio stars Ben Lyon and Bebe Daniels who might have been expected to ignore us because we were in direct competition.

Ben and Bebe had divided their time in the thirties between Hollywood and London, arriving back in London about three weeks before the outbreak of the war, where they stayed for the duration. The British public of that time never forgot that these two American performers, who could easily have returned to the US and lived out a safe war, chose to stay in England doing valuable war work as well as presenting a successful radio show, *Hi Gang* with Vic Oliver.

By the time the Bradens arrived, Ben and Bebe, with their two children Barbara and Richard, had embarked on the equally successful *Life with the Lyons*. We were surprised and delighted when they invited us to dinner and subsequently made a point of introducing us to people they thought could further our careers. Ben was free with his advice, and once warned me to "stay away from the gentry". I never quite understood that, but the problem never came up. The gentry, on the whole, stayed away from us.

Ben had starred in his first film in 1919, and even before that had appeared on the Broadway stage. Besides his performing activities in Great Britain, he represented 20th Century Fox in this country, and for a while became their casting director in Hollywood. Like many people, he claimed to have "discovered" Marilyn Monroe. He told Barbara that he'd been sitting in his Hollywood office one day, when an agent forced his way in, accompanied by an attractive girl to whom he said, "Show him, honey!"

Before Ben could react, the girl lifted her sweater and exposed her breasts. The sight almost blinded Ben, and all he could bring himself to say was, "Put them away! Please put them away!" He suggested a new name for her and arranged for her to appear in a film.

Years later Ben received a huge photograph of the lady which he used to keep on a wall in his office. It was inscribed, "To Dear Ben, You discovered me! You named me!" and it was signed, "Marilyn".

Earlier, when Ben was starring in the film *Hell's Angels*, the producer Howard Hughes, having almost completed the picture, decided it would have to be re-shot . . . in sound. The only trouble was that his leading lady was foreign, with a very strong accent. Someone new would have to be found . . . and Ben found her. He changed *her* name too and introduced her to Hughes as "Jean Harlow" . . . so Ben could truly be said to have discovered the two blonde bombshells of our time.

Bebe Daniels and Ben Lyon

256

For me, the real excitement of that first evening was meeting Bebe Daniels. My first fan letter was written to Bebe when I was about twelve, and I kept her signed photograph for years. I never missed one of her films and read everything that was written about her in the fan magazines. She was one of the few silent film actresses who could play both comedy and drama so you could tell the difference.

She'd been in pictures of course, since before I was born. At the age of fourteen, she was Harold Lloyd's leading lady, when he was known as "Lonesome Luke". At the age of nineteen she'd had her own production company at Paramount, her own writers, producers and directors.

The interesting thing was that by the time I met her she had no memory of any of it. The plots of the films, I mean. But she loved being reminded. It was like telling a little girl a story she'd never heard before . . . "Did I *really* do that?"

What she *did* remember was her favourite uncle, who, however innocently Bebe spoke of him, sounded suspiciously like a one-man Mexican Mafia. Bebe was a great friend of Marion Davies, and the two of them were constantly getting into hair-brained scrapes. Marion had William Randolph Hearst to get her out of trouble . . . Bebe had her uncle. One night Bebe, a major film star, but still a young girl, was indulging in her favourite pastime, driving much too fast in a powerful sports car, when she was overtaken by a motor-cycle cop and forced to stop. It never occurred to her to identify herself as a film star. She simply named her uncle and told the cop to send him the ticket. For the first time in her experience it didn't work.

At the police station she immediately called uncle and told him to sort things out.

"I'll put this dumb cop on the phone, and you can tell him where to get off."

"Just a minute, honey. Where are you?"

"I don't know . . . hang on. [Then to the cop] Where am I?"
She was told.

"It's a place called Bakersfield."

There was a long, low whistle.

"What's the matter?"

"I'm sorry, honey, but I can't help you in Bakersfield. It's outside my . . . ah . . . jurisdiction."

"Jurisdiction?"

"Well . . . you know . . . my sphere of influence. Outside the city limits."

The local judge decided to make an example of Bebe and

sentenced her to thirty days in jail, only to be embarrassed by *Bebe's* "sphere of influence". The cinema newsreels were there in no time. The Brown Derby insisted on providing all her meals on silver salvers and a local furniture shop measured up the cell, then cut and laid a wall-to-wall luxury carpet.

I've a distinct memory of seeing a picture of Bebe sweeping out that cell. The judge offered a pardon, but Bebe preferred to serve the full thirty days. Such publicity was too good to miss.

Bebe could tell a story like that in graphic detail because she remembered it as fun. Filming was work, and in her case almost continuous work. Each film blotted out the next. A typical conversation between us would run like this.

ME: Were you worried about adjusting to talkies?
BEBE: I don't remember my first talkie. (*Calling*) Ben, what was my first talkie? It was just after *Rio Rita*, wasn't it?
BEN: Bebe, *Rio Rita* was a musical. You studied with Signor Morandi for six months to be able to sing the title role.
BEBE: Oh, it must have been a talkie then.
ME: And when did you do *Counsellor at Law* with John Barrymore?
BEBE: (*calling*) Ben? *Counsellor at Law* . . . was that before or after that one I did with Doug Fairbanks Senior?
BEN: After.
BEBE: What was that called again? The one with Doug Fairbanks?
BEN: *Reaching for the Moon.*
BEBE: Oh yes, I sang a duet with that cute boy who was always getting drunk. What was he called again?
ME: Bing Crosby.
BEBE: (*as if I'd earned a medal*) That's right!

There was one memorable evening at the Lyons when Van Johnson was present and it emerged that he knew as much about Bebe's early films as I did, or so he thought. Bebe sat between us, fascinated, as we outlined the plot of *Senorita*, one of her silent films.

VAN: It began with your rich Mexican grandfather in a hospital waiting room looking at his watch.
BEBE: Where was I?
ME: In the next room waiting to be born. Your grandfather had to leave, but he wanted to be sure you were a boy.
BEBE: Why did he want a boy?
VAN: Because he wanted a male heir. The family was dying

out. Then a nurse came into the room and announced that the baby weighed fourteen pounds, and your grandfather rushed away without bothering to look at you.

BEBE: Why?

ME: Because he figured if you weighed fourteen pounds, you *must* be a boy.

BEBE: Listen, I think *I* weighed nearly fourteen pounds.

VAN: Now we skip twenty-one years. You've just arrived in Mexico to claim your inheritance, and you're met by your late grandfather's faithful old servant. He takes one look at you and nearly faints.

BEBE: Do I look that bad?

ME: You look great, but you're a girl.

VAN: And the inheritance can only be claimed by a male heir.

ME: So you decide to masquerade as a boy.

BEBE: How could I do that?

VAN: Well, the servant dresses you like a boy, then you take a pair of scissors, snip off two bits of his moustache and glue them to your upper lip.

BEBE: That wouldn't fool anybody. Besides, if he was an *old* servant his moustache would have been grey.

ME: Maybe he dyed it.

BEBE: Silly.

VAN: You have to masquerade as a boy because if you don't the estates go to your villainous cousin . . .

ME: . . . played by William Powell.

BEBE: William Powell? The "Thin Man"? What was he doing in one of my pictures?

VAN: It was long before he was a star.

ME: William Powell played the villain in all your pictures.

BEBE: I just remember him as the "Thin Man".

VAN: Anyway, in the end you and William Powell have a sword fight in the hacienda, and you use the point of your sword to flick all his clothes off.

ME: First you remove his burnouse, and then . . . (*starts to laugh*)

VAN: You catch his turban with the tip of your sword and give a pull . . .

ME: And as his turban unwinds, he spins round and round . . .

VAN: (*can hardly speak for laughing*) and he's left with just a pair of striped shorts.

ME: (*nearly choking*) And when the turban comes off he falls in a fountain.

BOTH: (*have hysterics*)

Bebe did not join in the laughter. She waited until we calmed down and then said, "They don't wear burnouses and turbans in Mexico."

"They did in this picture," said Van.

"It must have been Arabia."

We both shook our heads.

She thought a bit longer then said, "Who directed this picture?"

"Eddie Sutherland," we replied in unison.

"Well, you just wait till I see Eddie Sutherland. He's got some explaining to do."

The next time Bebe saw Eddie Sutherland Van Johnson wasn't there, but I was. Bebe asked him what the hell William Powell was doing dressed in a burnouse and turban in Mexico?

Eddie, quite willing to play the straight man said, "I don't know. What *was* William Powell doing dressed in a burnouse and turban in Mexico?"

He didn't remember the film any better than *she* did.

Difficult to explain to people who weren't around what it meant to be a silent film fan. I was in my teens when Bebe's daughter Barbara was born, and I decided to wait for her to grow up so we could be married.

While I was waiting I met another Barbara and changed my mind. When Bebe's Barbara was married, we were both invited to the wedding.

◆   ◆   ◆

Thursday was cook's day off, and on the Thursday before Christmas ours made her usual trip to London, where, we understood, she regularly visited her brother. She always carried two suitcases, and wouldn't let anyone help although they looked heavy. On this particular morning as she walked along the corridor from the front hall to the front door, I opened the door to let her out, and as I did one case snapped open. As she gazed down on the rich assortment of groceries from local tradesmen, she turned white, glanced at the other case then looked at me. Setting the second case down she looked accusingly in my direction again and said, "I've decided I don't like this job, and I won't stay a moment longer."

With me still standing at the open door she swept out, saying, "I'll send for my things," and began to run towards the Square. I suppose I could have chased her, but you don't behave rationally in these circumstances, do you? I closed the door and opened the second case. It too was packed with goodies. I then alerted the house and we joined forces, carrying everything back to the larder. Stricken as we were in the knowledge that two such cases had been added to our household bills every Thursday, for several months, and the contents carried away to London, it took us some time to realise that we were without a cook for Christmas and there was precious little time to find another.

Normally we'd have cooked Christmas dinner ourselves, but both of us had heavy work schedules leading up to December 25th, so advertisements were hastily placed in local papers, and I came home two days before Christmas to find a man ensconced in my flat over the garage.

"He's a cook," Barbara told me. "And comes highly recommended."

"By whom?"

"The army. He's just left the services."

Well, it was true. The army had given him an excellent reference, citing the fact that he was used to catering for two hundred or more at a time. He cooked a couple of meals that were reasonably satisfactory, although there were some rumblings from the kitchen about other people having to clear up after him. There was a tendency to leave potato peelings on the floor for the lower ranks to deal with.

We had, and still do in our family, a traditional Baltimore punch prepared by me on Christmas morning. Fred watched me making it and I think assumed that I was choosing bottles at random to fill the punch bowl. These included peach brandy, brandy, rum, and other liqueurs, carefully apportioned, along with double cream and beaten egg whites.

I gave him a glass before taking the bowl out of the kitchen. He pronounced it "very palatable". Then I left him to get on with the preparation of the meal. The only possible explanation for what happened is that Fred decided to make his own punch, using the ingredients I'd left behind and a few others he'd found in the cellar. About five minutes before dinner was due to be served there was an almighty crash from the kitchen. I rushed in to find Fred in the oven along with the turkey. Both were upside down. I managed to extricate him, but keeping him on his feet was something else. He muttered something about "being overheated" so I opened the kitchen door and let him into the fresh cold air. At this point he threw up for some time, and when I'd got him back on his feet I put him in a fireman's lift and carried him up to his quarters. There he stayed until the following evening.

It was our first Christmas at Creek House and our first with all three children. Chris and Kelly had rigged up the playroom/

261

theatre as a manger. Mr Fulton had built the crib and crooks for the shepherds, Mrs Fulton and Barbara had made costumes. In due course the audience was seated. (Barbara and I, Mr and Mrs Fulton, Gilbert Harding, Eric Nicol and an attractive intelligent girl called Elizabeth Cowley.) The house lights were dimmed, the footlights turned on and the curtains opened.

As the nativity play proceeded it emerged that Chris and Kelly were playing all the parts, alternating between Joseph and Mary, the three Wise Men and the Shepherds. A doll had been placed in the crib to represent the Christ-child.

Two-year-old Kim stood on a box which apparently was meant to represent the hills around Bethlehem. The two older children had decided she was too young to learn lines, but should be allowed to take part. From time to time one of them would nod a head in her direction. If it was Chris she would moo like a cow, and when Kelly nodded, she would say, "Baa baa". As the play progressed she grew perceptibly restless and as Chris and Kelly became more absorbed in their parts they forgot to nod in her direction. Finally Chris remembered and gave her a nod. She ignored him. Then Kelly tried. Still no response. There was a stage-whispered "Kim" to which she stamped her foot and said, "No!" . . . Consternation . . . Then she added, "Not fair, not fair . . . just baa baa and moo moo. Not fair."

Hastily, from her seat in the stalls, Barbara said to Chris and Kelly, "Perhaps it *is* a little unfair." Then to Kim, "Is there something you'd *like* to do, Kim?"

Kim gave a little curtsy and said, "Yes. I'd like to sing 'If I Knew You Were Coming I'd Have Baked a Cake'." Which she did.

A white Christmas

On that note the nativity play ended and the curtains were drawn.

During the afternoon, Gilbert and I went for a walk and discussed our respective futures. By now he was convinced he could probably earn a living as a freelance. He was still chairing the erudite *Round Britain Quiz* on radio, with only occasional ructions. He chuckled. "Had one only last week. Usually I'm with one team in, say, Scotland, and the other team comes from London or Ireland or Wales. The BBC do a splendid job of keeping the lines open so we can all hear each other. Well, last week, both teams happened to be in London, Christmas shopping I suppose, so we did the whole thing from different studios in Broadcasting House . . . and would you believe it, we couldn't hear each other at all. Now, no one knows better than you, Bernie dear, that there are occasions when I become slightly impatient, and after half an hour of wasted time I said, 'It seems very odd to me that when we're spread all over these sceptred isles we have little or no difficulty getting a feed on the lines, but when we're on two floors of our London headquarters the technical department is incapable of linking us together.'

"Then a girl's voice from central control said, 'I'm sure we're all doing our best, Mr Harding.'

"I said, 'What we want to hear, madam, is more of each other and less of your West Kensington accent.'

"Without a breath pause she said, 'Actually it's Maida Vale.'

"I could only laugh and arrange with the producer to send her flowers the next day. If only more people would realise that the only way to deal with me is to hit back. I can't help challenging

Barbara, Kim and Kelly

what I take to be inadequacy, but if they'd take up the challenge instead of moaning later about my rudeness, why then I'm putty in their hands."

He went on to complain about *Ignorance is Bliss* and Stewart McPherson in particular, but thought that Stewart's replacement, a young chap called Eamonn Andrews, might make the show more bearable.

"Such a programme demeans me. I'm intelligent, articulate and educated. I should be chairing a programme with a panel composed of my peers."

I had my doubts. Gilbert was everything he said he was, but lacked discipline. The following year he arrived for the first *What's My Line?* under the impression he was to be chairman. When he learned that Eamonn Andrews was to chair the panel, and he was to be one of the four panellists, he flatly refused to appear. Ted Kavanagh was brought in to take his place. There are many people who think they recall the panel on the first *What's My Line?* but most of them are wrong. It consisted of Jerry Desmonde, Marghanita Laski, Ted Kavanagh and Barbara.

The following week Gilbert took over the chair with disastrous results. Apart from forgetting to turn over the cards when the answer was no, he got the occupation of one of the contestants completely wrong, and kept contradicting the poor man every time he said, "yes" or "no".

On the third week, he took his rightful place on the panel, and was largely responsible for making *What's My Line?* the BBC's most popular show for many years. People used to compliment Barbara on the way she seemed to calm him down when he appeared to be on the verge of apoplexy. In fact her method was to encourage him to further mischief. "When the camera comes back on you for your next question, Gilbert," she'd say, "don't be here. Walk off the set now. It will really embarrass the director." Gilbert would chuckle and cool off.

In the hospitality room after his last appearance on *What's My Line?* Gilbert put his arm around Barbara and said, "This is the only woman I've never been able to fight with." The nearest they ever got to a scrap was on another panel game called *We Beg to Differ*. Gilbert suddenly turned to Barbara in the middle of the show and accused her of being "coyly Transatlantic". When the transmission was over she demanded an explanation. Gilbert smiled sheepishly. "Didn't mean a word of it, my dear," he said. "I just felt the show wanted livening up a bit."

As we continued our walk he said, "And what about you? You and Barbara? Are you going to stay here?"

264

"What do you think we should do, Gilbert?"

"Well, I lived in Canada long enough to know that the country abounds in talent, out of all proportion to its population. The trouble is that its own people don't recognise it . . . and in my far from humble opinion they won't in your lifetime. I'd stay where you are . . . but don't take success for granted. Nothing is quite so fleeting as fame."

We'd arrived at Shepperton Square and although Gilbert was Catholic he decided to pay a visit to the local Church of England on Christmas Day. It was locked.

His face darkened. He pointed to the house beside the church. "Is that the vicarage?"

"That's what it says on the gate," I told him.

He walked through the gate and rang the doorbell. It was answered by a middle-aged lady.

"I'd like to speak to the vicar," said Gilbert.

"You can't."

"Why not?"

"He's having his tea."

"That's no excuse. Fetch him."

The lady refused to do any such thing. Gilbert insisted. As their voices rose the vicar left his tea and appeared at the door to demand an explanation of the disturbance.

"Do you realise," said Gilbert, "that your church is locked on Christmas Day?"

"I do."

"May I ask why?"

"Because if it's not locked people go in."

Gilbert then launched into a tirade that was sharply cut off by the vicar shutting the door in his face. To my amazement instead of hammering on the door, he stepped back and looked again at the church. "That's a Norman tower," he said mildly. "I only wanted to see it from inside."

The rest of that day passed peacefully. The children went reluctantly to bed, Eric and Elizabeth left and, finally, so did Gilbert.

Barbara and I sat down to reflect on the last twenty-two months, and the incredible luck that had come our way . . . for luck it certainly had been. Luck and a lot of help from strangers. And yet there must have been some reason why we were welcomed so warmly by people we admired so much. Perhaps it was because we'd served a long apprenticeship in Canadian anonymity. Perhaps it was because, having lived a vicarious war, we radiated a kind of energy in the aftermath of the war that cut through a lot of the established concepts of traditional entertainment. In variety particularly, we liked to think that by querying the adage "to do your act", we'd given new importance to the status of writers, and new opportunities to British comedians who were looking for new ways to express themselves. Perhaps, with Norden and Muir and Pat Dixon we'd helped pave the way for a new kind of freedom in British radio. Certainly, before we came, there were talented British comedians knocking on the doors of agents, being admitted to the presence of secretaries, leaving their cards and hearing them being torn up and dropped in waste baskets before the door closed behind them.

On the night of December 25th, 1950 we certainly weren't thinking in those terms.

Pat Dixon had a reputation for moving quickly from one show to another. He always wanted to do something new. I count it a privilege that he stayed with me through *Breakfast, Bedtime, Brunch*, and *Between Times* right through to 1959. The same was true of Frank and Denis who, through those years, wrote *The Fletchers of England, The Encyclopaedia Bradenica, A Book at Bedtime with Braden*, and *The Braden Guide to Tin Pan Alley*. They did a lot more important things, but always left a corner for me.

Just as we were about to go to bed the phone rang. It was Bonar wishing us a Merry Christmas and telling Barbara he'd just seen a screening of *Tale of Five Cities* . . . "The film is lousy," he said, "but you come out of it great."

Bonar died tragically and, perhaps inevitably, young. Many of the people mentioned in this book have died, but I never became totally reconciled to the loss of Bonar. Sometimes if I'm walking at dusk in New Bond Street I'm convinced I've seen him just disappearing round a corner. But that night he was very much alive, and so were we . . . and just around the corner of the new year there were more good things to come.

◆   ◆   ◆

Robert Cannell (*Daily Express*): "Separately and together the Bradens have romped away with this year's show business laurels. Less than two years ago, the family reached London, unknown here, but radio famous in Canada. Their BBC audition guyed their own ordeal, and earned them immediate bookings. Then Barbara stepped into a West End stage lead, Bernard followed by appearing in *A Streetcar Named Desire*, then became nationally famous through *Breakfast with Braden*. Barbara countered her husband's progress by starring in radio drama. Bernard came back with star parts in Home, Light, and Third Programme plays. They played opposite each other and showed how easy it was. There wasn't a pin between them. Next, comedy in a successful variety series *Leave your name and number*. Now they share *Bedtime with Braden* and millions chuckle at this New Yorker of the Air. Barbara starred in the TV musical *Carissima*, and has just finished her first film, another step ahead. Lately they've appeared together on TV in *Kaleidoscope*. As a result there will be a series built round them in the New Year. My forecast is that they will be TV's 1951 find."

(From *BBC Year Book 1950*): "One of the more mobile, quick-firing units in the current invasion of British entertainment is a one-man blitz named Bernard Braden. Contrary to popular opinion, there is only one Bernard Braden but he is as ubiquitous as laughter and as likely or not responsible for it. So far nobody has explained whence he derives the energy that has rocketed him to stardom in only a year. In his home town of Vancouver he was at eighteen working for a local radio station and ready to do anything for the love of mike. One of his more successful engagements during this period was to Barbara Kelly, the 17-year-old actress who has since matched her husband's torrid pace and co-produced their three most important ventures, Chris, Kelly and Kim. Then there's Braden's 'Uncle Gabby', the garrulous old-timer whose mighty 'Hellooo – there!' has echoed across the Atlantic and penetrated into the corner of homes all over the British Isles. The Bradens passed with flying colours their BBC Dramatic audition, with Uncle Gabby sandwiched like a genie between impeccably portrayed extracts from Shakespeare, Strindberg and Shaw. From there they followed the old gentleman through the staid corridors of Broadcasting House into variety. It would be rash to suppose this was the end of the story."

Forty years later I picked up a cab at Euston Station one evening and noticed that the driver was peering at me in his mirror . . . knew the face, but couldn't place the name. He was still looking puzzled when I got out of the cab and paid him. As I turned away he said, "Don't think I didn't recognise you, Mr Lyon. Give my love to Bebe."

I promised to pass the message on and said I knew she'd be flattered.

ACKNOWLEDGMENTS

The photographs in this volume have been taken from the author's private albums, unless otherwise credited. The publishers have attempted to trace copyright holders but where inadvertent infringement has been made they apologise and will be happy to make due acknowledgment in any future edition.

The author and publishers should, however, like to thank Maurice Ambler, Olive Harding, Miriam Karlin, Eric Nicol and Irene Selznick for providing photographs from their private albums and Angus McBean (pp. 65, 78, 97, 98, 130 and 181), John Vickers (p. 36), the BBC Library (pp. 63, 107, 162 and 245) and the Hulton-Deutsch Collection (pp. 43, 94 and 139) for allowing them to reproduce copyright material.

INDEX

271

274

276